MEGALITHS, MYTHS & MEN

MEGALITH

AN INTRODUCTIO

with 142 illustratio

TAPLINGER PUBLISHING COMPA
NEW YO

PETER LANCASTER BROWN

MYTHS AND MEN

OF ASTRO-ARCHAEOLOGY

*Writing need not be the only
way of expressing thought.*

Baron Nordenskjöld

First published in the United States in 1976 by
TAPLINGER PUBLISHING CO., INC.
New York, New York
Copyright © 1976 by Peter Lancaster Brown
All rights reserved.
Printed in Great Britain

*To all pioneers of astro-archaeology
but particularly to C.A. (Peter) Newham (1899-1974)*

3-21-77
Library of Congress Catalog Card Number: 76-15090
ISBN 0-8008-5187-0

CONTENTS

070421

ACKNOWLEDGEMENTS

The author and publisher gratefully acknowledge the following illustrations and sources in addition to those acknowledged in the text:

Crown Copyright, Ancient Monuments Branch, Ministry of Public Buildings and Works 1, 19, 22, 66b, 69, 72-3, 96, 105a and b, 106; British Museum 16-17, 105d, 108a; *The Yorkshire Post* 48-9; C.A. Newham 56; *Antiquity* Tables A and B; Aerofilms Ltd 62, 83, 94a; *Science* 110.

The author would particularly like to acknowledge the unflagging assistance—both editorially and in the field—from his wife, Johanne.

PROLOGUE

In modern times, epoch-making discoveries in astronomical science are invariably made via the information received through the very largest optical and radio telescopes. Most of these fundamental discoveries concern bizarre stellar objects lying at the farthest regions of the Universe at distances measured in megaparsecs—a unit so large that its magnitude is beyond normal human comprehension.* Likewise, in archaeology significant discoveries in more modern times are usually the net result of painstaking excavations conducted by a group of specialists after several seasons of methodical digging at a site.

It was a general surprise to all then, when in 1963, the science magazine *Nature* carried an article evocatively entitled: 'Stonehenge Decoded' in which the British-born American astronomer Gerald Hawkins·claimed to have solved the long-standing astronomical riddle of Stonehenge—the most famous ancient monument in the whole of Britain. Hawkins claimed that the monument, whatever else it might be, also represented a sophisticated Neolithic observatory, built not simply to mark the point of sunrise of the summer solstice (an idea which had long been held) but also to keep track of the complicated vagaries of moonrise and moonset.

This was not the first time that Stonehenge had figured prominently in the pages of *Nature*. Sir Norman Lockyer—an early investigator of Stonehenge—had been its first editor, and in the early years of the twentieth century much had appeared in its pages concerning this enigmatic Megalithic structure. But Hawkins had been more fortunate than the earlier investigators, for he had at his disposal a powerful electronic computer; this combined with a few inspired scientific hunches indicated that

* One megaparsec ≈ 3 ¼ million light years (1 light year = 9·460 × 10^{12} km).

1

numerous alignments to the Sun and Moon could be interpreted in the various stone arrangements of the monument.

However, unknown to Hawkins, a British amateur astronomer, C. A. Newham, had sometime earlier been working on the same problem independently, and without the assistance of a computer he had arrived at very similar results. Newham had already published his preliminary report—second-hand—via the Science Correspondent of the *Yorkshire Post*, on 16 March 1963; Hawkins' paper did not appear in *Nature* until 26 October 1963. Newham's discovery announced through the British provincial press attracted no comment, and apparently not a ripple of interest. Hawkins' announcement via the established scientific press triggered one of the most publicized scientific controversies in modern times. . . .

In addition to Newham's work, the publication of Hawkins' paper brought to the forefront the work of Alexander Thom, Emeritus Professor of Engineering Science at Oxford. Thom had quietly been plugging away for several years without publicity in a long-term programme involving the survey and interpretation of solar, lunar and stellar orientations of a whole complex of Megalithic monuments (but not Stonehenge) which extend throughout the western half of the British Isles from Cornwall to the northernmost tip of Scotland and beyond.

Following a second paper in *Nature* by Hawkins which laid dramatic claim that one of the features of Stonehenge might have functioned as a computer-like device, the cult of so-called Megalithic astronomy suddenly came into full blossom in the mid-1960s. With it several astronomers stepped into the arena to offer their own interpretations of the newly published data. Fred Hoyle, better known as a cosmologist amid the realms of the megaparsecs, believed he could detect a level of sophistication in the Neolithic builders of Stonehenge which went much beyond the ideas of Hawkins. . . .

Meantime the archaeologists, stunned at first by the impact of the new astronomical findings, soon found their voice in R. J. C. Atkinson, one of the greatest living authorities on Stonehenge. In his review of Hawkins' work he considered that its results were 'unconvincing, tendencious, and slipshod'. Part of the initial antagonism created in the archaeologists was certainly caused by Hawkins' misinterpretation and sometimes blatant disregard for the achaeological evidence. But in part it was also owing to the archaeologists' traditional distrust for astronomical interpretations in alignments at Stonehenge and elsewhere—a distrust justified by some of Lockyer's hyperspeculative theories surrounding the purposes of British Megaliths.

The contentious Stonehenge debate has intrigued the layman and specialist alike. The field evidence *is* both conflicting and ambiguous; while not all archaeologists are unresponsive to the astronomical theories, not all astronomers are uncritical of them. Nevertheless, what is clear to all is that Stonehenge—designed and built two millenniums before the Romans set foot on British soil—is something specially unique in the history of mankind.

Stonehenge—at midwinter sunset.

INTRODUCTION

Nowadays the astronomical interpretation of archaeological monuments and other material has come to be known as astro-archaeology—for want of a better name. The amalgum of ancient astronomy and archaeology as a hybrid discipline may be traced back to the time of Napoleon's great scientific expedition to Egypt, and perhaps earlier to Isaac Newton's studies in ancient chronology. It was not, however, until Sir Norman Lockyer began his pioneer researches in Egypt and then in Britain that the English-speaking general readership, through his books *The Dawn of Astronomy* (1894) and *Stonehenge and other British Stone Monuments* (1906), were made aware of the wide possibilities of a novel approach to solving some of the puzzling problems inherited from the ancient world.

Criticism has been raised against the naming of the new interdisciplinary approach to ancient astronomy and archaeology. Some have considered astro-archaeology a rather ugly and misleading name; others have suggested an even uglier name 'archaeo-astronomy'. Some have rejected both hybridizations and refer to it as the astronomy of archaeology, astronomical archaeology, or the archaeology of astronomy—while in a fit of pique an anonymous archaeologist reviewer in the *Times Literary Supplement* once referred to it as 'astro-melodrama'.

In specialist studies confined to North-West Europe, the term Megalithic astronomy has wide usage.* Nevertheless, whatever its merits, the name astro-archaeology has now become generally accepted as the scientific activity which examines the nature of early astronomical knowledge via the interpretation of ancient monuments and other relevant archaeological data. A suggested sub-discipline, ethno-astronomy (although a more

* However, perhaps in the long term the name *Megalithic science* might provide the best compromise solution in this case—thus encompassing all aspects of interdisciplinary Megalithic studies.

exact name would be proto-astronomy), covers a closely allied field of research, but its purpose is that of specifically exploring the role which astronomy, myth and associated ritual played in historic societies and in neoprimitive societies such as those now found in Africa, Australia and Polynesia. But clearly the two approaches have considerable overlap.

This highlights the point that astro-archaeology is more than a simple amalgam of astronomy and archaeology. It represents an interdisciplinary approach which utilizes geology, anthropology, mythology, folklore, philology, paleography, ethnology, prehistoric and neoprimitive art, prehistoric and classical scholarship, biology, botany, geochemistry, nuclear physics—even pseudology—and a host of other ologies and arts. Each branch of learning has, of course, a bias towards its own special interests which may bring about a conflict of ideas, and this is nowhere more true than in relation to the problems of interpreting Stonehenge. . . .

The word *megalith* appears in the English archaeological vocabulary about the middle of the nineteenth century. It comes from the Greek words *megas* and *lithos* meaning 'great' and 'stone'. In 1912, when T. Eric Peet wrote his short minor classic *Rough Stone Monuments*, he posed the question of what defines a Megalithic monument. Throughout the world there are many monuments and structures of widely differing ages that can rightly be called 'megalithic'. In the widest sense a Megalithic structure embraces any structure or building made of large or very large stones, which would include Hadrian's Wall, the pyramids and the Great Wall of China, etc. Peet himself, however, limited its archaeological usage to a series of tombs and buildings constructed in certain areas of Western Asia, Africa and Europe.

European Megalithic tombs of the Neolithic and early Bronze Age are found predominantly in the lands bordering the Atlantic and the North Sea—in Spain, Portugal, France, Britain, Ireland, Holland, Germany, Denmark and Sweden. They do not occur in Central, East or South-East Europe or—apart from Palestine—in the east Mediterranean. In the west Mediterranean, except for Spain and France, they are not widely found. Ancient Megalithic structures in south Italy and the Balearic islands are of a later date.

Apart from those areas mentioned above, Megalithic

structures also occur on several Pacific islands and in Central and South America. Whereas the Egyptian pyramids are Megalithic structures, the contemporaneous Babylonian ziggurats are not, since they are constructed of man-made brick. For this reason the term Megalithic may sometimes be confusing in its astronomical context when discussing a particular period in history. This is why in contemporary astro-archaeology its usage generally has been restricted to monuments and structures of the Neolithic and Early Bronze Age in Western Europe and the Mediterranean. The monuments and structures involved in Old World Megalithic astronomy are broadly of three kinds: chambered tombs; single standing stones (menhirs or monoliths); and grouped standing stones. In the older literature these monuments and structures were frequently referred to under a Welsh-Breton nomenclature which nowadays has largely fallen out of fashion. In this older literature chambered tombs are often described as dolmens (from *dol* or *tol* 'table' and *men* 'stone'); single standing stones as menhirs (from *men* 'stone' and *hir* 'long'); grouped standing stones as cromlechs from *crom* 'circle' or 'curve' and *lech* 'place'.* These descriptions were frequently interchangeable and confused, and not all antiquarians were in agreement with their precise definition.

Archaeologists have now divided chambered tombs into several categories. Chambered tombs and their architectural subdivisions may be very significant in solving astro-archae-ological problems—since apart from the fact that many are probably (solar) orientated in some way, they provide more positive evidence than stone circles do about the social and cultural practices locally in vogue. The French word *alignement* is used to describe standing stones arranged in rows to form long 'processional' avenues. However, in British usage the term Avenue is often preferred, and 'alignment' is usually restricted to describe the azimuth direction between two stones or other features. Nevertheless, some archaeologists use the term as a synonym for 'arrangement'. The term Cursus (Latin for racecourse) is a name applied to a prehistoric earthwork with moderate-sized parallel banks. This term dates from the eighteenth century when it was introduced by the British antiquarian Stukeley, who is one of the key historical figures in

---

* Cromlech is a term still widely used in France.

1 The Trethevy Quoit, Cornwall. Megalithic funerary chambers of this kind are usually referred to as 'dolmens', but sometimes they may be referred to as 'cromlechs' or 'quoits'. Locally they often carry more colourful names such as 'the Devil's Den', 'the Druid Temple', or 'the Druids' Altar', etc.

the interpretation of British Megalithic monuments.

A henge monument may be a 'hanging' monument conceived like Stonehenge where the stone lintels are carried by stone uprights which comprise a circle or curve. The name Stonehenge probably derives from the Anglo-Saxon name for 'place of hanging stones'. However, it is likely that other 'ghost' henge monuments were probably Megaxylic—constructed with timber members now long rotted away. The usage of 'henge' is a misleading and unsatisfactory term, for it includes sites with no stones and/or no lintels, and in archaeology a henge monument has generally become known as a circular or oval enclosure surrounded by a bank and ditch with entrances. The British archaeologist Atkinson has introduced several henge classifications. In short: Class I henges have only a single entrance (Stonehenge, Phase 1); Class II henges have two or more entrances (Avebury); a Class II subgroup have a surrounding bank with a ditch both *inside* and *outside*.

Scattered round the British Isles are probably close on a hundred or more henges and hundreds more enigmatic earth-ring features—most of them only visible via the medium of air photography. Stone circles or ovals are found with or without an associated bank-and-ditch henge. Some smaller stone circles are known as 'hut circles', others are known as 'cairn circles', and these are likely associated with burial cairns no longer extant.

In Britain the names barrow and tumulus are names freely and indiscriminately applied to all manner of prehistoric and historic burial mounds whether they be long barrows, round or oval barrows, or earth-covered chambered tombs; descriptions by archaeologists are usually much more specific. Stone cists, or kists (the name is derived from the Welsh *cistraen*), are box-like, slabbed stone structures and were made to house the remains of the dead; they are frequently found under cairns. Cists vary in size; they may be covered by cap stones and may be large enough to house a fully extended burial, but others are smaller and were only intended for cremations or crouched-attitude burials.

Note: Dates used throughout this book (with some minor exceptions) are expressed according to astronomical usage so that dates BC and AD are indicated by the signs − and + respectively, viz − 1200 instead of 1200 BC. The plus sign is omitted from dates after + 1000.

CHAPTER I

Before the Megaliths

The archaeological record shows that in the immediate prehistoric period, civilizations developed in several centres. We can say that several societies can be recognized at this period: Sumer, Egypt, Anatolia, the Indus Valley, Shang China, Middle America and Peru. In this context civilization is accepted within the definition that a community has at least two of three things: towns of more than 5,000 inhabitants, the possession of a system of writing, and complex ceremonial centres. In the so-called Megalithic period of North-West Europe only the last ingredient is known to have been present. Certainly there were no towns of the order of 5,000 or more inhabitants, and as far as we can tell, writing was unknown. Yet if we interpret the nature and purpose of the complex British (and French) stone-built ceremonial centres correctly, we have civilized communities at work whose level of intellectual ability was little different from that of more contemporary societies.

The story of the British Megalithic culture begins with the first colonization of Britain by the Neolithic (stone-using) farmers before – 4000. Until recently it has always been fashionable for prehistorians to write about our Neolithic forebears as barbarians and savages. Gordon Childe, the great European prehistorian, always referred to pre-Roman northern and western Europeans as barbarians—perpetuating the myth put out by the imperialist Roman propagandists who chose to ignore the rich and complex native Iron-Age culture. This same blinkered view was adopted by European settlers in both the New World of the Americas and the New New World of the Antipodes.

The Neolithic farmers who colonized Britain in the fifth millennium were relatively sophisticated products of a long evolution of genus *Homo* dating back at least three million years. Richard Leakey's find of the so-called '1470' man and the finds of the joint French-American expedition in Northern Ethiopia carry man back in time long before the onset of the Pleistocene Ice Age.

The Pleistocene epoch, through which man evolved in his Paleolithic Stone-Age culture, marked a period in the Earth's geological history when at least four great ice sheets in turn advanced and then retreated. At times these ice sheets covered almost a third of the present land area of the Earth. In the late Pleistocene, during the last ice advance in Europe, the culture of Stone-Age man flowered as never before. This advanced Upper Paleolithic culture reached its peak between   −30,000 to − 10,000 and contains the earliest known art of prehistoric man. While a great deal is missing from the record of the prehistoric past, its art—with its classical simplicity and beauty—provides a firm past-to-present cultural bridge for *Homo sapiens* to seek out his roots.

During the nineteenth century the chronology of man's prehistoric past was based on a simple three-age system of stone, bronze and iron, taking into account the successive utilization of these materials for weapons and tools. The stone period was subdivided into the tripartite division of Paleolithic, Mesolithic and Neolithic, or the Old, Middle and New Stone Ages. From late Victorian times, when the Upper Paleolithic became accepted for inclusion as part of the overall reckoning of prehistory, these cultural divisions provided convenient chronological datum pegs to which ideas and theories might be related.

The Upper Paleolithic in Britain is generally assumed to range from *c.* − 50—30,000 to *c.* − 12,000; the Mesolithic from *c.* − 12,000 to − 4000 and the Neolithic *c.* − 4000 to *c.* − 2000. Elsewhere the demarcation between the Mesolithic/Neolithic may go back several millenniums earlier.

However, with the advance of archaeology this simplistic picture of culture sequences could not be maintained. Subsequently the three-age system has been subdivided and elaborated into a complicated and interrelated chronology which obscures a sharp, in-focus panorama of European prehistory. Fortunately for the purpose of establishing a relative chronology we can still fall back on an unobscured, broad-outline picture of the Upper Paleolithic and Mesolithic cultures based on a sequence established in caves and rock shelters in

South-Western France (below).

Late Middle Paleolithic		Mousterian
Upper Paleolithic	−32,000 to −28,500	Chatelperronian (Lower Perigordian)
	−28,000 to −22,000	Aurignacian
	−22,000 to −18,000	Gravettian
	−18,000 to −15,000	Solutrian
	−15,000 to −8000	Magdalenian

An even simpler history of man is the two-frame picture of man first as a hunter and food gatherer, and then from c. − 10,000 man as a pastoralist and food-crop raiser. These two periods are sometimes referred to as the Paleolithic food-gathering stage and the Neolithic food-raising stage. The change-over from hunting and gathering to agriculture has considerable significance for astro-archaeological studies. It was the adoption of farming and crop raising that stimulated a requirement for accurate calendrical devices in order that man might know when to sow and harvest his crops to best advantage.

The question has often been raised whether the proto-hominids possessed the innate ability to make use of celestial bodies in orientation in a similar way to that observed in several animal species which have been studied.

Some species of birds are uncanny masters of celestial orientation, but this innate ability seems motivated by evolutionary factors dictated by breeding and seasonal food supply. Some birds make journeys of several thousand kilometers, some even from the subarctic regions to subantarctic regions, and back again. Pigeons have been shown to have an innate ability in both directional and destination (target) orientation, and they may choose either the stars of the night sky, the Sun or the lines of magnetic force of the Earth—depending on which mechanism is most convenient in a given situation.

Orientation in its biological sense is of course a necessary feature with all creatures. Among the hominids, however, there appears to be little evolutionary stimulus to develop abilities to navigate long distances as occurred with birds, fish and sea mammals, since hominoid migrations are more limited in geographical range. Modern man generally needs a sextant, almanac and compass to find his way, but man in the primitive does possess high abilities in direction finding (*see* note 1).

Studies of neoprimitive societies such as the Australian Aborigines, and in particular the Polynesians, have revealed how these peoples made use of the Sun, Moon and stars for practical purposes. The Polynesians, without writing, instruments or charts, evolved an elaborate pre-scientific system of navigation which was superior to that of the Europeans who first encountered them. However, this was in no way an instinctive orientation art, but one *learnt* by the process of trial and error and applied to transoceanic navigation since their ancestors first set out on their Pacific voyages at the beginning of the first millennium BC.

Captain Cook, no mean navigator himself, was astonished at their skill and wrote in his *Journal*: 'These people sail in those seas from Island to Island for several hundred Leagues, the Sun serving them for a compass by day and the Moon and Stars by night; all the stars of which they distinguished separately by name and they know in what part of the heavens they will appear in their horizons; they also know the time of their annual appearance and disappearing with more precision than will readily be believed by any European astronomers.'

It is well to bear in mind this kind of proved achievement for neoprimitive man and be alerted to the probabilities that European Neolithic societies (and even earlier Upper Paleolithic societies) likely made good use of the Sun, Moon and stars.

Whether *Homo sapiens* has retained a biological vestige of a lunar-tidal rhythm inherited from his distant fish ancestors is conjectural. The rotation of the Earth in relation to the Moon occurs once in 24 hrs 50 mins; the Moon revolves round the Earth providing variable light and tidal conditions in 29·5 days; while the Earth and Moon revolve round the Sun in about 365¼ days. Because of these fluxional influences, the evolution of man and animals has been disciplined by the diurnal and seasonal (short- and long-term) changes brought about, and biologically man was adapted to these rhythmic cosmic influences long before he was able to take the first steps to intellectualize them.

It seems more than coincidence that the female menstrual cycle, on average, follows the monthly interval of the lunar cycle. It is true, however, that this menstrual range is *now* extended either side of the interval (in extremes of 20 to 120 days), and the female cycle as such does not any longer follow the phases of the Moon, but this in no way invalidates its likely evolutionary time-structured origins.

Several species of marine creature depend on the tidal rhythm and variable nocturnal light for successful breeding. The females of the Atlantic fireworm (*Odontosyllis*) shed their eggs, and the males rush in to fertilize them in an 18-hour lunar-dictated, time-factored slot. This occurs once a month on the night before the Last Quarter of the Moon. The ever-observant Aristotle noted the swelling of the sea urchins' ovaries at time of Full Moon. Among land animals, hares, long associated with the Moon in mythology, have a sexual cycle closely regulated to the phases of the Moon. The work of Soviet biologists has shown that if the period of the New Moon (dark nights) coincides with the innate sexual cycles in hares, it may radically upset the sexual process and appreciably increase sterility.

That man, albeit psychotic man, retains some affinity with the periodic swing of the Moon is still reflected by the influx of patients to psychiatric hospitals at time of Full Moon. In the eighteenth and nineteenth centuries, medical discourses were sometimes written at great length about relationship of illness to lunar changes. A discourse by a certain Richard Mead 'Concerning the Action of the Sun and the Moon on Animal Bodies' was typical of the *genre* in which actual cases were described in vivid style: '. . . The Girl, who was lusty full Habit of Body, continued well for a few days, but was at Full Moon again seized with a most violent Fit, after which, the Disease kept its Periods constant and regular with the tides; She lay always speechless during the whole Time of Flood, and recovered upon the Ebb. . . .'

Although archaeologists and astronomers would agree in principle with Pope's dictum that the proper study of mankind involves man, in archaeology, the reconstruction of a society begins with artefacts. These are the basic materials, but with artefacts there is the inherent danger in reading into them evidence beyond what is actually shown or what was intended to be shown. Indeed, speculative interpretation of artefacts is frequently the cause of a sharp division of opinion between those seeking proto-scientific-cum-notational content and those who only see in the same artefact ritualistic or abstract symbolism or other more mundane, pragmatic socio-economic information.

The earliest artefacts that *might* conceivably record cyclic processes in nature—recorded by man—date back to the Upper Paleolithic, to the period when cave art blossomed in several locales including North-West Europe. Many scholars have looked closely at Upper Paleolithic art for mythological and seasonal representations. Two kinds of art have been widely recognized: representational and non-representational. Representational art is considered unambiguous and easily recognizable for what it is. In cave art, animals are well represented: bulls, mammoths, rhinoceroses, lions, horses, goats, deer, bears, whales, fish, snakes, and birds frequently occur. In addition there are flowers, trees and plants. Non-representational art poses more difficult problems of interpretation, particularly the mystical Pan-like anthropomorphic figures and the various so-called signs and 'decorative' symbols. In addition to the representative cave and wall art we also have what their nineteenth-century discoverers lumped together and called 'fertility' symbols, which are represented characteristically by the buxom Venus goddess figurines of the Upper Paleolithic. These are generally agreed to be the proto-type sky—earth-mother or nurse goddesses of later archaeological periods.

Animal depictions have been widely attributed to cults involving hunting magic and fertility, but plant depictions may also involve fertility. Species identification by morphological detail provides an interesting guessing game for specialists, but this activity does not generally lead to a more significant understanding of Upper Paleolithic man, except that when a species is included in a seasonal representation, it provides clues to the parts of the year significant in the calendar—particularly so when known migratory species are cited.

The study and interpretation of Upper Paleolithic art is important in its possible influence in astronomical and mythological 'art' of later periods—shown in the seals of Sumeria, and so-called boundary stones (*kudurra*) of Babylonia, and the polychrome mosaics and vases depicting legend and mythology in the Mycenaean and Minoan civilizations. The Çatal Hüyük, Cretan and Mithraic bulls and the Egyptian Cow-goddess Hathor most likely derive from their Upper

2 Representative prehistoric cave art. A leaping cow and horses from Lascaux, Dordogne, France.

Paleolithic proto-types represented in the magnificent cave paintings of Lascaux. These paintings, discovered in 1940, are among the best publicized, and rightly so, since they represent the supreme height of Upper Paleolithic art in the representational form of 'seasonal hunting magic'. These animal depictions in cave and wall paintings of the Upper Paleolithic, particularly the bulls and bisons, may also represent the proto-type celestial images that later blossomed in Near Eastern zodiacs. Perhaps even more significant are the reindeer antler bone bâtons.

The reindeer horn bâtons have always been puzzling artefacts and subject to much speculation. No one has ever quite decided whether their prime function was practical or ceremonial. Over the years many theories have been put forward about them. Among suggestions ideas run to handles of slings, maces, tent pegs, dress fasteners, check-pieces of horse bits, instruments for dressing skins, magic sceptres or staves for ceremonial or sorcery, and shaft or arrow straighteners. For a long time they have been known in archaeological literature as '*bâtons de commandement*'. It is probably significant that the perforation of the holes in the reindeer horn has generally been the last operation in the manufacture of the artefact, since it frequently mutilates some of the overall decoration pattern.

As a possible dress fastener they appear to be much too

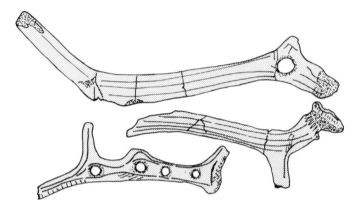

3 Batons de commandement (based on a photograph).

clumsy. If they were non-practical and ceremonial in purpose, a great many seem to be broken at one end. Indeed, the suggestion that they were employed as some kind of shaft or arrow straightening tool is more likely, for the perforated holes show distinct frictional wear. This idea is strengthened by comparison with analogous artefacts employed by modern Eskimoes to straighten arrow shafts.

One of the most interesting compositions engraved on a broken bâton is from Lorthet (Hautes-Pyrénées). This composition is made up of three deer, two of which are stags crossing a river in which several fish are leaping. The image has been interpreted as seasonal and probably intended to show the time of summer or autumnal salmon run and the time (in the summer) when stags leave the hinds. But the most intriguing part of the composition are the lozenge-shaped objects depicted above the back of one stag (Fig. 4).

It has been generally agreed that both are schematic representations; but what they are intended to represent is another matter. Opinion has ranged from the Sun and Moon—'the two eyes of the sky'—to various stellar-solar combinations and fertility symbols in the form of schematic representations of a

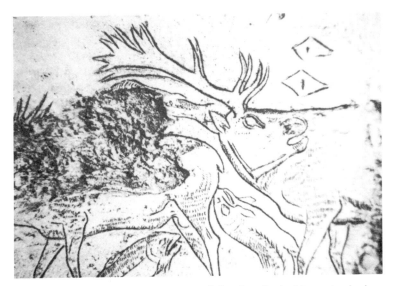

4 Antler bone from Lorthet, Hautes-Pyrénées, inscribed with two intriguing lozenge-shaped objects which may have astronomical significance.

vulva or the breasts of a mother goddess.

5 Prehistoric engraving from Fratel, Portugal, depicting two stars (or suns).

To an observational astronomer, symbolism of this kind could easily represent a configuration of two bright stars in close proximity (or two planets in conjunction). Such a stellar example is provided by the celestial Twins Castor and Pollux (Alpha and Beta Geminorum) possibly setting in the summer evening during the period in question. The choice of Castor and Pollux would not be without connections with fertility symbols in the ancient world, for twins have long been associated with this idea. On later Babylonian boundary stones celestial 'Twins' are frequently depicted, and in earlier times the twin stars were often considered 'the eyes of the night' as opposed to the Sun and the Moon 'the eyes of the day'. However, these ideas are no more than speculations; astronomically speaking they might also represent the flight of two brilliant meteors or fireballs; on a more mundane level they might perhaps be no more than a hunter-artist's representation of crude, flint-headed spears or arrows. Star asterisms, nevertheless, do seem to be depicted unambiguously at La Lileta in Spain—and again at Fratel in Portugal as a pair (Fig. 5). There is an unmistakable solar representation at Los Buitres containing symbolic images (human or plants?) within the solar disc, and at Pala Pinta de Carlao, two suns are set on a starry background.

The 'lozenges' also appear elsewhere at a later period; they appear significantly in association with two-eye 'oculi' and are typical of the decorative motifs at the Megalithic Newgrange chambered tomb in Ireland. Lozenge-shaped artefacts and decorative motifs are very common in Neolithic contexts, and they also turn up on Sumerian seals.

The so-called non-representational art of the Upper Paleolithic has attracted a good deal of attention for its possible astronomical/calendrical/notational content. The most publicized recent investigations into this question have been those by the American writer Alexander Marshack who has assembled what he considers positive evidence that pre-Neolithic man utilized a notation system to record the cycle of the Moon's phases. Marshack is no astro-archaeological scholar in the tradition of Epping, Strassmaier and Kugler, the trio of Jesuit priests, who by dints of brilliant scholarship cracked the astro-archaeological code of Babylonian cuneiform inscription, or like Neugebauer and Parker who continued this work in more contemporary times.

Marshack by training is a professional journalist who has worked and travelled widely in Asia and Europe. In turn he admits to having been a news writer, a book and drama reviewer, an art reporter, a photographer, a script writer, a producer and director of plays, as well as a popular science writer. Any one of these frank admissions is sufficient in itself to damn him in the eyes of many academics.

His working background echoes that of several others who in contemporary times have entered the domains of academic scholarship unabashed. In this particular context the name of Robert Ardrey, the American playright, is immediately brought to mind. His stylistically attractive books, aimed as personal investigations into man's origins and nature, have earned him a respectful and loyal international following.

Marshack became interested in ferreting out the problems of prehistoric science when engaged on a popular book about the path which had led man to his first landing on the Moon. In his later book *Roots of Civilization* (1972) he recounts his attempts to search out the origins of science and civilization. This proved to be much more difficult than he had first anticipated—he realized that there was 'something missing' from the archaeological record.

Marshack elaborates his arguments in an easy-flowing and sometimes vivid documentary style. He begins the story of his quest by relating how in April 1963 he was reading the June 1962 issue of the *Scientific American* which carried an article about a small scratched bone that had been found at Ishango—a site of the Mesolithic period—at the headwaters of the Nile. The article, by the Belgian, Jean de Heinzelin, described the bone and discussed what various interpretations might be put to the scratches. Similar scratched bones from the European Upper Paleolithic were well known, and the scratches had always been supposed to represent decorative patterns or, more imaginatively, some elementary numeration system such as hunting tally-marks, etc. The Ishango bone was dated $c. -6500$, some two or three thousand years before the first dynasty in Egypt and the appearance of the first known hieroglyphic writing there. In the article in question de Heinzelin believed the bone to be the handle of an implement used for engraving or tatooing. The most interesting feature, however, were groups of scratches, or notches, arranged in three distinct columns, which de Heinzelin at first was inclined to dismiss as simple decoration but later believed showed an arithmetical game devised by a prehistoric people who likely had a number system based on 10 as well as some knowledge of duplication and prime numbers.

With some dramatic Sherlock Holmsian colouring, Marshack relates that he looked at the photographs and drawings of the bone for perhaps an hour or so. Then he took a break for coffee. The dull, blackened bit of scratched bone puzzled him; there seemed something wrong with the accepted interpretation. Marshack was then deeply immersed in writing his popular book about the Moon. The Moon at this time was paramount in his thoughts. 'I decided to try a hunch,' he writes. Fifteen minutes later he claims to have 'cracked the code' of the bone scratches. He felt he was looking at a lunar notation—a system which could be read unambiguously to show the cycle of the Moon's phases and periods. . . .

Was this sudden inspiration a great breakthrough in scientific understanding with overtonal echoes of Newton's inspired discovery of gravity after watching that apocryphal falling apple—or of Kekule's sudden inspiration about the structure of the benzene molecule while dozing in front of the fireplace . . . ? We shall judge.

As a consequence of this seminal inspiration, Marshack travelled to Europe to search out more artefacts which had been gleaned from the Upper Paleolithic. His first stop was the Musée des Antiquités Nationales at Saint-Germain-en-Laye, near Paris, in order to browse through its twenty or so exhibition cabinets of engraved Upper Paleolithic materials—and double this number of objects locked away in various rooms and drawers.

Marshack, like some resurrected Schliemann, tells us in his finely tempered dramatic prose how he walked into the main exhibit room of the prehistoric period and experienced '. . . the sudden chill feeling of an intruder in an abandoned graveyard. There was a huge silence in the musty air of the high-ceilinged stone chamber . . .'.

During the course of his examination of various pieces from different archaeological horizons, he found several bones which he was persuaded showed similar lunar notations to the Ishango bone. The patterns were different, but they were not random as others had previously supposed. He was convinced that the marks inscribed had been made sequentially. When tested against a standard lunar notation model, they gave a reasonable fit.

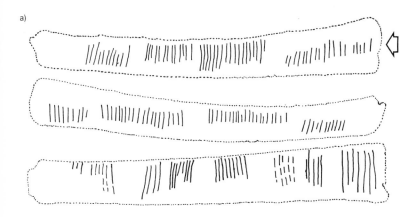

6 (a) Engraved marks on three faces of the Ishango bone-tool dated *c*. – 6500 (based on a photograph). (b) The engraved marks of the Ishango bone (top face) as interpreted by Alexander Marshack against his lunar model (simplified) showing possible sets and subsets of lunar-phasing notation (after A. Marshack).

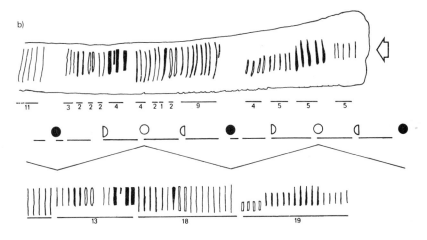

To facilitate the work of discovery and the counting of the minute scratches and grooves inscribed on many of the artefacts, Marshack had armed himself with a pocket microscope. He toiled daily among the bones, examining minutely the barely visible rows of dots and incisions, attempting to match each row to fit the lunar phase. Under the microscope several incised bone artefacts showed residual traces of red ochre lodged in the grooves. Marshack wondered whether this red oxide was added to each notational subgroup as it was inscribed—to act as a kind of printers' ink to ensure that the grooves or pits could be picked out against the stark-white of fresh bone. However, he was not wholly convinced about this idea, for he realized that ancient man also used red ochres to redden corpses, graves and his habitations. Ochre decoration is widely used by the Australian Aborigines for ceremonial purposes.

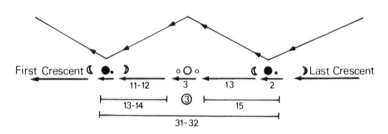

7 Standard lunar notation template used by Alexander Marshack showing the idealized periods in days of the observational divisions of the lunar month. In Marshack's standard (unequal) divisions he reckons the waxing period as 13 days; Full Moon 3 days; waning period 11—12 days; invisible (conjunction) period 1—2 days. In practice the count for one lunar month may work out as three periods of 15; 3; and 13—14 days respectively thus providing an anomalous lunar-month period of 31—32 days (as against a true period of 29½ days).

To appreciate and recognize the significance of the patterns of the Upper Paleolithic bone incisions, one must be keenly aware of the fundamental movements of the Moon in relation to time: The lunar month has nothing to do with the year, nor does it exactly fit into the year. The *sidereal month*—the time interval for the Moon to reach the same spot in the sky in relation to the star background—is 27 days 7 hrs 43 mins 11·42 secs; this period does *not* follow the phases of the Moon and therefore is of no consequence for the calendar. The *synodic month* is the interval between two New Moons and represents on average 29 days 12 hours 44 mins 2·98 secs; this is the *true* lunar month. Thus twelve lunar months, 12 × 29½, is about 355 days and falls short of the full year (expressed by the interval of time for the Earth to revolve in orbit round the Sun) by 10—11 days.

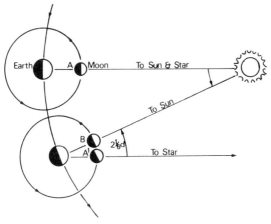

8 Drawing showing the *sidereal* and *synodic* periods of the Moon. Starting at conjunction with the Sun at New Moon (A), the Moon travels round the Sun in company with the Earth and makes one complete sidereal revolution (in relation to the stars) to A¹ (sidereal period) but must then travel an extra distance (to B) to arrive at conjunction (New Moon) about 2⅙ days later (synodic period).

Even ancient man recognized that it is impossible to combine the *months* with the *year* without adjusting one or the other. But in spite of this long-recognized incommensurability, the month became a conventional subdivision of the year. However, the 'month' is quite independent of the Moon, although as a reminder of its origin it keeps the name month (viz. *moonth* or 'moon time').

To ancient and primitive people the Moon afforded the only short fixed measure of the duration of time—apart from the very short measures of day and night. These people later tried to adjust the year by the Moon, and this could be done by adopting years of varying length of twelve and thirteen months respectively. But it was soon realized that for more accurate fixing, both of the seasons and of the months, the 'phases' of the stars were best employed, for these, being dependent on the Sun, keep pace with the natural year. It was also found possible to fix the solar year by the annual course of the Sun—especially by using the solstice positions.

Nevertheless, the use of the Moon must be the oldest form of time reckoning; its comparative rapid revolution provides an easily remembered time-unit and a natural step between the 'short' day and the 'long' year.

But the problem of using the Moon as a timekeeper is visually keeping track of it. The first difficulty is to catch sight of the new crescent in the evening sky after the Sun has set. The first opportunity when this can occur is influenced by several variable factors. First there are the obvious meteorological factors, such as cloud and fog; then there is an effect caused by the observer's terrestrial latitude, for the angle of the ecliptic (the apparent path of the Sun) to the horizon varies according to the season— lowest in winter and highest in summer. In addition there is the important factor involving the celestial latitude (declination) of the Moon. If, for example, the ecliptic is almost vertical to the horizon—as occurs at the spring (vernal) equinox, the effect of celestial latitude is negligible. However, at the time of the autumnal (fall) equinox this latitude effect exerts its greatest influence by bringing the Moon nearer to the horizon, or farther away from the horizon (Fig. 9).

To an observer—disregarding meteorological effects—no two consecutive reappearances of the new crescent Moon, after the Moon's invisibility in conjuction with the Sun, are ever separated by more than 30 days or by less than 29 days. Owing to the 29½-day odd-number period, an observer making a mark would have found that he had a different number for each lunation. In addition the Moon is 'lost' in the Sun for one, two or three days each lunation (conjunction); thus an observer keeping tally after seeing the first slender crescent (First Quarter) in the west after sunset might inscribe 27 or 28 marks until the slender crescent (Last Quarter) is lost in the east morning sky. But all things being equal the next notation period would give him a count of 29 or 30 marks. But taking into account realistic weather conditions, consecutive—actual observation—tallies might be highly variable. If the observer does not see the Moon after conjunction and continues a day notation past the last crescent towards the next first, the number of tallies in the cycle *might* sometimes be as high as 33.

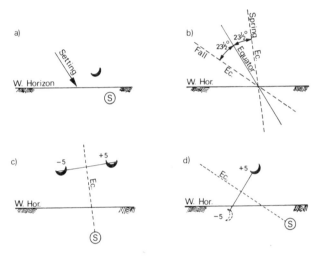

9 Sighting configurations for a new crescent Moon.
  (a) New crescent Moon in relation to the western horizon.
  (b) Varying angle of ecliptic (Ec) according to the season.
  (c) Configuration of the ecliptic in spring, high angle to the western horizon.
  (d) Configuration of the ecliptic in autumn (fall), low angle to the western horizon.

To understand Marshack's lunar notations one also has to think about periods of Full Moon measured in days—usually reckoned as three. It is the inequalities of the notation periods brought about by the difficulties of practical observation which allow Marshack's ideas some flexibility. If the Moon's phase periods could be noted exactly, it would be easier to draw firmer conclusions about the so-called notation periods he claims to have found on many artefacts. As it stands, the investigation of such interpretations involves playing an arbitrary numbers' game—a not too infrequent exercise in many facets of astro-archaeology as the reader will note later. Over a period of two lunations, or fifty-nine days, the inequalities can be somewhat ironed out. Marshack has demonstrated that some of the bone artefacts he cites show sequences running into many months by counts separated by gaps, angle marks and other devices. To help him solve these arithmetical sequences Marshack constructed for himself a standard lunar sequence model to which he could then apply his inscription finds as a kind of controlling number template (Fig. 7).

At this point one might mention several instances of more modern usage of lunar calendar sticks. These had been known about long before Marshack began his investigations into the Upper Paleolithic material. Marshack himself has looked closely at these in relation to his own ideas, particularly contemporary lunar calendar sticks from the Nicobar Islands. These are notched sticks which take the form of white wood shaped to appear like a knife or scimitar with notches on the edge and on the flat. The months are recorded by cheveron marks; when all the space is used up, further months are engraved across earlier ones, resulting in a cross-hatched pattern (Fig. 10). Inscribed marks on these particular sticks clearly denote the days of the waxing and waning Moon.

10 Part of a lunar calendar stick from the Nicobar Islands (based on a photograph).

The Pawnee and Biloxi Indians of North America had analogous systems and utilized notches cut in a stick for computing nights or even months or years. A similar system is used in the Balak calendar, which has 12, sometimes 13, × 30 squares. As a way of chronological control it is used with a buffalo rib with 12 × 30 holes (four times repeated). Every day the soothsayer calendar-keeper draws a string through one hole. In New Guinea a system was once used where the months were counted by means of notches cut in trees. Not far removed from rigid calendar sticks is the use of knotted cords for counting days; this method is used by primitive cultures such as the Negritos of Zambala, the Solomon Islanders, and in Nauru west of the Gilbert Islands. The Peruvians also utilized this idea with their quipus.

Besides being used as part of lunar and calendric notations, sticks have been used in other guises. The Australian Aborigine uses message sticks which convey various kinds of information, sometimes citing numbers of Moons. In North-West Australia, Aboriginal artefacts of wood, churungas, may sometimes contain schematic maps of a region. At first glance these inscribed patterns appear to be expressions of abstract native design, yet further—more critical—examination has shown that they may very well map out the principal rivers of a region and their confluences. In North-West and Central Australia wooden churungas also depict astronomical objects such as the flights of meteors, fireballs and comets. Somewhat different again are the contemporary Aboriginal bark paintings which depict constellations and other astronomical subjects and their associated mythology.

In the context of these latter ideas it can be seen that Marshack's ideas about Upper Paleolithic lunar notations are not unreasonable assumptions. Of course, resort to the comparative method—present to past—is no proof that an idea is correct; but these cited examples show that meaningful inscriptions by non-literate primitive peoples are not unique to a particular locale. Marshack's claims, however, have attracted strong criticism from several quarters, in particular from archaeologists and anthropologists (rather than astronomers), who have specialized in the field of Upper Paleolithic non-representational art and therefore feel qualified to offer constructive criticism. Some have disputed the whole idea that the scratch marks are notational. But in his study of the Blanchard plaque of the Aurignacian period $c. -27,000$ (Fig. 11) Marshack claimed that the various specialists with whom he discussed the evidence had, almost without exception, agreed that the sequence was notational. These specialist opinions covered disciplines such as anthropology, ethnology, linguistics, semantics, cognitive psychology, and brain neurology—as well as archaeology.

One of Marshack's ideas which has been criticized is his claim that scribed marks on bones were made consecutively by the same hand and at one time. Also criticized is his idea that adjacent groups of marks were made with different tools and were intended to represent separate subjects and separate

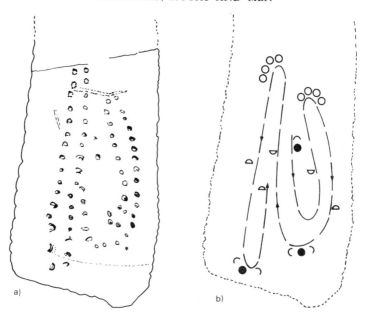

11 (a) The engraved bone plaque from the rock shelter of Blanchard, Dordogne (based on a photograph). (b) Schematic representation of a 2¼ lunar month notation traced out on the Blanchard bone according to the ideas of Alexander Marshack.

properties. Marshack believes that such groups were purposely made distinctly separate. Another point strongly criticized has been the so-called sequential microscopic marks—or 'invisible scratches' as one reviewer called them—which were only visible to Marshack under magnification. His answer to this latter criticism was that because the bones were now discoloured and their surfaces partially deteriorated, marks which were once plainly visible were not now seen without optical aid. However, one of the principal arguments against Marshack's interpretations is the question of where he decides a particular sequence of marks begins, and how to count the marks. Several critics of his ideas maintain that almost any number can stand for a lunar phase of some kind, since the reading of marks can start anywhere, move in any direction, and allow quite arbitrary decisions to break the phase-markings which are to be recognized.

Marshack emphasized firmly that the notations he claimed to

have found on Upper Paleolithic objects need not necessarily be arithmetic abstractions, but were more likely a record of actual observational data of the Moon's phases. He presumed that night to night observations were memorized—yet this seems unlikely—or noted in some form which has not survived (perhaps wooden 'diaries'), and that the final calendric notation or related groups of marks was executed only when a batch of observations had been completed.

The least convincing artefacts showing so-called sequential pattern markings are Upper Paleolithic bone tubes used by prehistoric cave artists for containing paint like those found in the Grotte des Cottes (Vannes) which still contain traces of red ochre, and thus *their* use is unambiguous.

Marshack's lunar-notation months vary from 27 to 33 days; the first and last quarters vary from 5 to 8 days and periods of Full Moon and New Moon from 1 to 4 days—plus an allowance of ±1 day for errors in observation. From these very flexible parameters the lunar model used by Marshack can be made significant for any number or sequence of numbers between 1 and 16 and between 26 and 34. The difficulty in accepting Marshack's ideas is that for each example he has studied, each seems to require assumptions to be made about 'cloud-outs' or it requires other adjustments to account for inconsistencies. With good reason critics have claimed that his ideas are too glib and allow too much manoeuvring or arbitrary jiggling of numbers to suit circumstances.

However, in spite of the hostile reception Marshack's ideas received from some archaeologists and anthropologists, they do provide an excellent pioneer study in Upper Paleolithic astro-archaeology. But whether Marshack has indeed made a significant discovery and a breakthrough in finding a scientific-based Upper Paleolithic culture, as he indirectly claims to have done, cannot yet be finally assessed. His theories need to be bolstered with more supporting evidence; his work needs repeating and extending by other astro-archaeologists—perhaps by the so-called ethno-astronomers—with specialist knowledge of Upper Paleolithic art. Perhaps the very piece of unambiguous evidence needed to clinch his theory is still languishing unrecognized in some museum store-room (*see* note 2).

There seems little doubt that Upper Paleolithic man had a fairly sophisticated knowledge of the 29—30 day movements of the Moon, coupled with a profound knowledge of the seasons. However, the question which arises is why he decided to inscribe it somewhat ambiguously on bone implements. Admittedly bone is more durable than wood. One can accept a moon-count being inscribed on durable bone implements, but a baton made of wood would provide a more practical medium for daily use in recording a count mark. If some of the bone implements Marshack cites were intended as more definitive forecast standards, they are not particularly accurate as day-count gauges.

Marshack divides Upper Paleolithic art into two main categories. The one including his so-called lunar counts and seasonal elements he refers to as 'time-factored' art—a description he uses frequently in his writings. Likewise Upper Paleolithic art which is considered to contain elements relating to myths and tales is referred to as 'storied'.

Marshack's investigations were focused primarily towards the non-representational art of the Upper Paleolithic, but he has also directed his attention to representational cave and wall art. Cave and wall art interpretation is, of course, a well established discipline in its own right.

Among the artefacts considered by many to be fertility symbols are the now famous Upper Paleolithic Venus figurines—'mother goddesses' or 'nurses'—which have attracted much attention and given rise to an extensive literature. Archaeologically they are known from the earliest horizons of the Aurignacian and extend to the end of the Magdalenian. Venus figurines have been found in Britain, France, Italy, Spain, Austria, Germany, Czechoslovakia, the Ukraine, and as far eastwards as Lake Baikal.

Venuses are found in association with non-representational bone artefacts (including those described by Marshack as notational). In appearance most are plump little creatures with exaggerated female characteristics: large breasts, thighs and buttocks. Many are carved from mammoth tusks, but one of the best known is made of limestone and known generally as the Venus of Willendorf, named after the locale where it was discovered in 1908, by a labourer engaged in road repairs. No more than 100mm (4 inches) high, it portrays a female with enormous breasts and thighs, tiny arms and a strange, featureless face.

Many of the known Venuses are so grotesquely distorted in proportions that it is believed they are intended not as lifelike sculptures but as objects used in some cult of fertility, for they exaggerate the parts of the female form relevant to child-birth and seem to regard the rest of the female figure as irrelevant. In several instances Venuses are baton-type figurines consisting of no more than a pair of breasts, and the figure is straight-formed and marked in groups and sets.

Human and animal birth *must* have been one of the great mysteries of Upper Paleolithic man. The Venus female images might be expected to reflect the biological miracle of birth. Neither can it have escaped notice that the lunar and menstrual cycle of women had a similar time span. It is not unreasonable to expect to read symbolic meanings of birth and rebirth in the Venus figurines and seminal connections with lunar and solar seasonal rites which were gradually elaborated and later became very important in the Neolithic cultus.

12 The Venus of Willendorf.

13 A faceless Venus figurine from Dolní Věstonice (Moravia), probably of Gravettian age.

According to Marshack the engraved Middle Magdalenian bâton from Le Placard (Charente) is inscribed with a lunar notation count which may probably refer to a menstrual cycle day-count (Fig. 14). In almost similar vein to the Venus

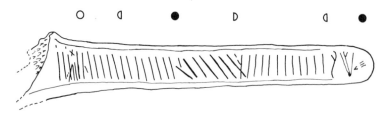

14 Schematic representation of engraved marks on the main face of the Le Placard (Charente) bâton against a (simplified) lunar phasing (after A. Marshack). It has been suggested that the inscribed 'lunar sets' may sometimes also refer to menstrual or pregnancy records or periods involved with initiation ceremonies.

figurines is the equally well known bas-relief from Laussel depicting a naked, faceless female holding in her right hand a bison horn inscribed with thirteen lines (Fig. 15). This sculptured Venus, figured out of a block of limestone, was originally painted red. The incisions claimed as significant used to be called *marques de chasse* and believed to be records of the number of animals killed in a hunt. From an astro-archaeological point of view this relief may be interpreted several ways. Since the number thirteen is correct for a lunar year, it *may* indeed be a lunar calendar depiction; it might also be half a lunation period—viz. from New Moon to Full Moon or Full Moon to New Moon. But it is still very conjectural whether the horn is indeed intended to represent the lunar crescent or simply something more mundane.

This numbers game is only too easily played in astro-archaeology. Numbers have provided a kind of magic to man since the earliest times, and magic numbers have been with us since the earliest writing inscribed on Sumerian clay tablets. Soviet scholars, in particular (with the help of computers), seem prone to playing numbers games in attempts to crack the language structures of the ancient world. The Soviet scholar Boris Frolov has played a numbers game in an article entitled

15 Bas-relief from Laussel. This faceless Venus holds a bison horn inscribed with thirteen lines and these may have astronomical significance.

'Stone Age Astronomers' in which he asserted that the number seven is what he calls a 'preferred' number which can be traced back to earliest times. This thesis, however, is no new idea, and the number seven theme has been explored by many writers and scholars—particularly since several prominent groups of stars contain seven significant members, e.g. The Plough (Ursa Major), Orion, and the Pleiades. To the ancients, the five planets plus the Sun and the Moon provided the most highly significant cosmic 'seven' number of all, and this number seven is thematic in Sumerian astro-mythology c. – 3000. To the later Babylonians, the Ziggurat of Nabu, at Barsipki, was known as the 'House of the Seven Bonds of Heaven and Earth' and was believed to have been painted in seven different colours.

To the Sumerians and Babylonians, the Sun, Moon, planets and stars all represented sky gods and goddesses. In Sumerian script the picture of a star represents *an*, 'heaven', and the same sign signifies *dinger*, 'god'. Similar ideas were common also to Egypt, Anatolia, the Indus Valley, Shang China, Middle America and Peru. But long before these civilizations developed, Upper Paleolithic man had evolved a sky-father cultus overlapping with the earth-mother cultus. The Venus figurines, bâton decoration, and cave and wall art clearly symbolized the seasonal-cum-fertility concept of the earth mother. The sky-father ideas might be represented separately by the Sun, Moon, planets or stars—or by all of them together. Solar symbols were often anthropomorphic representations. These figures have disproportionally large hands, and the fingers are spread out ray-like. The ring and cup petroglyphs and circle and spiral motifs which characterize European Megalithic art also likely symbolize the sun god or other sky gods.

The sound of the sky father—the extraterrestrial high god— was well known to the Australian Aborigines and American Indians through their bull-roarers and churungas. The bull-roarer as a mystic device was swung round the head at the end of a string when was heard a weird booming noise— interpreted as a manifestation of the high god himself. Aboriginal bull-roarers are made of wood, bone or stone, and remarkably similar-shaped objects in bone and stone have been found at several Upper Paleolithic sites such as the Pin Hole Cave in Derbyshire, England, in association with Mousterian-type implements, and at Laugerie-Basse and Laugerie-Haute near Les Eyzies in the Dordogne.

The association of bull-roarers with the high god, or gods, is a significant one and a sure example of primitive peoples attempting to make sense of natural phenomena. When a meteorite falls from the sky, practically identical noises are sometimes heard by eye-witnesses. This noise phenomenon is explained by the retardation of the meteorite's high cosmic velocity when it hits and then screams through the Earth's atmosphere. A sonic boom also occurs similar to that heard when a high-speed aircraft breaks the sound barrier. In addition to the sonic boom the flight of a meteorite gives rise to a spectrum of sound varying from claps of stage-thunder, roaring express trains, and swarming bees to quiet eerie swishing noises (known as electrophonic noises) which have been likened to the sound of wind playing through telegraph wires. Several of these latter noise descriptions can be reproduced by the swing of a bull-roarer.

There can be little doubt that in ancient times the event of a meteorite fall—with all the accompanying and frightening displays of brilliant light and uncanny sounds—made a deep impression (as it still does today) on those witness to it. The recovered meteoric stone, or a much rarer meteoric iron, carrying the sound of the high god, would certainly be treated as a fetish object and much revered. It is only a short step to attach a string to such an object, or later a similar-looking substitute object, to recreate the same noise—the signature of the cosmic god—when whirled about the head.

Within recorded historical times there is a solid corpus of evidence to support the idea of holy and universal reverence held for meteorites. At Epheus, the great mother goddess of Asia Minor was symbolized by a stony meteorite, and it was supposedly St Paul who related that this was a star which fell down in the sky from Jupiter. A black meteorite stone that fell in the seventh century is still preserved in Mecca, built into the south-eastern corner of the Kaaba, the Great Mosque. This stone, framed in silver, has remained the principal object of veneration since it was believed to have been received from the angel Gabriel.

During the eighteenth century a stony meteorite that fell in Japan was made an annual offering in a temple of Ogi, while a stone that fell in India during the nineteenth century was cloaked in fresh flowers each day and annointed with ghee, and the site of its fall was preserved as a shrine.

Another well-known example is the toad-shaped meteorite noted by Cortes which fell on the Pyramid of Cholula and was treated as a sign by the Aztecs that the cosmic gods were angry because the pyramid had been built.

Even today meteorites are still widely confused with thunderbolts, and it was natural that in the ancient world the two were considered facets of the same phenomenon. The Egyptian hieroglyph for thunderbolt *and* meteorite, which significantly contains a star, shows this unequivocally. In this way the European sky gods Zeus, Thor and Dyaus Pitar were associated with meteorites and thunder.

It was the rarer iron-nickel meteorites that were truly significant objects, for many ancient and modern races have converted them into tools and weapons. To many races they were the only readily available source of metal. Earlier, stony meteorites, because of their sometimes unique pear-shaped form (caused by their flight through the atmosphere), were utilized as axe-heads which gave rise to them being known as 'thunder-stones'. As flints were used for the same purpose, the same name, confusingly, was applied to them (as with fossils also). The early axe cultus and double-axe cultus are certainly associated with meteorites. The axe symbol frequently appears on painted rocks and walls, and in Neolithic Western Europe it was undoubtedly a symbol of the sky god—representing the 'thunderbolt' hurled by the sky god.

In China two puzzling ancient iron axes dated *c.* – 1000—almost half a millennium before iron working began in China—were finally identified as meteoric nickel-iron. In ancient Mexico, Indian ploughshares were made of meteoric iron, and the Greenland Eskimoes had a long tradition of using meteoric iron for harpoons.

In ancient Egypt it is likely that the knife used in the rite of opening the mouth of the deadman was meteoric—for sky iron was magical. The hieroglyph for the name of this knife again shows a star. In Assyrian, meteorites were referred to directly as 'the metal of heaven'. The Pyramid Texts discuss unequivocally the deadman himself becoming cosmic iron and sent back among the stars. There is also the Egyptian cosmic link with iron associating it with the Children of Horus who formed the four corner stars (Alpha, Beta, Gamma and Delta) of the Ox's Foreleg (Ursa Major) Figs. 17 and 37. The Pyramid Texts also relate that the Double Doors of heaven, through which the deadman passes, are of iron.

Thus, through the spectrum of time we can see how man has been closely associated with ideas of the cosmos and heaven. It began from the time he fashioned his first bull-roarer—in a distant period long before he invented writing and committed his first cosmic and creation myths to clay tablet, papyrus, stone or oracle bone.

The ancient Egyptian texts provide clear examples of what Neolithic man felt about the gods and the cosmos. Osiris was a supreme god. His son Re, the sun god, had power over darkness—equated with the powers of life and death. Osiris himself was sometimes considered to live on in the annual sprouting of the grain or in the Nile floodwaters which personified fertility of the land; he also was the Moon or the constellation of Orion, and his sign is depicted with Orion.

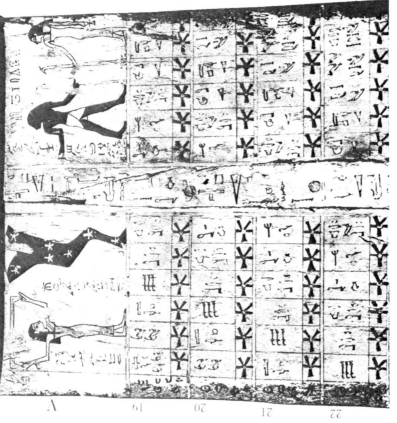

17 Diagonal clock asterisms (the Decans) found on an Egyptian coffin c. – 2100. Depicted (top, left to right) are sky goddess Nut, the Bull's Foreleg (Ursa Major), Orion, and Sothis (Sirius).

16 Sky goddess Nut, a direct descendant of the mother goddesses of the Upper Paleolithic.

Osiris was also associated with the nether world. It was the deadman's greatest wish that he be absorbed into the great rhythm of the Universe—either as an eternal passenger aboard the Sun boat Re; or among the circumpolar stars; or to seek rebirth with the Moon in his boat which like that of Re sailed over the sky-back of Nut, the great sky goddess (Fig. 16).

The nether world was usually an unseen place, but it was also sometimes referred to as the 'Field of Rushes'—a place where Re fought his nightly battle against darkness. The Pyramid Texts tell that the Field of Rushes was synonymous with the Cosmic Heavens and a place of beautiful roads where the dead king accompanies Orion who is guided by Sirius, the Dog Star (Fig. 17). A coffin text relates:

> *I pass through Heaven, I walk upon Nut*
> *My mansion is the Field of Rushes*
> *My riches are in the Field of Offering*

There is much cosmic poetry in Egyptian texts which was echoed again by the Egyptian astronomer Ptolemy *c.* +150 when he wrote: 'I know that I am mortal and the creature of a day, but when I search out the many rolling circles of stars, my feet touch the Earth no longer, but with Zeus himself I take my fill of ambrosia, the food of the gods.'

It is in the Egyptian texts where we can glean insights into how ancient man was totally and emotionally involved with Nature's processes. The course of the Sun, the rising and setting of the stars, and the swing of the Moon became firmly ingrained in him as part of a farmer's theology and unshakable creed.

CHAPTER II

Stonehenge:
Early Scribes and Speculations

Among the ancient monuments of Britain, certainly none is more famous than Stonehenge, and as a premier tourist attraction it ranks second only in popularity to the Tower of London. As an ancient monument Stonehenge was never discovered in the sense that the ruins of Babylon were discovered. Its stones—the drab grey sarsens*—forming the now ruined structure, have existed as an integral part of the Wessex landscape for thousands of years and go back in time far beyond the earliest which folk memory can recall.

Seen from any distance the remaining stones appear dwarfed into insignificance and almost lost in the open, featureless skyline of Salisbury Plain. Even the official guidebooks warn that Stonehenge is one of those historic monuments possessed with the disadvantages of a reputation, and the first impression for a visitor is always one of disappointment.

The Plain itself, which someone once nicknamed the cemetery of ancient Britain, is anything but level and rolls on like a great undulating ocean of green—its numinous quality evocative of all things past. When John Evelyn, the diarist, travelled across the Plain in 1654, he considered its 'evenness, extent, verdure, and innumerable flocks, to be one of the most delightful prospects in nature', while Samuel Pepys, the other diarist, encountered 'great hills, even to fright us'. Indeed, to different people the Plain suggests different things. To travellers with literary fancies its often broody atmosphere suggests the novels and poems of Thomas Hardy. The Plain also provided the backcloth to the nature-poetry of Wordsworth

---

* The name sarsen, according to one account, is a corruption of Saracen, 'foreigner'. Another version opts for the Anglo-Saxon *sar* 'troublesome' and *stan* 'a stone'.

who as a disturbed young man at three-and-twenty wandered its length and wrote in his *Prelude*:

> To have before me on the dreary Plain
> Lines, circles, mounts a mystery of shapes . . .

To the musical, it echoes and underlines the very Englishness of Vaughan Williams' symphonies, and to ex-servicemen of many nations, its now deserted airstrips and camps nostalgically recall part of lost youth.

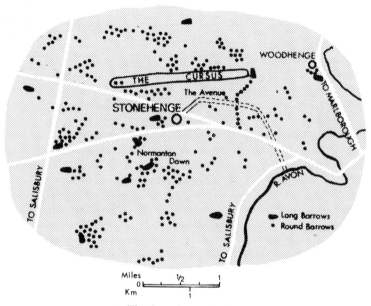

18 The Stonehenge Region.

Not until the visitor to the monument is standing almost within the shadow of the stones can he appreciate the massive unique quality of the man-made arrangements. It is only then he is likely to pause—to speculate and conjecture the whys and wherefores that led ancient man to conceive and then erect the greatest architectural work of prehistoric Europe.

Nowadays, Stonehenge to the casual uncritical eye presents a spectacle of large stones in considerable disarray. Even in the early eighteenth century it was so when William Stukeley, the antiquarian, neatly described it as in 'rude havock'. Nevertheless, even from its ruined chaotic state it has been

19 Stonehenge seen from the north-east.

possible—through excavation—to reconstruct its basic architecture and see it the way its ancient constructors knew it at its various building phases.

It is the outer circle of grey stones which first catches the eye (Fig. 19). This circle once consisted of thirty upright sarsens, each one worked to a rectangular section. On each pair of stones rested a matching horizontal lintel block of which now only five survive in their original positions. These lintels probably formed a continuous architrave—all shaped to fit part of the circle curve and all gripped and held in place by a double jointing consisting of a mortise and tenon and a tenon and groove. These skilfully executed joints show that the Megalithic artisans who laboured at Stonehenge were well versed in traditional carpentry techniques which the master designer of the monument had no hesitation in applying to the less-familiar stone-fixing problem.

The outer sarsen circle has a diameter of 29·25m (97·5 feet) measured across the inner 'polished' faces of the sarsens (the outer faces were apparently left rough). Each of the upright sarsens has an average weight of 26 tons and an average height of 4m (13 feet); the longest have a total measure of 5·4m (18 feet)

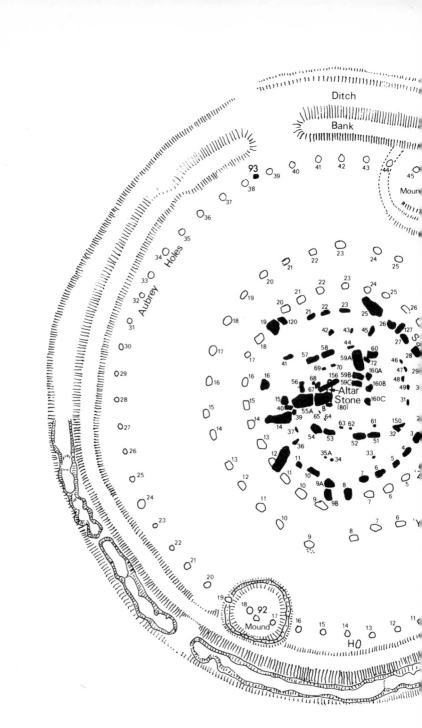

Ditch

Bank

Aubrey Holes

Mound

93

Altar
Stone
(80)

92
Mound

H O

42

20 Descriptive Plan of Stonehenge.

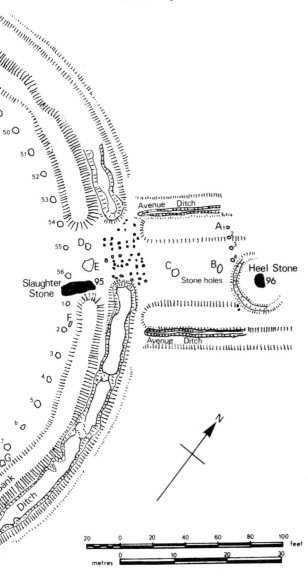

of which about 1·2 to 1·5m (4 to 5 feet) is buried. The sarsen stones that form the circle are frequently referred to as 'Grey Wethers'—a local Wiltshire name for the blocks of tertiary sandstone which lie scattered on the Downs—alluding to their suggestive appearance to flocks of grazing sheep (*see* note 3). These blocks of sandstone are still to be found on the surface to the north of Stonehenge, and buried remnants stretch far east-wards and form part of the Reading Beds of the London Basin (Fig. 101).

Within the outer sarsen circle stood a circle of bluestones 22·8m (76 feet) in diameter. Opinions expressed about the number of stones intended to form the circle range from fifty-nine to sixty-one. Only nine stones remain in an upright position, and many are missing. These bluestones are foreign to the Wessex landscape.

Farther towards the centre of the monument stood five massive sarsen trilithons ranging from 6 to 7·5m (20 to 25 feet) in height above ground level and arranged in the form of a horseshoe with its open side orientated north-east. Each

21 Detail of the sarsen ring and interior stones existing at Stonehenge *c*. 1975. Centre of sarsen circle (Sc); centre of Aubrey circle (Ac).

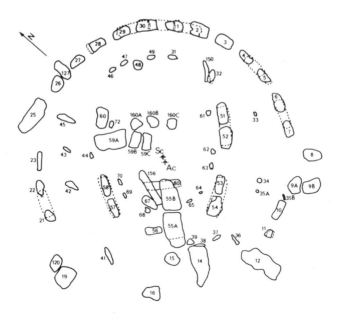

22 General view of Stonehenge looking north-east. Trilithon sarsens 52—51 (left); outer sarsens 7—6 (right); bluestone stump 34 (left foreground); bluestone 33 (in shadow, centre).

trilithon—as the name implies—consisted of three stones, two forming the uprights and the third being horizontal, laid lintel-fashion across the top and fixed by a mortise and tenon joint similar to the outer sarsen ring. Between each trilithon upright the width of opening is about 30 to 33cm (12 to 13 inches), but the opening of the central trilithon (55—56) may have been slightly wider. The central trilithon collapsed before 1574; the fourth trilithon (57—58, now repaired) fell on 3 January 1797, probably as a result of the rapid thaw of frozen ground. The partly ruined state of the fifth trilithon (59—60) occurred before 1574.

Within the area confined by the great trilithon horseshoe and close up against it, stands the remains of an inner, lesser horseshoe of foreign bluestones. This horseshoe was once believed arranged as nineteen slender stones to stand in height between 1·8 to 2·4m (6 to 8 feet). Only twelve of the stones now remain on site.

The foreign bluestones have long provided one of the many Stonehenge mysteries. How they arrived there—and from where—has given rise to many theories. However, in 1923, by a remarkable piece of detective scholarship, H. H. Thomas finally traced their *in situ* home to the Prescelly Mountains in South Wales (Fig. 45).

Within the horseshoes, close to the geometric centre, lies the so-called recumbent Altar Stone, so named by Inigo Jones (below). This 6-ton stone is also a foreigner to Stonehenge, but although it too is a native Pembrokeshire stone, it differs from the volcanic Prescelly bluestones being formed of micaceous sandstone—probably derived from the standstone beds near Milford Haven. Disturbances round the Altar Stone provide mute evidence of the numerous activities of a long history of treasure hunters—all doubtlessly seeking the supposed gold horde of a long-dead British chieftain once believed interred near the centre of Stonehenge.

Within the boundary of the monument defined by a large surrounding earthen rampart and outer ditch (vallum) are four highly significant features—the four Stations—which have considerable bearing on the astronomical theories connected with Stonehenge. Only one of the four Stations (93) still retains a stump of stone defining its exact position; the exact position of stone 94 is uncertain; stone 91 has fallen, and 92 is known only by its stonehole. Two of the Stations (92 and 94) are located on mounds (often alluded to as 'tumuli' or barrows in the older literature) and two (91 and 93) are at ground level.

Other significant features of the monument are three circles of holes: the fifty-six Aubrey holes lying just inside the surrounding earth rampart, some of which are visible at ground level; and the Y and Z holes radiating spoke-like from the larger sarsen circle, but not easily recognizable at ground level.

Towards the north-east the earth rampart is bridged to form the feature known as the Causeway Entrance. Across it, straddling the first and last holes of the Aubrey circle, lies a large recumbent sarsen, measuring lengthwise 6·3m (21 feet). Although this was known as the Slaughter Stone by the earlier antiquarians, at present there is no evidence to justify such an evocative name.

Outside the large sarsen circle and bank-and-ditch feature sits the most important and conspicuous of the single stones: the

23 Sketch of the central area at Stonehenge looking from the west *c.* 1958 before the re-erection of the trilithon stones 57—58.

24 Station Stone 93, Stonehenge. This is the only Station whose exact position is known.

Heel Stone, or the Friar's Heel. It consists of a leaning monolith of unworked stone now standing 4·8m (16 feet) high in a position 76·8m (256 feet) from the so-called geometric centre of Stonehenge. It is very near the pinnacle of the Heel Stone, as viewed from the centre of the monument, that the Sun appears to rise at the time of the summer solstice on or about 21 June. The alternative name 'Friar's Heel' is associated with an ancient Stonehenge legend involving the devil and a friar. The story relates the outcome of an affray between them which resulted in the huge stone hitting the friar. The stone struck the friar on his upright heel just at the moment when the Sun rose, and so the devil had to flee. The visitor today cannot find this idention on the Heel Stone, thus spoiling a colourful legend. However, R. J. C. Atkinson believed it to be located on stone 14. An earlier name for the Heel Stone is 'Hele' stone, which is supposed to take its origin from the Anglo-Saxon verb *helan* 'to conceal'. The name was allegedly applied to the stone because it concealed the Sun at its rising on the day of the summer solstice.

Other notable features of Stonehenge are the Avenue and Causeway. The Avenue, an earthwork extending approximately north-eastwards for a distance of over 120m (400 feet), was first noticed by William Stukeley in 1723, and he named it after a similar avenue of standing stones at Avebury near by. However, unlike Avebury there are *no* standing stones within the Avenue at Stonehenge, and because of this it has been suggested that 'Processional Way' might be a more apt name.

The Causeway feature leads from the earth rampart to the start of the Avenue and contains the remains of many postholes whose presence in this part of the monument has considerable bearing on the astronomical theories of Stonehenge. Scattered round the monument are several other significant stone and postholes whose alignments are also important in the astronomical theories.

All the above features were approximately those of the final development of Stonehenge. How the monument appeared in its different construction phases is outlined later in relation to modern interpretations and theories.

Ignoring obscure and doubtful classical references, Stonehenge did not generally invite comment until Henry of Huntingdon in the twelfth century referred to it in his *Historia Anglorum* as one

25 The Slaughter Stone, Stonehenge.

26 Looking north-east towards the Heel Stone from the centre of the Stonehenge circles.

27 The Heel Stone, Stonehenge. A side view of this stone shows it now tilted, whereas originally it was likely intended to sit in a true vertical position.

of the four wonders of England (the other wonders were apparently natural features). Geoffrey of Monmouth also referred to it in the twelfth century in his *History of the Kings of Britain*. It is believed that Geoffrey was a Welsh monk. His apocryphal history was written in the vein of an historical novel—part fact but mostly fiction. It is Geoffrey's book which has provided the definitive source for all Arthurian legends. To Stonehenge, however, he attached the colourful story of Hengist and Horsus who led a Saxon invasion of England in the fifth century. But this story also involves the legendary Merlin who, after 460 British nobles had been slain and then avenged by Aurelius Ambrosius, had been retained to give advice about erecting a monument to them.

Merlin told Ambrosius of the Dance of the Giants in Ireland where lay a collection of stones possessing unique healing qualities against many ailments. It was supposed that the Giants of old had taken these from Africa and laid them to rest in Ireland. In Merlin's opinion no other stones suited the intended purpose better, and Aurelius despatched his brother Uther Pendragon to Ireland with an army to capture them. This mission was successful. The stones were moved to the coast—then aboard ship to England—and finally erected at Stonehenge.

In 1624 a certain Edmund Bolton suggested that Stonehenge was the tomb of Boadicea, the colourful British pagan queen who led a bloody revolt against the Romans in the first century. Four years earlier King James I, himself very curious about the monument, instructed Inigo Jones, the surveyor-general of the royal buildings and the innovator of the Palladian style of architecture in England, to prepare him a detailed report.

In the mid-seventeenth century four important books appeared which argued various theories about Stonehenge. The first was Inigo Jones' *Stone-Heng Restored* (1655) in which were dismissed the Arthurian claims and all prehistoric theories for the reason that the ancient Britons either before or following the Romans were considered much too bestial by nature to have created such a monument . . . *therefore it must be Roman.* Next, in 1663, was *Chorea Gigantum* by Walter Charleton who opted for Stonehenge as a ninth-century Danish monument—using the Danish megaliths as a parellel example. Charleton had also suggested that the purpose of nearby Avebury might

28 An early print (caricature-style) of Stonehenge *c*. 1575 depicting a fictitious castle on the skyline. The caption alludes to the story of Uther Pendragon and the Irish origin for the bluestones.

29 Stonehenge restored—showing six trilithons—according to the ideas of Inigo Jones *c*. 1621 (*see also* Fig. 44).

be discovered by digging round its stones. The other two books were Webb's *Vindication of Stone-Heng Restored* [to the Romans] and Gibbon's delightfully entitled *A Fools Bolt soon Shott at Stonage* (*see* note 4).

Both the well-known seventeenth-century diarists, Evelyn and Pepys, recorded their comments after visiting the monument. John Evelyn called it 'stupendous . . . appearing at a distance like a castle', and he posed the perennial question when he wrote: 'As to their being brought thither, there being no navigable river near, is by some admired; but for the stones, there seems to be the same kind about 20 miles distant Marlborough Downs, some of which appear above ground.' Samuel Pepys' account is more laconic, but he found the monument 'as prodigious as any tales I ever heard there of them', and he wondered enigmatically: 'God knows what their use was.'

Within historical times, it was supposedly the Duke of Buckingham who was the first curious enough to begin the exploration of the monument. John Aubrey (1626—97) records in his *Antiquities and Folklore*: '. . . In 1620 the duke, when King James was at Wilton, did cause the middle Stonehenge to be digged, and this underdigging was the cause of the falling down and recumbencie of the great stone there.' This is the first reference in the literature to the feature now known as the great central trilithon (stones 55—56).

Aubrey also recounts that in the process of digging 'they found a great many bones of stagges and oxen, charcoal, batter dashes, arrow heads, and some pieces of armour eaten out with rust. Bones rotten, but whether of stagges or of men they could not tell.' Aubrey tells us that, according to Philip, Earl of Pembroke, an altar stone which was found in the middle of the area was carried away to St James Palace. John Camden, another chronicler, refers to it in his plans: 'Place where men's bones are dug up.'

Aubrey, one of the greatest of the early Stonehenge antiquarians, was born at Easton Percy only a short distance from Stonehenge. He tells us that from an early age he had a love of antiquarian pursuits and in particular 'Salisbury-Plaines and Stonehenge'. It was Aubrey who first discovered the outer circle of holes, or pits, which now bears his name. He was an influential figure in contemporary society; a Fellow of the Royal

Society of London and a friend of the King. Somewhat unfairly he has been described by some of his biographers as 'gossip monger and hanger-on of the great'. In 1663 he revisited Stonehenge for the benefit of Charles II, and it is from about this time we have the Druidic folklore-and-fancy element of his nature entering into the scheme of things. But Aubrey's *magnum opus*, the *Monumenta Britannia*, the manuscript of which is now at the Bodleian Library at Oxford, was never published owing to insufficient interest then shown by the public at large in antiquarian findings.

Aubrey tells us in his manuscript: 'There have been several books writt by learned men concerning Stoneheng, much differing from one another, some offering one thing, some another. . . .' Aubrey submitted that Stonehenge and other circle monuments he had inspected 'were Temples of the Druids'. Exploiting an early usage of the comparative method in archaeology, he wrote: 'When a traveller rides along the Ruines of a Monastry, he knows by the manner of buildings, etc Chapell, Cloysters and etc, that it was a Convent, but of what Order, Benedictine, Dominican and etc, it was, he cannot tell by the bare View. So it is clear that all the Monuments, which I have recounted were Temples. Now my presumption is, That the Druids, being the most eminent Priests or order . . . 'tis odds, but that these ancient monuments, etc Avbury, Stonehenge, Kerring, Druidd etc were Temples of the Priests of the most eminent Order, viz Druids, and it is strongly to be

30 Walter Charleton's *Chorea Gigantum . . . Stone-heng . . . Restored to the Danes* (1725 edition).

presumed that Avbury, Stonehenge and etc are as ancient as those times. . . .'

Aubrey admits that his theory is conjectural, and with a nice turn of phrase concludes: '. . . but although I have not brought it into a clear light; yet I can affirm that I have brought it from an utter darkness to a thin mist, and have gonne further in this Essay than any one before me.' Aubrey justifies his general speculations, noting: 'These Antiquities are so exceedingly old that no Bookes doe reach them, so there is no Way to retrieve them but by comparative antiquitie, which I have writt upon the spott, from the Monuments themselves. . . .'

Aubrey's attitude to the matter can be summed up by his Latin postscript: *Historia quoquo modo scripta bona est* (In whatever way history is written, it is good). Aubrey was certainly not devoid of a sense of humour, for he tells us that the first draft of his text 'was worn out with time and handling; and now, methinks, after many years lying dormant, I come abroad like the Ghost of one of these Druids . . .'.

Aubrey had many Druidical fancies, for example, he noted how the common sparrow frequently nested in the natural cavities contained in some of the weathered sarsens. As a consequence he proposed the idea that the mortises belonging the joints for fixing the sarsen lintels at Stonehenge might have been purpose-built nesting-boxes for the holy birds of the Druids ('the Aves Druidum of the Templa Druidum').

Before Jones' and Aubrey's time there had been no mention of the Druids, but from hereon to this day the monument was never to be free from their ubiquitous presence.

The Druid Celtic priesthood was not established in Britain until the La Tene phase of the Iron Age (*c*. − 300) at the earliest. Of the old Celtic nations—their culture and their religion—we have no native account. No Celtic language has any literary remains earlier than the seventh century (usually glosses), and the oldest manuscripts of connected works cannot be traced back beyond the eleventh century. Roman and Greek writers left contemporary accounts of Celtic history, religion and customs. These accounts of religion and customs are very scrappy and are usually restricted to generalized statements about the Celts in relation to the favoured races of Rome and Greece.

Stuart Piggott, in his authoritative book *The Druids* (1968), posed the long puzzling question of why a priesthood within the barbarian pre-Roman Celtic religion, attested only by a handful of some thirty scrappy references in Greek and Roman authors, many little known and obscure, had come even to be remembered at all except by scholars nearly 2,000 years after its official suppression by the Roman authority. And Piggott noted: '. . . instead of the Druids-as-known we have been landed with the Druids-as-wished-for.' (*See* note 5.)

The earlier colourful Druid theme was again taken up by William Stukeley in 1740 when he published his *Stonehenge, a temple restored to the British Druids*. Aubrey's ideas had been somewhat cautiously worded with qualifying remarks such as '. . . This Inquiry I must confess, is a groepeing in the Dark . . .'. Stukeley, however, had none of Aubrey's reticence and declared firmly that it was certain that the Druids had worshipped at Stonehenge and in similar locales, and the object of their worship had been the serpent.

Stukeley, beginning his thesis with the solid biblical figure of Abraham, wove a tale which, incurring as it does Phoenician voyagers to Britain, is a classic exposition of the traditional hyperdiffusionist migration theory. Nevertheless, for all its conjectural flights of fancy, his theory greatly influenced later investigations at Stonehenge and elsewhere and much influenced the attitude to British prehistory generally.

Stukeley certainly made an excellent survey of Stonehenge, and he was an observant field antiquarian. His work called to attention some features which had apparently gone unnoticed before. Several of his novel lines of enquiry stimulated others in related fields—but sometimes disastrously. Stukeley, for example, believed he had discovered the fact that the builders of Stonehenge had utilized a unit measurement which he liked to call a 'Druid cubit', supposedly a measure of 20·8 English inches (which is actually very close to the length of the Egyptian royal cubit 20·67 English inches, or 525mm). There can be little doubt that Piazzi Smyth first received stimulus for his notion of the 'Pyramid inch' from Stukeley, and it is possible that the ideas for Flinders Petrie's 'Etruscan foot' and Thom's so-called 'Megalithic yard' have the same antecedents. Stukeley also speculated that the Druid builders may have used a magnetic compass to set the geometry of Stonehenge, and from a study of the monument's orientation he deduced that the building had taken place about —460. Subsequently several enthusiasts have applied Stukeley's magnetic orientation ideas to finding construction dates for British churches and other alignments, leading to some very doubtful results. He also brought to notice an earthwork feature known as the Cursus (Latin for racecourse) often interpreted in the older antiquarian literature as the 'hippodrome', along which the Romans (or other earlier tribes) were supposed to have held chariot races.

But Stukeley's work at Stonehenge is of special interest, for he refers to the fact that the principal axis of the monument pointed to the north-east and the midsummer-day rising of the Sun. This appears to be the first 'astronomical' reference on record (discounting some apocryphal ones). Several investigators following Stukeley took up the threads of the Druid theme. In 1747, John Wood's *Choir Gaure Vulgarly called Stonehenge, on Salisbury Plain, Described, Restored, and Explained* appeared; this work contained the first accurate plan of the monument but was steeped in the same Druidic fancies.

Another Druid convert was Dr John Smith, who in 1771 published a pamphlet entitled *Choir Gaur the Grand Orrery of the Ancient Druids* in which he wrote: 'From many and repeated visits, I am convinced it to be an astronomical temple; and from what I have recollected no author has as yet investigated its uses. Without an instrument or any assistance whatsoever, but White's "Ephemeris", I began my survey. I suspected the stone called *The Friar's Heel* to be the index that would disclose the uses of this structure; nor was I deceived. . . .'

Smith related how he drew a circle round 'the vallum of the ditch' and divided it into 360 equal parts—then setting a 'right line' through the Friar's Heel and marking the Sun's summer solstice point. '. . . Pursuing this plan, I soon discovered the uses of all the detached stones as well as those that formed the body of the temple.'

Smith's astronomical speculations are of great interest. He maintained that Stonehenge functioned as an orrery, but instead of a mechanism to show planetary motions it was a calendar of stones. Plausibly he supposed that thirty stones in one of the circles multiplied by the significant figure of twelve—because there are twelve signs of the Greek Zodiac—gave a total of 360, the 'round' number of days known in the ancient solar year. Smith also endorsed the ideas of Stukeley that the axis of the monument was aligned to the midsummer sunrise.

In spite of its false conclusions and briefness of reference, one of the best nineteenth-century studies of Stonehenge (and other megaliths) is contained in James Fergusson's *Rude Stone Monuments in All countries their age and uses* (1872). The greatest puzzle to all Stonehenge investigators was the origin, the age, and the purpose of the monument. Fergusson weighed the evidence carefully and came to the definite conclusion that (wrongly) it was post-Roman. He paid particular attention to the Cursus and Hippodrome theories and remarked: 'That these alignments were once race courses, appears to me one of the most improbable of the various conjectures which have been hazarded . . . No Roman race course that we know of, omitted to provide for horses returning at least once past the place they started from, and no course was ever a mile, much less a mile and three-quarters long . . . But if not a race course what were they?'

Fergusson's own idea favoured the battlefield theory, and indeed perhaps Stonehenge itself was a monument erected by the victor of the contest in memory of a slaughter as Geoffrey of Monmouth's tale would have everyone believe.

Flinders Petrie, later to become the greatest ever British Egyptologist, surveyed Stonehenge in 1880 and produced the first really accurate drawing, which was supposed (but is not) accurate to ± 1 inch. Petrie himself wrote in his *Stonehenge: Plans, Descriptions and Theories* that he was sure that the monument predated Roman times, but he believed that perhaps some of its stones had been erected during Roman times to Aurelius Ambrosius and other local chieftains who were doubtless buried in or near Stonehenge. Petrie's date for the monument was arrived at by some faulty reasoning about changes in the obliquity of the ecliptic—an error subsequently detected and corrected by Lockyer.

It was to be expected that sometime in the nineteenth century someone would put forward a theory which connected Stonehenge and its mysteries with the so-called lost continent of Atlantis. The first on record is attributed to W. S. Blacket in 1883. Since then hardly a year passes without some new crank theory involving Stonehenge with the Atlantids or the Lemurians—or the equally bizarre Buddhist monk ideas which followed hard on the heels of the Atlantids.

Since World War II, there has been a considerable ouput in pseudo-scientific literature that often cites fantastic theories hinged on Stonehenge, but consider the following comment: 'Every kind of theory has been proposed and so regularly combated. And so it will be till the end of time. Each generation considers itself wiser than the preceding, and better able to explain those matters which to their fathers and grandfathers only appeared more difficult of explanation as they advanced in their inquiries. And thus it has come to pass that more books have been printed about the much-frequented Stonehenge than about all the megalithic structures, collectively, which the world contains; and the literature of this, the best known of them all, would fill the shelves of a small library.'

Surprisingly, the above comment was *not* written by a contemporary reviewer of Stonehenge theories but (by William Long) as far back as 1876.

By 1896 there was hardly a theory about the nature and purpose of Stonehenge which had not sometime been aired. Chief contenders listed that year in H. N. Hutchinson's *Prehistoric Man and Beast* were:

A temple of the Sun.

A temple of the serpent.

A shrine of Buddha.

A planetarium, or astronomical model of the planets.

A calendar in stone for the measurement of the solar year.

A gigantic gallows on which defeated British leaders were hung in honour of the Saxon god Woden;

or

A memorial set up by Aurelius to commemorate the British nobles treacherously slain by Hengist, the Saxon, at a banquet.

CHAPTER III

Stonehenge and Lockyer

Norman Lockyer (1836—1920) began to study the alignments at Stonehenge after his first successful astro-archaeological ventures in Egypt in the 1890s.

Lockyer, a brilliant self-taught astronomer, had been a pioneer in astrophysical studies of the Sun, but his interests were many and wide-ranging. In his now classic seminal astro-archaeological work *The Dawn of Astronomy* (1894) he recalled how he first became interested in early astronomical orientation: '. . . It chanced that in March 1890, during a brief holiday I went to the Levant. I went with a good friend, who one day when we were visiting the ruins of the Parthenon, and again when we found ourselves at the temple of Eleusis lent me his pocket compass. The curious direction in which the foundation at Eleusis revealed by the French excavation were so striking and suggestive that I thought it worthwhile to note their bearings so as to see whether there was any possible astronomical origin for the direction to which I have referred. . . .'

Lockyer was not the first to be curious about possible astronomical alignments in Greece and the Middle East. However, since he was not a specialist scholar like most of the French and German archaeologists or Egyptologists who had earlier looked into this question, he was able to cast his net wider. In his study of Greek temple orientations he enlisted the help of the archaeologist F. C. Penrose, who directed the British School in Athens in the 1880s. Penrose had made a special study of Greek temples and indeed before Lockyer approached him, he had independently thought about the problem of possible astronomical orientations (*see* note 6).

The success of Lockyer's studies in Egypt and with the Grecian temples stimulated him to extend his searches even further. He realized that by finding possible astronomical orientations in Britain, in a more northerly latitude than Egypt, he would be able to separate out changes in the obliquity of the ecliptic (traced out by the Sun), since over a given period such changes show more readily in northerly (or southerly) latitudes.

Lockyer began his work at Stonehenge in 1901 with the help of Penrose and others. The midsummer solstice alignment was measured, and this led to his detecting an error in Flinders Petrie's earlier calculations. Lockyer's and Penrose's date, derived from measured changes in the obliquity of the ecliptic, took the origins of Stonehenge far back into prehistoric times and indicated a construction date of about − 1680 (± 200 years).

When Edmond Halley had visited the monument briefly in 1720, he had shrewdly guessed, from the general appearance of the stones, that it must be at least 3,000 years old. Godfrey Higgins in his *Celtic Druids* (1827) had suggested, on astronomical grounds, an even earlier date reaching as far back as − 4000, but no one until Lockyer and Penrose came along truly believed that the monument was much older than Celtic-Roman times. Lockyer and Penrose announced their discovery in a paper addressed to the Royal Society. But to popularize his early and subsequent sorties at Stonehenge and elsewhere, Lockyer wrote his book *Stonehenge and Other British Monuments* (1906; 2nd expanded edition 1909).

In measuring the midsummer solstice alignment,[*] Lockyer, like those before him, came up against the problem of what features of the monument one should choose to determine this: the mid-line of the Avenue; the axis determined by the stone circles; or the Heel Stone? The mid-line of the Avenue and the 'axis' lie approximately on the same azimuth, but because of the general ruined (and partly restored) condition of the monument, the determination of a true axis and a geometric centre is a somewhat arbitrary exercise, and in addition different features have different centre points or centre lines.

The so-called axis line is considered to be the line passing midway between stones 55—56 (of the central trilithon) and the midway point of stones 30—31 and 15—16 (in the outer sarsen circle). After measuring the azimuth of the mid-line of the Avenue, deriving a mean figure of 49° 35′ 51″, Lockyer decided instead to adopt the azimuth 49° 34′ 18″ which defines the mean axis of Stonehenge through the Ordnance Survey bench

* *See* p. 66

mark on Sidbury Hill 13km (8 miles) to the north-east and on the same line passing through Grovely Castle 10km (6 miles) to the south-west. Lockyer's choice of the Avenue azimuth incurred much subsequent criticism and is not now generally accepted.

Lockyer, when he took his azimuth from the Avenue, ignored the Heel Stone whose centre line lies 1·8m (6 feet) east of the Avenue mid-line. Although, as seen from the axis line inside the stone circles, the Sun now appears to rise (approximately) over the Heel Stone, in ancient times, because of changes in obliquity, it rose to the north of it (Fig. 31). Nevertheless, whatever the merits for the Heel Stone as a doubtful ancient solar marker point, it seems beyond all doubt that it was used as some kind of celestial marker point.

At Stonehenge, after examining what he called 'the orientation theory' involving the Heel Stone and Avenue, Lockyer believed that there were other considerations to be taken into account. He wondered whether there had been an earlier circle on the site. He then examined the 'tumuli' and the Station stones and noted that a line drawn from 91—93 marked the sunset on about 6 May and 8 August and in the reverse direction marked the sunrise about 7 February and 8 November. These he believed represented the mid-quarter days of the year, or about forty-five days before and after the solstices. The line 91—93 almost passes through the centre defined by the large sarsen circle which is about 1m (3 feet) north of the centre defined by the Aubrey circle. However, in his consideration of the Station stones he missed making the significant discoveries of those who later followed him. Had he been alert to the monument's possible connections with the Moon from clues already in print in Godfrey Higgins' *Celtic Druids* and other sources, he might well have tested out a lunar hypothesis.

Over the question of a possible earlier circle at Stonehenge, or alternatively somewhere near by, Lockyer noted the opinion put forward by the geologist J. W. Judd (*see* note 8) which considered that the bluestones had been transported from an earlier circle in some district local to Stonehenge and had been moved either as trophies of war or as the sacred treasure of a wandering tribe. But as the bluestones were recognized as foreign to Salisbury Plain, their presence there needed some

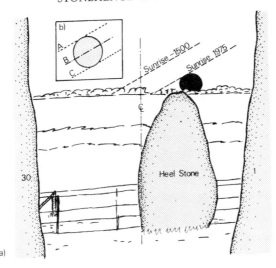

31 (a) A view to the north-east at Stonehenge as seen from the centre of the sarsen circle about four minutes after the first light of sunrise on 20 June at two different epochs. Note how the arbitrary choice of different parts of the Sun (inset b), i.e. first gleam, half risen, fully risen, makes a difference of at least 2,000 years to a significant horizon azimuth point. Note that the azimuth point at which midsummer sunrise occurs is at present shifting *eastwards* along the horizon at approximately 1° per 4,300 years.

explanation if the apocryphal tale of Geoffrey of Monmouth was to be discounted. Judd favoured the glacial idea. By the middle and late nineteenth century everyone had fully realized the tremendous carrying power of ice; they could see with their own eyes the vast lumps of Ice Age debris strewn across the British landscape—left behind when the last great glaciers had retreated northwards. Everyone readily appreciated that ice could pluck great masses of stone from a native mountain bedrock and subsequently deposit it hundreds of miles away. It was natural within the climate of opinion which then reigned to attribute the presence of the foreign stones to glacier action. Judd summed up the problem: 'I would therefore suggest as probable that when the early inhabitants of this island commenced the erection of Stonehenge, Salisbury Plain was sprinkled over thickly with the great white masses of Sarsen stones ("grey wethers"), and much more sparingly with darker coloured boulders (the so-called "blue-stones"), the last relics of the glacial drift, which have been nearly denuded away. From these two kinds of materials the stones suitable for the contemplated temple were selected. It is even possible that the abundance and association of these two kinds of materials so strikingly contrasted in colour and appearance, at a particular spot, may not only have decided the site but to some extent have suggested the architectural features of the noble structure of Stonehenge.'

Nevertheless, present-day archaeological opinion conflicts with Judd's plausible glacial idea—especially in respect to the origin and presence of the bluestones. Indications are that it was a more fundamental criterion—such as choice of latitude—which influenced the Neolithic builders to adopt Stonehenge as a site.

Lockyer's investigations of the various alignments persuaded him that Stonehenge was closely associated with the ancient May year and May worship—a thesis which constantly recurred in his writings about Megalithic monuments almost to the point of obsession. He believed that there was good evidence for supposing that May worship preceded solstitial worship at Stonehenge. He readily drew comparisons between Stonehenge and the Megalithic structures of Carnac in Brittany. Like Stonehenge many of the Carnac menhir alignments had been shown to be solstitial. To support his ideas Lockyer quoted the work done by F. Gaillard who had been one of the pioneers in developing what was then generally known as 'The orientation theory of Carnac'.

One of the most interesting sections of Lockyer's Stonehenge book are his two chapters devoted to 'Astronomical Hints For Archaeologists' in which he sets out what he believed were model principles that should be followed in investigating Megalithic sites. Here we read his views on possible stellar orientations for North-West European sites—similar to the star alignments he believed he had proved in connection with his earlier work on Egyptian monuments and what he believed Penrose had proved in Greece.

He wrote: 'In continuation of my work in Egypt in 1891 and Mr Penrose's in Greece in 1892, I have recently endeavoured to see whether there are any traces in Britain of star observatories, including those connected with the worship of the Sun at certain times of the year. We both discovered that stars, far out of the

Sun's course, especially in Egypt, were observed in the dawn as heralds of sunrise—''warning-stars''—so that the priests might have time to prepare the sunrise sacrifice. To do this properly the star should rise while the Sun is still about 10° below the horizon. There is also reason to believe that stars rising not far from the north point were also used as clock-stars to enable the time to be estimated during the night in the same way as the time during the day could be estimated by the position of the Sun.'

From then on Lockyer was chiefly concerned with his obsessional search for traces of May-day worship. The major section of the latter part of his Stonehenge book is much concerned with the folklore elements of his theories. He believed that the May-year worship came to an end when the monument was redesigned in −1680.

He posed the question that if Stonehenge and other British stone circles could be proved to have used observations of warning stars, the date when such observations were made could be determined perhaps within 200 years of the truth. This is because a comparatively rapid movement of the stars in declination is brought about by *the precession of the equinoxes* (Fig. 32). Changes in the Sun's declination due to *changing obliquity of the ecliptic* by comparison are very slow. But Lockyer's assumptions about warning stars are a trifle too glib which he afterwards realized. There are factors entering into the problem that cause uncertainties and confusion. For example, one first needs to assume a date for a monument in order to identify a given star correctly. It can be shown that for a particular alignment several bright stars may be associated with it *at different epochs.*

Lockyer believed—optimistically—that the star-dating method had enormous advantages over the solar-dating method. At that time no one had tried to apply the method rigorously as a scientific tool, although others had applied analogous stellar-based methods to stars of the southern hemisphere in attempts to date the origin of the constellation figures.

Lockyer related how he obtained clear evidence in different parts of Britain of sites used for night work and sites constructed in relation to the May year which he repeatedly emphasizes was an underlying theme in the whole of Europe in early times and

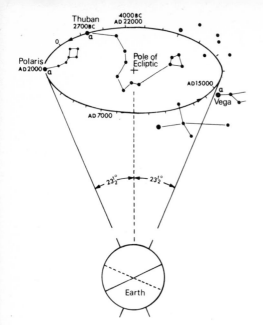

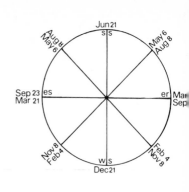

33 Astronomical and vegetation calen[dar] divisions of the year (after Lockyer). Note summer and winter solstices (ss[s]) and equinox rising and setting (er, [s])

32 Precession of the Earth's axis (precession of the equinoxes) brings about a slow shift of the star sphere over a period of *c*. 26,000 years so that the celestial coordinates of all stars, viz. Declination (Dec) and Right Ascension (RA) change with time and need to be related to a given epoch, e.g. 1950. One effect of precession is to change the pole stars, thus about the time the Egyptians built their pyramids (*c*. – 2700) Thuban (Alpha Draconis) was the northern pole star.

34 Bearings of summer and winter solstice risings and settings (ssr, wsr, sss, wss) for latitude 51°N expressed (a) the amplitude method (b) the azimuth method.

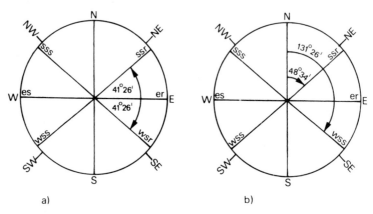

a)   b)

* The summer solstice (solstice meaning Sun standing still) is defined (at Stonehenge) by the farthest sunrise along the horizon northwards; the winter solstice by the farthest sunrise southwards. At the equinoxes (meaning day and night of equal length) 21 March and 21 September, the Sun rises due east (*see also* note 7).

was still directly evident in the determination of the quarter days in Scotland. In his book he purports to demonstrate the methods employed by ancient British 'astronomer-priests' in respect to their stellar observations.

Lockyer considered that the easiest way for the astronomer-priests to carry out stellar observations in a stone circle would be to erect a stone or barrow indicating the direction of the place on the horizon at which the star would rise as seen from the centre of the circle. If the stars to be observed at dawn were to herald the summer, the stone or barrow itself might be visible. Lockyer believed there was a good reason why they should not be too close and remarked with wry humour: '. . . in a solemn ceremonial the less seen of the machinery the better.'

Stones and barrows would be illuminated in the dark by a light placed strategically near by, and later Thom echoed the same idea. Lockyer noted that cups which hold grease or oil are known in connection with such stones, but these would be suitable only in good weather when there was no wind. He believed that in windy weather a cromlech or some other similar structure must have been provided for a priest's shelter.

Lockyer stressed the need for the importance of accurately scaled plans and remarked: 'not slovenly plans with which Fergusson and too many others have provided us.' He recommended the old 25-inch to 1-mile Ordnance Survey maps which he supposed (optimistically) showed menhirs sufficiently accurately so that azimuths could be read off to one minute of arc.

Lockyer discussed the question of obtaining accurate star declinations as these showed ever-changing values owing to precessional shifts. Tables for precessional shifts are now more easily obtainable than in Lockyer's day, but for specific stars they can be easily computed using simple tables found in standard astronomical text-books. Lockyer used both the *azimuth* and *amplitude* methods, the angular distance from the north (or south points) and the angular distance from the east or west points respectively. Today a field surveyor would use the simple azimuth method measured from true north turning clockwise 0° to 360° (Fig. 34). This is the use of azimuth as adopted by surveyors, navigators and engineers; in astronomy azimuth usually refers to the angular measure round the horizon zeroed from the observer's true south point, increasing in angle westwards.

Lockyer delivered plenty of practical advice for would-be astro-archaeologists. He provided a clearly set out graph for determining the declination of a star (for latitudes 49° to 59°) from the measured azimuth (Fig. 35). He rightly emphasized the importance of horizon elevation and how refraction enters into the calculations; he noted that elevations along the horizon could be found approximately from the study of the contour lines on the 1-inch Ordnance maps or their equivalents. Other useful figures provided show the changing declinations of the brightest stars which may have entered into the reckoning of the ancient astronomer-priests. These show star declination changes (due to precession) calculated for the years −2150 to −150 (2150 to 150BC). Examination of these figures (Fig. 36) shows at once the problems previously alluded to (above), viz. that one really first needs to know the approximate date(s) when any star observation took place. For example, although star number 26 (Spica, Alpha Virginis) and star number 25 (Betelgeuse, Alpha Orionis) were well separated in declination in the year −2000, at about −650 their declination values were the same.

Lockyer, although himself highly optimistic about the use of stars in determining construction dates, later recognized there was a problem when he wrote: '...After determining the azimuth of the sight lines and having found (from the tables) the declination; we may find more than one star occupying that declination at various dates. Which of these stars, then, must we consider?'

Lockyer says that we should choose the star (or stars) most conveniently situated for enabling the time to be estimated during the night, or those which could have been used as warning (heralding) stars. He provided a summary of dates which may be critical times, i.e. May (May year), August, November and February and for the solstices. (Note that for different epochs and months Lockyer cites different stars; for Star Guide see Fig. 37.)

Lockyer also deals with the question of Sun observations, and immediately we encounter one of the most vexing and controversial questions concerning both solar and lunar alignments (in particular with Stonehenge): What part of the solar or lunar disc was supposed to indicate the azimuth at time of rising or setting: upper limb (first glimpse (gleam) or upper tangent); centre (half orb); or lower limb (lower tangent, or full

	−1900	−1400	−800
May	Castor rising N 41°E Antares setting S 75°W	Pleiades rising N 77°E Antares setting S 72°W	Pleiades rising N 71°E
Aug	Arcturus circumpolar (hill 3° high) Rising Date 2170 BC.. N 11° 15′ E Date 2090 BC.. N 14°18′E Date 1900 BC.. N 18°44′E	Arcturus rising N 17°E	Sirius rising S 63°E
Nov			Betelgeuse setting N87°W
Feb	Capella rising N 36°E	Capella rising N 28°E	Capella rising N 21°E

And for the solstices of June and December:

	−1900	−1400	−800
Summer Solstice	Betelgeuse rising N 87°E. Arcturus setting N 18°W (hill 3° high)	Betelgeuse rising N90°E Arcturus setting (late) N 16°W Alpha Serpentis setting N 53°W	Gamma Geminorum rising N 68°E
Winter Solstice	Scheat rising (early) N 72°E Markab rising (late) S 89°E	Castor setting N 37°W Pollux setting N 42°W	Alpha Capricorni rising S 66°E

In the above tables, note that Lockyer's azimuths follow the old system. To convert these to modern surveyors' 0° to 360° usage *see* Fig. 34 (e.g. N 41°E = 49°; S 72°W = 198°).

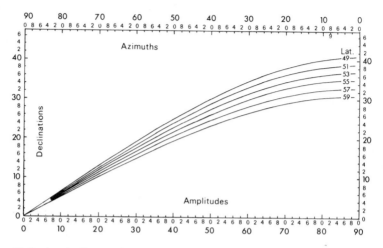

35 Lockyer's diagram for the graphical determination of star declinations for latitudes 49° to 59° (*see also* note 7).

orb)? Lockyer himself seemed under no misunderstanding in this matter when he wrote: 'It is frequently imagined that for determining the exact place of sunrise or sunset in connection with these ancient monuments we have to deal with the Sun's centre, as we shall do with the Sun half risen. As a matter of fact, we must consider that part of the Sun's limb which first makes its appearance above the horizon; the first glimpse of the upper limb of the Sun is in question, say, when the visible limb is 2' high; and we must carefully take the height of the hills over which it rises into account.'

Lockyer also provided a convenient figure for finding the azimuth of the summer solstices between latitudes 47°N to 59°N (Fig. 38).

Lockyer visited many Megalithic sites throughout Britain in order to extend and develop his astro-archaeological work begun at Stonehenge. Several of these sites have been intensively studied by later students of astro-alignment theory, in particular by Alexander Thom.

One of the most interesting sites visited by Lockyer on several occasions is known as the Hurlers, some 8km (5 miles) north of Liskeard in Cornwall. In his Egyptian work Lockyer believed he had detected precessional changes in particular star risings and settings which were reflected by the axis of temples. Now he supposed that similar changes in sight lines could be seen in three stone circles of the Hurlers complex. Locally these circles are popularly known as 'Cheese-wrings', and the name frequently crops up in South-West Britain in connection with Megalithic circles and similar field monuments.

In plan the Hurlers consists of three large circles composed of granite stones orientated in nearly a straight line in a north-north-east and south-south-west direction (Fig. 39). The middle circle is the largest c. 40·5m (135 feet) in diameter; the northernmost one is c. 33m (110 feet), and the southern one c. 31·5m (105 feet). All three circles are now greatly disturbed, and at least half the stones are out of their original positions. Thom, who later surveyed the site, classified them—within the framework of his own theories—among his Type II egg-shaped rings (see Fig. 61).

The outcome of Lockyer's early investigations at the Hurlers was to persuade him that the sight lines could be established for Arcturus (Alpha Boötis) in −2170, −2090 and −1900; Antares (Alpha Scorpius) −1720; Betelgeuse (Alpha Orionis) −1730; Sirius (Alpha Canis Majoris) −1690; midsummer Solar Solstice; November sunset; and November sunrise (Fig. 39). Lockyer supposed that Arcturus was used as a 'clock-star' to serve as a warning star for the month of August—'and perhaps', he conjectured, 'for the Cornish Harvest festival'.

Following up the idea that folklore might have the confirmatory answer, Lockyer checked up local saints since 'a local festival in the old days was often associated with the local Saint'. Consulting the Calendar of the *Annuaire* of *Institut de France*—'because Cornish Saints are common to both Cornwall and Brittany'—he noted that the days dedicated to Sts Justin and Claire were the 9th and 12th of August. This Lockyer believed was convincing evidence to assume that the Hurlers monument incorporated at least one warning clock-star for the August festival.

The Hurlers was also used by Lockyer to further his ideas of the importance of the May year, this time using the apparent alignment of Antares from the northernmost circle to a tumulus which lies approximately south-west of it. He added this to some of the observations he and Penrose derived earlier in Egypt and Greece and remarked: 'We have, then, now a third term in the

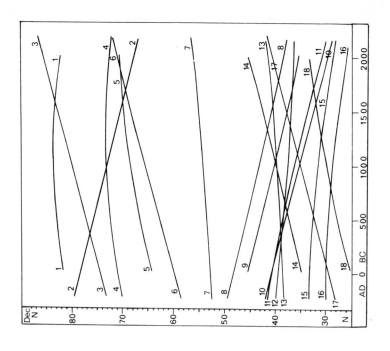

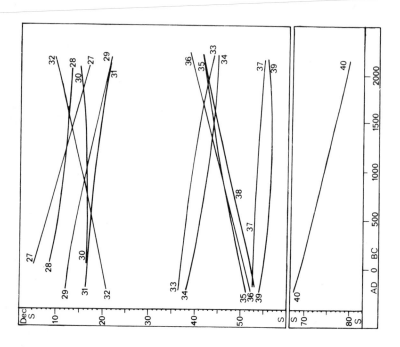

72

Key to stars:

Note that the genitive form of the constellation name is used.

1 β Ursae Minoris
2 α Ursae Minoris (Polaris)
3 α Draconis (Thuban)
4 α Ursae Majoris (Dubhe)
5 γ Ursae Majoris
6 η Ursae Majoris (Benetnasch)
7 γ Draconis
8 β Cassiopeiae
9 α Cassiopeiae
10 α Persei

11 α Aurigae (Capella)
12 α Cygni (Deneb)
13 α Lyrae (Vega)
14 α Corona Borealis
15 α Geminorum (Castor)
16 β Geminorum (Pollux)
17 α Bootis (Arcturus)
18 β Leonis
19 α Leonis (Regulus)
20 α Andromedae

21 η Tauri (Alcyone)
22 α Tauri (Aldebaran)
23 α Canis Minoris (Procyon)
24 α Aquilae (Altair)
25 α Orionis (Betelgeuse)
26 α Virginis (Spica)
27 α Ceti
28 α Aquarii
29 β Orionis (Rigel)
30 α Capricorni

31 α Canis Majoris (Sirius)
32 α Scorpii (Antares)
33 α Columbae
34 α Piscis Austrini (Australis)
35 η Argus (η Carinae)
36 α Centauri (Rigel Kent)
37 α Argus (α Carinae; Canopus)
38 α Crucis
39 α Gruis
40 α Eridani

36 Diagrams (after Lockyer) for the determination of changing star declinations between − 2150 and − 150 (2150 BC and 150 BC) brought about by the precession of the equinoxes.

73

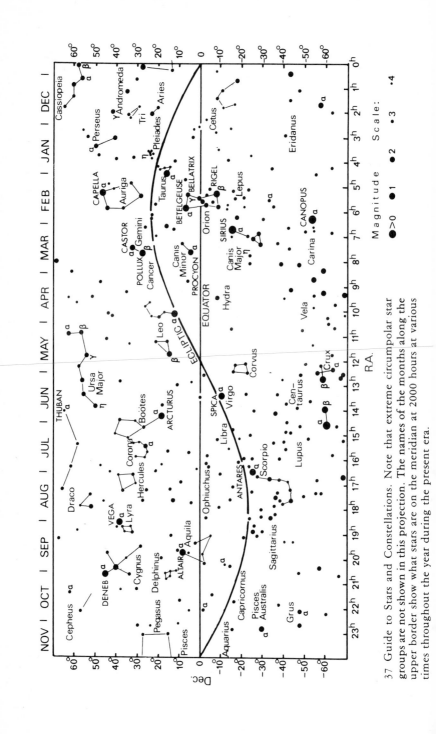

37 Guide to Stars and Constellations. Note that extreme circumpolar star groups are not shown in this projection. The names of the months along the upper border show what stars are on the meridian at 2000 hours at various times throughout the year during the present era.

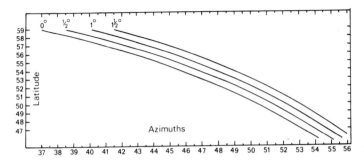

38 Lockyer's plot for finding the azimuth of the summer solstice for any site between latitudes 47° to 59°N. Note the plot shows values for true horizon (0°) and horizon heights of ½°, 1° and 1½°, which may result because of ground slope, distant hills or obscuring vegetation.

39 The Hurlers circles, Liskeard, Cornwall, showing Lockyer's supposed alignments at different periods.

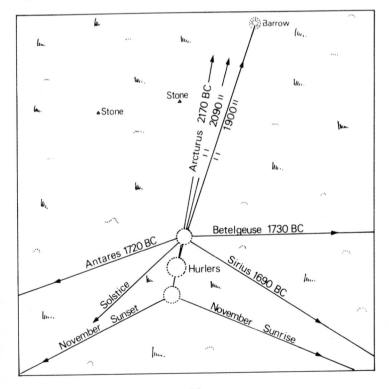

astronomical use of stars to herald the sunrise on May morning.'

Temple of Min	Thebes	−3200	Spica
Temple of the Hurlers	Liskeard	−1720	Antares
Older Erechtheum	Athens	−1070	Antares

Lockyer's attempt to resolve the problems of the Megaliths also embraced the Megalithic avenues—particularly those on Dartmoor. These Megalithic avenues may be marked out by single, double or multiple rows of stones; some straight and some crooked which follow any number of directions of the compass and sometimes several within the same monument. Earlier French work on the alignments in Brittany had persuaded him that these were monuments connected with the worship of the Sun of the May year. This Lockyer believed had been the earliest attempts of ancient man to measure the calendar by the Sun after they discovered the Moon unsatisfactory as a measure of time. Applying his ideas on Dartmoor and using the comparative method (made fashionable by nineteenth-century pioneer anthropologists such as Tylor and Frazer), he concluded: 'The equivalents of the Brittany alignments are not common in Britain; they exist in the greatest number on Dartmoor, whither I went recently to study them. The conditions on high Dartmoor are peculiar; dense blinding mists are common, and, moreover, sometimes come on almost without warning. From its conformation the land is full of streams. There are stones everywhere. What I found therefore, as had others before me, was that as a consequence of the condition to which I have referred, directions had been indicated by rows of stones for quite other ceremonial purposes. Here, then, was another possible origin. It was a matter of great importance to discriminate most carefully between these alignments, and to endeavour to sort them out. My special inquiry, of course, was to see if they, like their apparent equivalents in Brittany, could have had an astronomical origin. The first thing to do, then, was to see which might have been erected for worship or which for practical purposes.'

   Lockyer dismissed as non-astronomical those stone rows and avenues which are very long and crooked and which follow several directions. He supposed, in some cases, they may have provided useful guides at night, or in mist, in difficult country with streams to cross, but added cautiously that their possible utility must not be judged wholly by the present conformity of the ground or the present-day beds of the streams. Indeed, since Neolithic times both the climate and the terrain have certainly deteriorated following the climatic optimum which occurred c. − 4000.

Over the question of the straightness of the avenues, Lockyer believed that those astronomically orientated must not necessarily always be assumed to be *exactly* straight. Straightness he considered would only be true for level ground, but if the avenue passed over ridges and furrows, the height of the horizon must be taken into account when determining azimuth.

Lockyer was puzzled (as we still are) about the *real* practical purposes of some of the multiple avenues—although elsewhere he wrote—'we know how such Avenues were used in Brittany for sun worship'. Lockyer too was greatly puzzled why avenues and circles were found in association with barrows and burials.

It is at this point Lockyer provided a word of cautionary advice concerning stone alignments to future field workers plus a brickbat for authority—counsel and criticism which is still highly relevant today. He wrote: 'We must not take for granted that the stone-rows are now as they left the hands of the builders. The disastrous carelessness of the Government in the matter of our national antiquities is, I am locally informed admirably imitated by the Devonshire County and other lesser councils, and, indeed, by anybody who has a road to mend or a wall to build. On this account, any of the rows may once have been much longer and with an obvious practical use; and those which now appear to be far removed from circles may once have been used for sacred processions at shrines which have disappeared.'

Among several of the avenue structures Lockyer investigated, which serve to illustrate his working method, are two notable double avenues of upright stones at Merrivale (near Walkhampton in Devonshire). These double rows of stones run parallel from west to east (azimuth 82°; or 262°). The northern row is 181·8m (600 feet) long and the southern 263·8m (870 feet), and both are blocked by a triangular stone at the eastern end (Fig. 41). Near the centre of the southern row is a round barrow with a circle of stones surrounding it. Leading from the south-west corner of this barrow is another with a single stone row leading south-west to a distance of 42·7m (140 feet). South

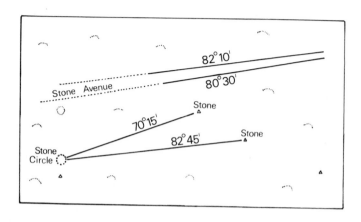

40 Avenues, circles and stones at Merrivale near Walkhampton, Devonshire, showing Lockyer's supposed astronomical alignments (after Lockyer).

41 The Merrivale Avenue showing a blocking stone.

of the last stone row is a stone circle of 91m (300 feet) and a single stone alongside a cairn. There are several other barrows near by. The avenue stones range in size between 0·5 to 1m (2 to 3 feet); in each row the stones are spaced about 1m (3 feet); the distance between the rows measures 24m (80 feet).

It will be recalled that Lockyer believed that a long avenue directed to the rising point of a star over undulating ground would not necessarily be exactly straight. And if two avenues are directed to the rising place of the same star at different epochs, then they *cannot* be parallel. These two factors Lockyer utilized to counter what he referred to as the 'curious arguments of critics of the astronomical theory'. These critics maintained that the absence of parallelism was a strong argument which could be used *against* the avenues once having had an astronomical use. At Merrivale the two avenues are most certainly not parallel, and there is a decided kink in the alignment of the most southern one.

At Merrivale, Lockyer fancied that the Pleiades (the Seven Sisters) were sometimes involved as warning stars to herald the rise of the May Sun at azimuth 75°—82°. Variations in azimuth could be brought about by differing heights of the observer's horizon towards which the sight lines are directed. At Merrivale, Lockyer determined that the height of the horizon was 3° 18′. Then assuming that the Pleiades were the warning stars in question (which announced the May sunrise) and armed with data gleaned from the 25-inch to 1-mile Ordnance Survey map (and additional survey data supplied by Mr Worth), he derived the following results:

	Azimuth (modern style)	North Declination	Date BC
North Alignment	83°15 (Mr Worth)	6° 47′47″	−1710
	82°30 (Mr Worth)	7° 16′20″	−1630
	82°10 (Ordnance Survey)	7° 32′ 0″	−1580
South Alignment	80°40 (Mr Worth)	8° 26′ 0″	−1420
	80°30 (Ordnance Survey)	8° 30′ 0″	−1400

From the above, Lockyer believed that the case for the Pleiades was well proven, and it was strengthened even further by the fact that according to Penrose's Greek determinations of various stellar orientations, the Hecatompedon at Athens was also orientated to the Pleiades in − 1495. Lockyer noted that the

Cursus at Stonehenge is very nearly parallel to the Merrivale Avenue, and consequently believed that like the Merrivale Avenue the Cursus was used as a processional road to watch the rising of the Pleiades. The stone at the eastern end of Merrivale is referred to as a 'blocking stone', and Lockyer supposed that its purpose was that of a sighting stone. He noted that the end stones are longer than the rest and believed that this assisted in providing clues to the true direction of other avenues.

In summarizing his study of the Cornish and Dartmoor stone monuments, Lockyer poses several questions and remarked that in some future period he hoped that they would be carefully considered by students of orientation. He wondered, for example, whether the avenues consisting of two rows of stones were a reflection of the Sphinx Avenue of Egypt. Was there a double worship going on in the avenues and the circles at the same time . . ? Did all the cairns and cists in the avenues represent late additions? He commented: 'I have always held that these ancient temples, and even their attendant long and chambered barrows, were for the living and not for the dead . . . There was good reason for burials after the sacred nature of the spot had been established, and they may have taken place at any time since; the most probable time being after 1000 BC up to a date as recent as archaeologists may consider probable.'

Lockyer does not gloss over the objections to the astronomical theory by his contemporary critics who came out strongly against the avenue-alignment ideas because there were too many of them—one critic cited a personal count of fifty. Lockyer's answer was that he believed that the avenues were dedicated to different uses 'some practical and others sacred, at different times of the year'. In favour of his astronomical theory he wrote: '. . . the results obtained in Devon and Cornwall are remarkably similar . . . Among the whole host of heaven from which objectors urge it is free for me to select any star I choose, at present only six stars have been considered, two of which were certainly used, as in Egypt, as clock-stars as they just dipped below the northern horizon, and another two afterwards at Athens; and these six stars are shown by nothing more recondite than an inspection of a precessional globe to have been precisely the stars, the "morning stars", wanted by the astronomer-priests who wished to be prepared for the instant of sunrise at the critical points of the May or solstitial years.'

Lockyer's ideas have been much criticized both by archaeologists and astronomers, but it was his later, uninhibited excursions into the realms of hyperspeculative prehistory and folklore which subsequently attracted the most adverse and damaging criticism of all. In his Stonehenge book he devotes a substantial part of it to a rambling discussion showing how folklore and tradition provided 'dim references to ancient uses of the stars'.

Today such a modus operandi for a physical scientist, purporting to work via the scientific method, is almost unknown and would be a disastrous methodology except perhaps for a few isolated exceptions. Lockyer as the undisputed Editor of *Nature* was never plagued with the problem of meeting the requirements of critical and anonymous scientific referees appointed by editors of scientific magazines. Consequently he was self-indulgent and frequently allowed his ideas to degenerate into undisciplined flights of hyperspeculative fancy. Today many archaeologists, unaware of Lockyer's great contributions in several fields of pioneer solar and stellar science, place him among those in the lunatic fringe along with the Velikovskys and the von Dänikens.

However, it can be plausibly argued that Lockyer's excursions into mystical folklore shows his true mettle as a polymath* and a searcher after truth much in the traditions of the great nineteenth-century master-polymath Humboldt. Lockyer's astro-archaeological interests from the 1890s onwards were only a small part of his wide-ranging interests in the Cosmos. For example, in 1903—one of the busiest years of his life and then at the summit of his scientific fame—his chief overriding interests were in meteorology.

Lockyer had a well-developed sense of humour—an attribute that does not always go hand in hand with those unable to suffer fools gladly. Typical of his humour was his beautiful apt quip: 'I thought the change in the obliquity of the ecliptic was the most majestically leisurely movement known to us, but certainly the Sun has something to learn from a printer's office.'

As one of the great men of science, Lockyer had greatly

* Lockyer even found time to write a book *The Rules of Golf* (1896) in conjunction with W. Rutherford.

impressed Tennyson, and in turn Lockyer was greatly impressed by the breadth of the poet's knowledge and close acquaintance-ship with astronomical detail. Tennyson once wrote gushingly to Lockyer '. . . in my anthropological spectrum you are coloured like a first-rate star of science'. Lockyer, as part of his wide-ranging interests, was later to write a book (his last) in collaboration with his daughter Winifred, entitled *Tennyson as a student and a Poet of Nature* which set out to show to the public the extent and accuracy of the poet's scientific knowledge.

Lockyer was never content to examine only the obvious facets of any subject and marshalled *any* evidence likely to have relevance. One must not forget the kind of intellectual atmosphere in which Lockyer operated at the beginning of the twentieth century. Not long before, there had been a vigorous revival of interest in folklore and mysticism, particularly in the hands of the powerful world-embracing scholarship of Tylor, Frazer and Max Muller—especially the latter whose solar myth theories have echoes today. Anthropology was a brand new science which was still unsure of its direction and its limitations; it had not yet been systemized like the traditional natural sciences inherited from the Hellenic world.

Frazer was a pioneer of the interdisciplinary approach. At the height of his fame he was labelled as the leader of the 'new humanism'. He invaded several scholastic domains to root out the facts. Like Lockyer, it was Frazer's firm belief that one should not let the ignorance of a particular discipline of learning stop one from taking it by the throat to see what it had to say for itself. He was often criticized for his emphasis on a library-based approach to anthropology, and because he was sensitive to this criticism, he considered the greatest compliment ever paid him was when a home-leave visitor from a distant shore once exclaimed in admiration: 'Why you know my blacks better than I know them myself!'

Frazer's methodology was to imagine himself as an intel-lectual savage faced with the problem of explaining to himself natural and human events. This later gave rise to his method being nicknamed the 'If-I-were-a-horse' approach, alluding to the apocryphal story of an American farmer who lost a horse (*see* below). It also had parallels with the method which Conan Doyle made fashionable with Sherlock Holmes: 'You know my methods in such cases, Watson. I put myself in the man's place, and having first gauged his intelligence, I try to imagine how I myself should have proceeded under the same circumstances.'

Frazer is now academically in eclipse, but *The Golden Bough*, in its abridged paperback edition, enjoys a remarkably healthy sale and is still the most widely read work on anthropology (*see* note 9). It remains a book that anyone claiming knowledge of literature is expected to have read. Freud, and several others, borrowed heavily in factual material from Frazer—but placed on it a different interpretation. Frazer was also a translator of Ovid's *Fasti* which contains some of the earliest literary references to astronomical phenomena, but Frazer always admitted that his ignorance of astronomy was as great as that of the poet's. One of the principal criticisms against Frazer was his overemphasis on the vegetable element in mythology—which later Andrew Lang called the Covent Garden school of mythology.

Lockyer was often much too fanciful and naive in his views. In the period since Lockyer published *Stonehenge*, much has come to light which invalidates many of his ideas. Archaeology is now a fast evolving science and is at present caught up in its own revolution of rethinking. The so-called New Archaeologists are rapidly purging archaeology's own store-cupboard of obsolescent ideas. Much of this new thinking has wide-reaching repercussions in the current problems relating to astro-archaeology (*see* Chapter XI).

Lockyer's methods in Egypt, at Stonehenge and at other British Megalithic sites provide a valuable historical perspective to astro-archaeology. Anthropology, in the guise of ethnographic parallels, is again becoming fashionable as an ancillary scientific tool in astro-archaeology. Although misguided, Lockyer was undoubtedly a pioneer in this field. When he began his British survey he related: 'It is not my task to arrange the facts of folklore and tradition, but simply to cull from the available sources precise statements which bear upon the questions before us. . . .'

One of his first tasks had been to establish the importance of time relations, in particular the quarters of the year—the four important occasions in the Gregorian, Greek and Roman calendars. Lockyer drew attention to the significance that all these dates fall roughly half-way between the solstices and equinoxes, and later he was to relate these to Megalithic alignments.

Lockyer, like Aubrey and Stukeley before him, deeply involved himself with ideas about the Druids. He recounts that the earliest information about festival days in Great Britain can be gleaned from Cormac, Archbishop of Cashel, in the tenth century (via Hazlitt's *Dictionary of Faith and Folklore*), and that according to Vallancey 'in his time four great fires were lighted up on the four great festivals of the Druids, viz. in February, May, August and November'.

Much of Lockyer's thesis was derivative of Frazer's *The Golden Bough*. Lockyer acknowledged his great debt to Frazer; in his chapter on 'Sacred Fires' he wrote: 'The magnificent collection of facts bearing on this subject which has been brought together by Mr Frazer in *The Golden Bough* renders it unnecessary for me to deal with the details of this part of my subject at any great length.'

Lockyer then briefly reiterated a record of the fire festivals:

(1) In February, May, August and November of the original May year.
(2) In June and December on the longest and shortest days of the solstitial years . . .
(3) A fire at Easter.

Direct from *The Golden Bough*, the reader is treated to a chapter on 'Sacred Trees,' 'Holy Wells', and 'Streams' before a chapter on the origins of British worship and the similarities of Semitic and British worships.

The comparative method is freely invoked by Lockyer. He found that the Semitic Baal was also common to Western Europe; its equivalent supposedly being Bel, Beal, Balor, Balder and Phol, Fal, Fail—citing too that Balus is named as having been the first king of Orkney. The May, Beltaine fire-festivals of the Druids are now long familiar themes to readers of Frazer's best-selling abridged version of *The Golden Bough*.

Still plugging away at the May theme, Lockyer regarded the cursus at Stonehenge and the avenues on Dartmoor as evidence of ceremonial and social processions, and supposed: '. . . feasts, games and races were not forgotten . . . so far as racing is concerned, is proved, I think, by the facts that the cursus at

Stonehenge is 10,000ft long and 350ft broad, that it occupies a valley between two hills, thus permitting of the presence of thousands of spectators, and that our horses are still decked in gaudy trappings on May Day. . '

In pursuing the origins of British worship he fancied that the ancient coast-following voyager-prospectors to Britain in search of tin might have been trading in Cornwall as early as −2500. Citing so-called similarities between Middle Eastern and the Celtic languages (via the influence of Max Muller) and other supporting evidence given him by contemporary anthropologists, he concluded: '. . . the bulk of the population of these islands, before the arrival of the Celts, spoke dialects attuned to those of North Africa.'

Lockyer's ideas of contacts between cultures of the eastern Mediterranean and Britain were not so very far removed from the later modified diffusionism of Gordon Childe, whose influence on British prehistory in more modern times was tremendous. Gordon Childe (among others) believed that there was very strong evidence for contacts between the Wessex culture and Mycenae '. . . resembleness that may be individually fortuitous, but their cumulative effects are too remarkable to dismiss . . .'. Although contact between the two probably occurred, it is well to bear in mind that its impact is *now* believed to have been relatively insignificant. Nevertheless, there are several archaeologists who still maintain that the final development of Stonehenge (Stonehenge III) *must*, on several counts, have derived from a significant Mycenaean contribution.

In the final chapter of *Stonehenge*, Lockyer summarized his ideas in a reconciliation of his Egyptian findings with those derived from Britain and Brittany. He related that his British observations were based on observations made at a large number of monuments 'made in the course of three or four years, by the help of a great many friends in different regions, who find it a very pleasant occupation for their holidays'.

This evidence consisted of over a hundred positive alignments which he tabulated as follows:

Sun:	May	15
	November	9
	Summer Solstice	17
	Winter Solstice	11

Stars:	North clock-stars,	Arcturus	24
		Capella	13
	South clock-stars,	Alpha Centauri	6
	Warning stars,	Pleiades	16
	Warning stars,	Antares	2

Lockyer described his evidence as 'overwhelming' and believed that blind chance had nothing to do with the setting out of the various alignments for he stressed how well they fell into definite groups. But he did not subject this work to any kind of telling statistical analysis as did Hawkins and Thom with their own findings in more recent times.

In his chronology Lockyer considered that the avenues and cromlechs formed the earliest, primitive stage, and the stone circles came later—representing a more advanced practical astronomical knowledge. The avenue was single purpose, and could only be orientated towards the rising (or setting) of a single astronomical object, whereas the circles in combination with several outliers were multipurpose and may have marked several different astronomical events. The earliest sunrise observations related to May—the vegetation year (closely associated with growth and fertilization)—which Lockyer believed had probably been Paleolithic man's first solar mark point on a distant horizon. Much later the orientations were associated with the solstitial year beginning in June. At Stonehenge Lockyer suspected there had once been circles associated with May which preceded the present-day solstitial circle. Thus perhaps Stonehenge had begun as a May temple—a British Memphis— and had ended as a solstitial one like that of Amen-Ra at Thebes (*vis-à-vis* Lockyer's Egyptian ideas).

Lockyer concluded (correctly) that the British circles were in full operation 'more than a thousand years before the Aryans or Celts came upon the scene'. But he supposed that the Druids of Caesar's time were undoubtedly the descendants of the astronomer-priests of more ancient times, and through the Druids he believed one could study the achievements of the earlier astronomer-priests.

There can be no doubt that some of Lockyer's Celtic-cum-Druid interests were fostered by what French archaeologists had told him about the origins of the Lockyers—supposedly descended from the Ligures—an early Celtic swarm—who settled near the Ouse. The temptation to attribute some astronomical knowledge to his immediate forebears was perhaps subconscious, but nevertheless it does appear to have coloured his ideas about the Celts (*see* note 10).

Between the years which followed Lockyer's pioneer writing and the appearance of Hawkins' novel paper 'Stonehenge Decoded', little was done at Stonehenge to follow up Lockyer's ideas. His work suffered criticism from all sides. But it was his later, rather extravagant, speculations which lost him most support. His earlier work in Egypt and at Stonehenge had indeed won many champions even among archaeologists of the stature of Wallis Budge, Flinders Petrie and Gaston Maspero. Scholars such as Max Muller and J. G. Frazer saw in Lockyer's practical field work much to confirm their own library-researched mythological and folklore writings. Frazer was no doubt delighted to read what he considered confirmation of his ideas about midsummer fire mythology when he read in Lockyer's *The Dawn of Astronomy* '. . . just as surely as the temple of Karnak once pointed to the Sun *setting* at the summer solstice, the temple of Stonehenge pointed nearly to the Sun rising at the summer solstice . . . Observations indicated to priests that the New Year had begun, and possibly also fires were lighted to flash the news through the country. And in this way it is possible that we have the ultimate origin of the midsummer fires . . .'.

After the publication of the first edition of his Stonehenge book in 1906, Lockyer had persuaded the Royal Society to set up a committee to carry out an astronomical survey of ancient monuments in Britain. Although he professed himself too old to undertake the new work, it was at this very period he began to look into Welsh stone circles and to immerse himself deeply in Celtic mythology.

These mythological investigations went beyond the boundaries of what most present-day archaeologists and astronomers think relevant to scientific astro-archaeology. His hyperdiffusionist ideas which advocated an early link between Britain and Egypt were interesting enough but had little real evidence to support them. His belief that an astronomer-priesthood class familiar with Egyptian methods began their work in Britain as early as $c. -3600$, and the Druids were lineal descendants of a Semitic people who migrated to Britain had all the flavour of an eighteenth-century Romantic like Stukeley but none of the cautionary scepticism one expects from an Editor of *Nature* and an influential Fellow of the Royal Society to boot. His grand synthesis approach, utilizing a combination of archaeology, astronomy and mythology, was pioneering and praiseworthy so long as it was disciplined by the strictures of scientific method. His early supporters were perfectly willing to go along with the idea that the Egyptians *and* the ancient Britains had orientated their buildings and monuments to the heavenly bodies, but the Druidical overtones—derivative of Aubrey and Stukeley—were not so easily digested.

Lockyer died in 1920. Soon after one of his friends—and a sympathetic biographer—wrote: 'The Sun is our supreme historian, and the astronomer is his prophet. Lockyer's astronomical interpretations, often tentative in suggestion, often based on defective measures, and at best but holiday work, are a legacy left by a great interpreter of the Sun himself to students of archaeology and anthropology which they cannot afford to ignore.'

CHAPTER IV

Stonehenge:
Later Scribes and Speculations

A principal criticism against Lockyer's Stonehenge theories was the method he adopted for determining sunrise at Stonehenge in relation to the estimated age of −1680 (± 200 years). Sunrise at Stonehenge he considered was the instant when the first gleam of the Sun's disk appeared, while at Karnak (in his Egyptian studies) he defined it as the moment when the Sun's centre (half orb) reached the horizon. Lockyer was accused by his critics of arranging the facts in arbitrary fashion to suit his different theories.

In 1912, T. E. Peet, in his brave little monograph *Rough Stone Monuments*, attempted to find who the builders of Stonehenge were, and from where in history its builders had so suddenly and so mysteriously sprung and then apparently later disappeared without a trace. But Peet had no more success than Lockyer.

During the following years articles and books about Stonehenge continued to appear regularly, but most of them simply rehashed the previous archaeological material. In 1927 a review article appeared in the very first volume of *Antiquity*. This particular journal was to become deeply involved in the Stonehenge and other Megalithic controversies of the 1960s. The article 'Stonehenge as an Astronomical Instrument' by A. P. Trotter set out to re-examine the astronomical claims about Stonehenge. Trotter's intention was, he wrote, 'to examine facts rather than discuss theories'. Straightway he declared his interests, or rather his lack of partisan interest, for he approached the problem of Stonehenge neither as an archaeologist nor as an astronomer. The article chiefly discussed the implications of Lockyer's attempted method of dating and reiterated the three possible sun-rise positions of first gleam, half risen (half orb), and fully risen (full orb) which might be significant. First gleam gave Lockyer a date of *c*. −1700. Alternatively a half risen Sun will give *c*. −3500 and a fully risen *c*. −5200. Standing on Lockyer's designated central axis, he noted that the difference of position between an observer's right eye and his left makes a difference of 500 years to a date, and he concluded that consequently Stonehenge is a very unsatisfactory astronomical instrument for the purpose of setting out dates.

Trotter offered an opinion on how the Stonehenge midsummer-alignment idea might have worked in practice. He remarks that the eastern point of sunrise makes long hops in spring, then it slows down and creeps to nearly north-east. An observer standing midway under the great trilithon (55—56) would see the Sun one morning rise close to the north side of the entrance, and its rising point would change less and less each day, and for a period of about three weeks the position of the Sun on the horizon at sunrise would move only the width of the Sun. Thus he considered that the builders of Stonehenge may well have been able to tell the *week* when the summer solstice occurred, but that they could hardly have known the exact *day*. Because of this Trotter concluded that Stonehenge was useless for calendar purposes except to fix one 'date', namely the week of midsummer time.

Although snippets of evidence accumulated over the years, it was not until the early 1950s that a much clearer picture began to emerge about Stonehenge when the archaeologists Stuart Piggott, R. J. C. Atkinson and J. F. Stone attacked the problem.

By this time it was clear that Stonehenge indeed had a long history. The post-Roman dating of Fergusson had long been soundly dismissed. Excavations of the ditch had given up pottery shards and other artefacts that could be dated − 1900 to −1700, very close indeed to Lockyer's earlier perhaps somewhat highly fortuitous astro-based estimate. Piggott and Atkinson showed that the monument had grown and developed in later Neolithic times from a simple arrangement—comparable to other British henge monuments—to one of much greater complexity.

In what is now called Stonehenge I *c*.− 2350 to − 1900,* the monument consisted of a circular ditch and inner bank 2m (6 feet) high and 96m (320 feet) in diameter with a 10·5m (35 feet) entrance gap facing north-east (Fig. 42). From this period

* These are Atkinson's own uncorrected dates. The latest radiocarbon dates indicate a more ancient chronology.

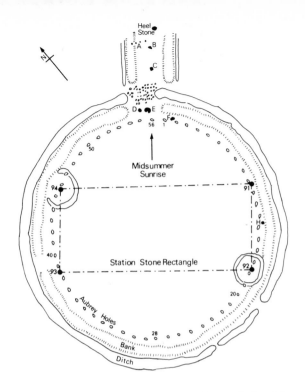

Heel
Stone

A   B

C

D   E
56   1

50

Midsummer
Sunrise

94   91

H

40 0   92

Station Stone Rectangle

93

20 0

Aubrey Holes

28

Bank
Ditch

42 Plan of Stonehenge I. The Avenue feature is dated later.

there are also several other significant features: the Causeway
postholes and other scattered groups of post and stoneholes B, D
and E; the fifty-six Aubrey holes which were dug and then
refilled shortly after; three large postholes in the visitors' car
park (Fig. 60) and possibly others yet undiscovered; the four A
postholes; probably timber posts at Stations 92, 94 and Heel
Stone 96, with the later erection of stones at Stations 91 and 93.
In this period stone D was possibly moved to C position, and
stone E was dismantled and subsequently buried alongside its
original position.

In what is known as Stonehenge II *c.*– 1900 to – 1700 (*see*
footnote, p. 90), a structure which is no longer extant, several
additional changes came about: The construction of the
Avenue; the filling of the Heel Stone ditch; the arrival at the site
of the bluestones, and the beginning of their erection in the
form of a double circle at the centre of the enclosure (Fig. 43).
However, the double-circle scheme was never apparently
completed, and only about two-thirds of the stones were erected
in position. When they were later removed, the holes were

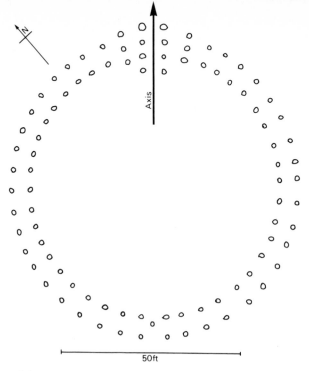

43 Plan of the Stonehenge II scheme. The erection of stones in the southern quadrants was never completed.

44 Stonehenge III depicting the lintelled sarsen circle (SC); the five sarsen trilithons (ST) forming a horseshoe; the bluestone circle (BC); the bluestone horseshoe (BH); and the Y and Z hole arrays. The key refers to the condition of stones *c*. 1975.

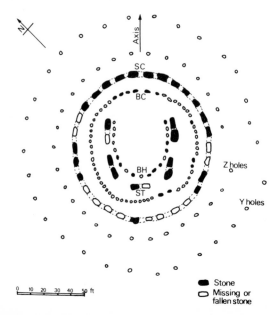

■ Stone
□ Missing or
   fallen stone

refilled with tightly packed chalk in preparation for the erection of the later sarsens.

During Stonehenge III *c.* – 1700 to – 1350 (*see* footnote, p. 90), the larger sarsen stones arrived on site from the Marlborough Downs and were erected: (*a*) as the five trilithons in the form of a horseshoe layout, (*b*) as a circle of thirty upright stones capped with lintels to form a complete architrave, or connecting ring. The bluestones, dismantled from building phase II, were re-erected to form (*a*) a circle of fifty-nine to sixty-one (the precise number is debatable) stones arranged in a circle 2·4 to 2·7m (8 to 9 feet) inside the sarsen circle, (*b*) a horseshoe layout consisting of nineteen stones positioned inside the five trilithons. The fifty-nine Y and Z holes were dug and then later allowed to fill up again naturally.

The fifty-six Aubrey holes—first noted by Aubrey in 1666 and then overlooked by subsequent commentators on the monument—were rediscovered by R. S. Newall during excavations supervised by Colonel Hawley in the period 1919—26. These holes consist of roughly circular pits varying from about 0·6 to 1·2m (2 to 4 feet) in depth and are filled with an assortment of chalk rubble, burnt material and organic topsoil. At one time it was supposed that they had once held stones or timber posts; but excavations have disproved this and indeed have indicated that they were deliberately refilled after digging.

The presence of the foreign bluestones incorporated in the Stonehenge structure has stimulated many speculations since the earliest published accounts. Judd, it will be remembered, considered that they had been transported to Stonehenge from another site, but that they originally had come to the general area via glacier action. Much earlier Geoffrey of Monmouth's apocryphal story recounted they had been brought over from a mountain in Ireland to be raised as a cenotaph to 460 slain British warriors. But how the stones had been transported in ancient times was a great puzzle. No one could really be sure which agency to invoke: Man or Nature. One thing was certain, no bluestones except for a few tantalizing fragments—associated with remains from the Wessex Culture—could be found in the district round Stonehenge in modern times; neither do any appear to be incorporated in local buildings or other modern structures—contrary to frequent reports that this occurs.

Fergusson, in 1872, believed the old Irish legend to be substantially true and related that this idea was corroborated by geologists because very similar stones were well known in Ireland. Fergusson asked:'Why may we not suppose that these were erected in memory of the kings or others who were buried in front of them?' Others, however, held the opinion that the bluestones were more likely to be spoils of war and had been brought to Stonehenge by the victors to perpetuate the great occasion. In 1923, H.H. Thomas put an end to the Irish story, at least, when he proved by a remarkable piece of petrological analysis that those stones long recognized as varieties foreign to Salisbury Plain all came from a relatively confined area in the Prescelly Mountains in South-West Wales. These foreign stones proved to be varieties of spotted dolerite or preselite, rhyolite and volcanic ash; the so-called Altar Stone and other foreign stumps and debris probably came from the Cosheston (sandstone) Beds at Milford Haven immediately south of the Prescelly Mountains.

The route by which these stones arrived at Stonehenge has vexed both archaeologists and geologists. Much has been written about the probable methods and techniques employed by ancient man to transport these massive stones to Salisbury Plain. These efforts have even been re-enacted for television audiences. Most now believe it was the hand of Man rather than the hand of Nature which brought them to Stonehenge. But the geological mechanism has not been entirely discounted, and in 1971 the geologist G. F. Kellaway argued again a very plausible case for ice (*see* below).

Although the distance involved is not great, the sarsens incorporated at Stonehenge have also been subject to transportation (probably from Marlborough Downs to the north, but this is not absolutely certain, *see* also Kellaway below). At several sites throughout Great Britain other Megalithic monuments are composed of stones locally foreign to the immediate vicinity.

In spite of the modern field work of Piggott, Atkinson and Stone, which threw fresh light on the construction sequences at Stonehenge, there were still many inexplicable puzzles. For example, what purpose had the Aubrey holes and the Z and Y holes served, and were there still undetected significances in the outlying Station stones? The Heel Stone and Avenue direction

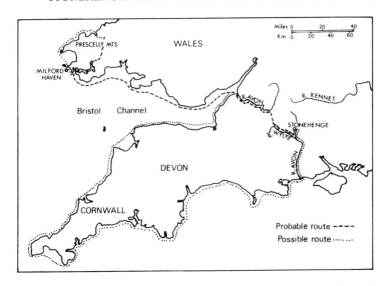

45 The possible alternative routes for the transport of the bluestones from the Prescelly Mountains in South Wales to Stonehenge in Wiltshire.

was accepted as astronomically—or leastwise seasonally—important, but there was little or no evidence round the monument to provide for more than the simplistic picture of it being some kind of prehistoric ceremonial centre linked with the summer and winter solstices.

Stonehenge by its location is closely associated with a remarkable cluster of round barrows. These and the exotic grave goods contained in some of the barrows had been assigned to the Wessex culture of the early Bronze Age dated, from its apparent links with Mycenae, to around − 1550 to − 1400. In the early 1950s some charcoal gleaned from the Aubrey holes (Stonehenge I) and submitted to radiocarbon analysis provided a date of − 1848 (± 275). But it was not until 1959 that the first radiocarbon dates for Stonehenge III were announced. A discarded antler pick, used in the construction of Stonehenge, had been found in association with one of the trilithons. This provided a date of − 1720 (± 150); more recent tree ring calibrations alter this figure by a substantial margin and places it at an earlier period.

An unexpected and exciting discovery, which at the time appeared to clinch the theory linking Stonehenge with

Mycenaean Greece, was a dagger carving found by Atkinson on one of the sarsen monoliths in July 1953. This was seen when he was attempting to photograph for a tourist some graffiti carved by a seventeenth-century visitor to Stonehenge. It was while gazing through the finder of his camera he suddenly saw the shadowy outline of a dagger and a single-bladed axe engraved in the stone (Fig. 46). Quickly moving his eye from the camera, he stared intently at the ancient weathered surface. The engravings were real enough, still plainly visible and quite unmistakable in the slanting afternoon light. Atkinson recounts that when he called his colleague J. F. Stone to see the marks for himself Stone became so excited that he bit his pipe hard and broke a tooth, which at least goes to prove that some archaeologists are not as phlegmatic as they would often lead us to believe!

Both to Atkinson and Stone the axe looked familiar. Irish weapons practically identical to it had been found in the Wessex barrows near by. This dagger intrigued them. It had a large knobbled pommel and a long, tapering straight-edged blade. Nowhere in Western Europe were such daggers found, but similar ones had been found among the ruins of Mycenae. If the dagger was truly Mycenaean, it would be very powerful evidence indeed to connect Stonehenge with the 3,500-year civilization of Mycenae, and with it the strong implications that the master architect of the later Stonehenge was himself an Aegean. . . .

46 Dagger, axe and assorted graffiti engraved on trilithon 53.

The discovery of the first prehistoric carving led to further discoveries. Carvings, and a whole miscellany of graffiti, dating from recent historic times were already well known at Stonehenge. There is hardly a sarsen which does not bear at least one inscription. The very sarsen photographed by Atkinson for a visitor that fateful afternoon (stone number 53) has one of the best known and deepest inscriptions, and probably one of the earliest, which reads IOH: LVD: DEFERRE (Johannes Ludovicus (or John Louis) de Ferre), positioned slightly above eye level (Fig. 46). There are also several other axe heads on this stone, shown with the cutting-edge upwards; some of these axe carvings (sky-god symbols?) have been subject to severe weathering, and there are traces of vague, more conjectural markings, too much affected by weathering for them to be deciphered.

Atkinson in his book *Stonehenge* (1956) related how, a few days after the first discovery, the ten-year-old son of one of the excavation helpers found the first of an even larger group of axe carvings on the outer face of stone 4 (Fig. 47). During the following week R. S. Newall, the veteran Stonehenge excavator, discovered a number of shallow, very weathered axe carvings on the same stone, plus another three, more clearly defined, axes on stone 3, near by.

Indeed, the first discovery was only a beginning and served to alert everyone to the possible existence of additional carvings. Several other traces of axes, daggers and rectangular designs have been noted since. Stones known to contain designs include 3, 4, 23 and 57. According to Atkinson, stone 156, which carries a carving once claimed to be prehistoric, was actually cut by an itinerant stone worker in about 1829. Another interesting carving is one discovered by Newall on the face of stone 57 which supposedly resembles carvings that occur in chambered tombs in Brittany and are known as 'shield-escutcheons'. The carving on stone 57 is very indistinct and has almost been entirely obliterated by continued abrasion from visitors' footwear.

Atkinson in his Stonehenge book made a special appeal to visitors not to finger any of the stones, and in the interest of posterity I pass on his request.

47 Axe engravings on stone 4.

CHAPTER V

Who 'Decoded' Stonehenge?

The discovery of the carvings had been one of the most exciting post-war finds and especially significant to archaeologists who firmly believed that the Stonehenge III construction phase owed much to cultural diffusion via Mycenae. However, a decade later the carving discoveries were overshadowed by Gerald Hawkins' spectacular ideas published in *Nature* on 26 October 1963. These ideas brought an immediate and interested response from many quarters.

Hawkins' first paper was a relatively short contribution. It set out to show that not only were Lockyer's summer solstice ideas correct, but that this was only the tip of the astronomical iceberg. Many of the stone alignments could be shown to indicate, quite unambiguously, rising and setting points of the Moon in its rather complicated path round the ecliptic, in addition to which there were several other highly significant Sun and Moon marker points 'hidden' in the monument.

Hawkins had first assumed a construction date of -1500, then with the help of an IBM 7090 electronic computer he determined significant horizon positions for the rising and setting points of the Sun, Moon, stars and the planets. Following this, various positions of stones, holes and midpoints were measured, using as a basis the existing survey of the monument published by the British Ministry of Public Buildings and Works; this survey has a scale of 20 feet to 1 inch.

One hundred and sixty-five recognized positions were fed into the computer. Primed with the coordinates of each one, the computer was commanded to perform three tasks:

(*a*) Extend lines through 120 pairs of surveyed positions (both ways, thus $120 \times 2 = 240$ positions).

(*b*) Find the true azimuths of these lines.

(*c*) Work out the declination* at which these lines extending outwards would intercept the sky-line.

This was of course only a modification of the basic method adopted earlier by Lockyer. However, since there are more than 27,000 possible alignments at Stonehenge, it can be seen that without resort to the modern computer the task of calculation is a Herculean one.

Hawkins recounts his methods and ideas in his subsequent book *Stonehenge Decoded* (1965). The program for the computer took about one day to work out. The basic card information was transferred to magnetic tape, and then the computer took over. In less than a minute the machine had its answer. Hawkins relates that he estimated that a human calculator would have been kept busy performing the same task for about four months.

From these results it was immediately apparent that the declinations provided by the computer showed a large number of duplications. Hawkins was set wondering. Were they significant? What did the repeated approximate declinations +29°, +24° and +19° and their analogues −29°, −24° and −19° mean?

First Hawkins and his assistants checked the planets. He noted that Venus was the only one which might show declinations of this kind. However, since Venus' maximum declination is ±32°, this seemed too big a discrepancy to provide a convincing fit. Saturn was then tried and found equally wanting since its maximum declinations are only ±26°. The rest of the brighter planets were also unlikely candidates.

Next the brighter stars were tried. Hawkins, of course, was familiar with Lockyer's work at Stonehenge and elsewhere, and it was inevitable that some of the stars frequently cited by Lockyer such as Capella, Arcturus, Sirius, Canopus, Vega and Alpha Centauri should be checked out. Since Hawkins had adopted −1500 as the chosen epoch for investigation, it was necessary to compute the various star declinations for this time (because of the effects of precession). But this done, he again drew a blank. Although Arcturus nowadays has a significant declination of +19° 21', in −1500 it was about +42°; Sirius

---

* Celestial equivalent of terrestrial latitude (*see* note 7 and Star Chart Fig. 37).

now has a declination of $-16°$ $39'$ in -1500 it was $-19°$. Although Sirius' declination in -1500 looks significant and a close fit for -1500, Hawkins considered that this particular fit was pure chance. None of Lockyer's other stars gave significant declinations. (The reader can verify this for himself for epoch -1500 by resort to Lockyer's star plots, see Fig. 36).

If then the planets *and* the stars could be discounted, what about the Sun? Hawkins wondered. He had already suspected that some of the extreme declinations would roughly fit the Sun; this was to be anticipated in view of the long established mid-summer solstice alignment. But then what about the Moon? Now Hawkins relates he went back to the computer, this time to determine the extreme declinations of both the Sun and the Moon at epoch -1500 and the extreme directions of their risings and settings at this time. It was not known of course (except for Lockyer's *a priori* assumption) how the Stonehenge observers in ancient times might have interpreted risings and settings, viz. which part of the Sun indicated the alignment (see Fig. 31). Hawkins believed that this problem might also be resolved by the computer.

The Sun has two extreme positions for rising (i.e. winter and summer solstices), but the Moon, owing to its more complicated movement, has four. These factors were taken into account when the computer was reprogramed. This new task was performed by the computer in a few seconds. When Hawkins and his assistants compared the figures, he relates that they were left with no doubts. The supposition that the Stonehenge alignments followed the paths of the Sun and Moon in relation to their horizon movements was 'all but complete'.

Hawkins confessed that he was prepared for *some* Stonehenge Sun correlations but not for a *total* Sun correlation; neither had he suspected that there might also be a total Moon correlation as a bonus. Lockyer had never once hinted at a Moon correlation for Stonehenge or any other British or French alignments, and Hawkins himself least expected any. However, had either carefully read all the available (but voluminous) apocryphal Druid literature, both might, indirectly, have been alerted to this intriguing possibility. A later reference (post-Lockyer) is that provided by Vice-Admiral Boyle Somerville in 1912. In a paper published in the *Journal of the British Astronomical Association*, Boyle Somerville had suggested that there was a lunar line in the Callanish Megalithic monument in Scotland. . . .

Alexander Thom subsequently followed up both Lockyer's and Somerville's work. Over several years, working slowly and methodically with little or no publicity, he had already by the 1950s come to the firm conclusion that many of the stone circles investigated and surveyed by him showed (in addition to other astronomical and novel metrical features) positive lunar orientations. But, for personal reasons, his work had not included Stonehenge and did not do so until much later (1974).

C. A. (Peter) Newham, a British amateur astronomer, had a year or two previous to Hawkins investigated both lunar and solar alignments at Stonehenge. However, by one of those quirks of fate that beset scientific discovery, and which has some disturbing echoes of the controversy that occurred in British astronomy surrounding the discovery of Neptune in 1846, his work was passed over or ignored until Hawkins' first paper appeared in *Nature* and stirred up the long-dormant Stonehenge astro-debate.

Newham's involvement with Stonehenge began in 1957 when visiting the monument with his wife. He then became interested in Lockyer's ideas after discussing the various astronomical theories with a warden. Being advised to read Atkinson's doubts about Lockyer's findings (set out in Atkinson's book *Stonehenge*), he was soon set to thinking about possible new approaches to the whole problem. It was not long after this that two events occurred in his life which influenced his subsequent actions: His wife died and shortly afterwards he retired. Now inactive after forty-six years as a gas industry engineer, he found himself at a loose end. It was (as an engineer himself) that he decided to recheck Lockyer's axis and alignments which he ingenuously believed might be done in a few days. In this, he later related, he was sadly misled; there was more in the monument than met the eye, and he returned home after two weeks 'not much wiser than when he went'. But this first reconnaissance had not only been to examine the problems involved in finding an accurate axis alignment, but also to re-establish, search out and settle doubtful measurements and differences in various published plans of the monument.

During the following three years, from his home in Yorkshire, he visited Stonehenge many times—always accompanied by his old theodolite. As time went by, his practical knowledge about Stonehenge increased. Then one day he began to suspect that the alignment Station 92 to disturbance G was positively aligned to the extreme northerly moonrise (one of the four extreme Moon positions). It was now that one of those odd quirks of fate enters the story. Because his ideas and his arithmetic were only tentative, he wrote to a professional astronomer friend at London University Observatory for confirmation of his own calculated positions. In the letter he requested what the true azimuth of the Moon should be for this particular alignment. In the reply to his query this figure was given as 45°. Newham was disappointed, for this was several degrees different from what he considered himself as correct. But being only an amateur astronomer, who was he to argue with a professional? He now temporarily put aside the Moon-alignment ideas and looked further into possible Sun and star alignments.

In November 1962 he received a list of possible stellar, Sun and Moon risings from an amateur astronomer friend, F. Addey, then Director of the Solar Section of the British Astronomical Association, who knew about Newham's interests at Stonehenge. The list was composed of risings which might have been observable in early times over the Heel Stone. It was late evening when Newham casually cast his eyes over the list just before retiring to bed. However, for some inexplicable reason he found sleep impossible that night; subconsciously his brain was working overtime. Somehow the arrangements of numbers seemed vaguely familiar, but yet so elusive. Then quite suddenly the mist of doubt evaporated. Around midnight the problem of his previous anomalous Moon alignment had been solved; the figure given to him by his friend at London University should have read 40°.5 and not 45°.0. Clearly a stupid, unchecked typing error had misdirected the whole of his subsequent work. Now fully aroused, all ideas of sleep that night were forgotten. By 4 a.m. not only was the alignment 92—G confirmed time and time again, but also two new Sun alignments.

Newham, who along the way had been much influenced by the findings elaborated in Atkinson's Stonehenge book and also by Newall's role in pre-war excavations, wrote immediately to both of them to present his results. Newall himself had always had an eye open for possible astronomical significances at Stonehenge. Earlier he had suggested that the *most* significant alignment might be midwinter sunset, and he was sceptical of all but Newham's new idea for an equinox alignment. Atkinson, however, was in general accord with all the ideas and advised Newham to seek publication, suggesting *Antiquity* as the appropriate journal.

An outline communication setting out his results was duly submitted to Glyn Daniel, Editor of *Antiquity*, along with a query whether Daniel would be willing to accept a more extended treatment. Newham sat back to await reaction. But for two months Newham's communication apparently languished on the Editor's desk. Then, at last, in March, Newham received a letter rejecting it. In reply Daniel wrote that since he was not an astronomer, he did not properly understand it—but in any case he did not believe it to be suitable material for his journal. What is still unclear is whether or not Daniel, while fearlessly admitting his own inability to judge its astronomical merits, had submitted it to a referee who could assess it.

Newham himself always felt that his communication was rejected simply because he was an amateur astronomer rather than a man of recognized academic standing. It seems more likely, however, it was because he was an astronomer of *any* kind. For although now dead some fifty years, the nightmare *bête noire* spectre of Lockyer and his Druids still haunted the chambers of the Society of Antiquaries at Burlington House W.1.

Meanwhile in Leeds, where Newham was active in the University Astronomical Society (and had served as its President), he had publicly discussed his ideas with astronomical friends. One of them, the Science Correspondent of the *Yorkshire Post,* was sufficiently impressed that Newham was on to something truly original and as a result wrote up a popular account of Newham's work as a three-column article which appeared in the pages of this influential but provincial North Country daily on 16 March 1963, a full seven months before Hawkins' own original paper in *Nature.* Newham's work—to satisfy journalistic taste—was written up under the eye-catching title: 'The Mystery of Hole G' (Fig. 48). In many ways this subject title is still relevant because archaeologists, particularly R. A. Newall, have good reason to doubt that this particular hole (among others) was man-made. But hole G was not the fundamental issue raised by the article. What it set out to show

The Mystery of Hole G

BY DOUGLAS EMMOTT

Attention this week has once again been focused on Stonehenge, where one of the uprights was blown down in a gale. In this article, The Yorkshire Post Science Correspondent discusses an amateur astronomer's intriguing theories which may add a new chapter to the story of Stonehenge.

STONEHENGE, that mysterious monument which rises above Salisbury Plain, may be a little less inscrutable than had been supposed. An amateur astronomer, Mr. Peter Newham, 63, of Tadcaster, has formulated an intriguing hypothesis which, if proven, might open up whole new fields of inquiry in a subject which has yielded very little significant new information since the last major excavation nearly 40 years ago.

If Mr. Newham's line of reasoning is sound, the positions of certain hitherto inexplicable features of Stonehenge would be explained For the purposes of this inquiry the plan of Stonehenge given here is reduced to the elements bearing upon the new theory.

In 1846, the Rev. E. Duke discovered that the North mound 94 lined up with a stone numbered 93 at the last light of the setting sun on the shortest day of the year. Conversely, a line drawn from the South mound (92) to stone 91 aligned with the rising sun on the longest day of the year.

It was discovered, too, that the axis of the Sarsen stone circle was similarly aligned In fact, the positions of sunrise and sunset are slightly different today owing to the progressive shift of the earth's axis.

So much, then, is established. What follows is speculation. On several occasions in the past few years Mr. Newham has visited the site and made careful observations of his own.

The first remarkable discovery he made was that a line drawn from mound 94 to 91 would appear to coincide with the point on the horizon where the moon rises at its most southerly point during its 19-year cycle.

Conversely, the line from 92 to 93 marks the moonset at its most Northerly setting point. The suggestion that these two alignments are of significance is bolstered by the curious fact that the main Sarsen circle of stones is about a yard off-centre with the outer Aubrey circle of burial holes.

Had it been quite concentric, the 92-93 sighting would have been obscured. Is this the reason for the off-centredness which has puzzled generations of archæologists?

It must be remembered that the layout of Stonehenge has been drawn up generally with remarkable precision. The ancient architects were evidently knowledgeable geometricians: indeed, the feat of measurement would tax a modern surveyor with the most up-to-date instruments and techniques.

Unusual feature

From this point, attention is turned to another unusual feature. This is catalogued as " hole " G, the middle of three equally spaced " holes " lying to the East and just beyond the Aubrey circle, and for which there is no convincing explanation.

Most Stonehenge authorities

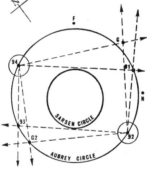

have dismissed these disturbances as natural or " shrub-holes." Their disconcerting symmetry and the absence of similar features within the whole of the area that has been uncovered have prompted doubts in more cautious minds.

Mr Newham has noted that a line drawn from 94 to G appears to mark the rising sun on the shortest day of the year. Mound 92 to G marks the moonrise at its most Northerly point.

Thus, six of the eight major solar lunar events of the year are apparently accounted for within the theory. To complete the octet, Mr. Newham has postulated the existence of a further marker hole in the unexcavated part of the site, about 16 yards South of 93. This he has provisionally designated G2.

Now, a line drawn from 92 to

Mr. Peter Newham: A new theory about Stonehenge.

G2 would mark the setting sun on the longest day, while 94 to G2 would mark the moon set on its most Southerly point. Thus, the hypothesis has the added merit of inviting confirmation. If the hypothetical G2 should, in fact, be discovered the possibility of coincidence could be virtually eliminated. The key which now seems to fit the lock would surely turn.

Advanced culture

It would seem, therefore, that Stonehenge might be a far more comprehensive calendar in stone than has been supposed. This, in turn, would suggest that the builders of the later portions of the monument were of a more advanced culture than the native inhabitants of Britain at that time says Mr. Newham. There is supporting archæological evidence for this view.

A few years ago, there would have been no difficulty in obtaining permission to search .or positive confirmation of the existence of G2. One would simply have dug about the point indicated and sought the necessary proof.

Today, however, archæologists tread with infinite care. In the past, crude pickaxe excavating has destroyed a wealth of detailed information which modern science would have been capable of deciphering Such brutal methods have wrought such havoc with the " shrub-holes," for example, that it is now almost impossible to determine their real significance even with advanced techniques.

Reluctant to dig

Conscious of this fact and realising that future generations of investigators will read much greater meaning into undisturbed evidence than we might hope to do, the custodians of Stonehenge are reluctant to dig. Nearly one half of the site remains virtually unexplored below ground and only in exceptional circumstances will the Ministry of Works sanction further excavation.

It is conceivable, however, that archæological advisers will recommend a search for Mr. Newham's ghost-hole, G2 by preliminary above-ground detection methods. Encouraging soundings would indicate a call for spade and trowel—and, perhaps, the opening of a new chapter in the story of Stonehenge.

48-9 C.A. Newham's ideas about Stonehenge were first published in the *Yorkshire Post* on 16 March 1963. Note the hypothetical G2 hole.

was that the Station stones could be used to indicate several alignments—particularly lunar ones.

Back in 1846, the Rev. E. Duke had discovered that the North mound (94) lined up with stone number 93 at the last light of the setting Sun on the shortest day (Fig. 49). Conversely, Duke noted that a line extended from the South mound (92) to stone 91 aligned with the rising Sun on the longest day of the year. Duke's discovery can be considered the first real step in solving the astronomical problems of Stonehenge.

Newham had discovered an equinox alignment, 94 to stone hole C, but he also noted that a line extended from mound 94 to 91 appeared to coincide with the point on the horizon where the Moon rises at its most southerly point during a nineteen-year cycle. Conversely, the line from 92 to 93 marked the moonset at its most northerly setting point. Newham believed that these two alignments were significant by the curious fact that the main sarsen circle is about 1m (3 feet) out of true centre with the Aubrey holes. Had they been concentric, the 92—93 sight line would have been obscured. This off-centre puzzle of the monument had long been a contentious discussion point among archaeologists.

Newham's view on the controversial G hole (possibly a natural hole or a hole left by the rotted stump of a long dead shrub or tree) was that it could be considered very significant since a 94 to G alignment marks the rising Sun on the shortest day of the year. Mound 92 to G marks the moonrise at its most northerly point.

Thus it was Newham's contention that six of the eight major solar/lunar events of the year could be accounted for within the theory. But speculating further (and speculation is a genuine and useful scientific tool if handled in a disciplined way), Newham introduced a hypothetical marker hole in the unexcavated part of the site about 10·5m (35 feet) south of 93 which he provisionally designated G2 (Fig. 49). From this the hypothetical alignment 92 to G2 would mark the setting Sun on the longest day, while the assumed alignment of 94 to G2 would mark the moonset on its southerly point. Newham believed that if the hypothetical G2 were later discovered by excavation, the chance of sheer coincidence having influenced the arrangement of Stonehenge alignments could be very nearly eliminated.

Atkinson, following discussions about this idea with Newham, later searched for G2 using a primitive, but effective, surface-bumping technique ('bosing'), but with negative results. Newham, however, was correct in his intuition about looking for a southerly moonset point. Although it still appears he was wrong about the particular hypothetical 92 to G2, such a true azimuth exists elsewhere in the monument which later finds confirmed (*see* below).

This G2 ghost hole drew attention to the point that only half the site had been excavated. The remaining half was unexplored below surface level, and only in very exceptional circumstances would the Ministry of Works, who administered the monument, wave the embargo on further excavation. Post-World War II field archaeologists were acutely embarrassed by their nineteenth-century and pre-war colleagues whose excavation techniques were not always above criticism. In the future, some believe traditional field excavation may be superseded; newer sub-surface exploration techniques might even resolve problems without disturbing the valuable—and irreplaceable—four millenniums of debris buried underfoot.

The same week that Newham's findings appeared, Stonehenge had been in the news following the collapse of one of the sarsen uprights in a gale. The public might be greatly interested in one of the sarsens tumbling over in the wind, but Newham's work created not a ripple of response. The seminal message that the sarsens perhaps formed part of a complex of stones of an advanced prehistoric culture, perhaps unique to Britain, had fallen on very deaf provincial ears.

Newham was again bitterly disappointed. But convinced that his ideas were sound, he did what no professional literary adviser would have recommended: he decided, at his own expense, to print and publish his findings in full.

Yet even now the Fates were still against him. A local printer promised delivery of the booklets ready for sale by June 1963. Three days after receipt of Newham's manuscript, the print shop was razed to the ground by fire. Although new premises were promptly found, it was not until late October (three days before Hawkins' paper 'Stonehenge Decoded' appeared in *Nature*) that Newham received the first galley pulls for correction. Newham's booklet, *The Enigma of Stonehenge and its Astronomical and Geometrical Significance*, finally saw light early in 1964.

On the same day that Hawkins' paper appeared in *Nature*, the whole world knew about the new Stonehenge theories, and his ideas were given the widest publicity by the press, radio and television. Atkinson, as the chief authority on Stonehenge, was asked by the media for his comments, but surprisingly failed to mention Newham's work. He did later apologize to Newham in a letter, giving the reason that the TV interviewer had failed to ask a previously agreed leading question. Such indeed is the spontaneous method by which fact and truth reaches a wider public!

Nevertheless, Hawkins' own work was highly original, and although following up the same basic ideas as Newham, he had taken them much further which he was able to do mainly because of his superior technological resources. With the help of the computer, Hawkins and his team had verified several puzzling Stonehenge alignments. The $\pm 24°$ declination of the Sun was there, but more frequently were the very significant $\pm 29°$ and $\pm 19°$ extreme declinations traced out by the Moon during its nineteen-year swing round the ecliptic. Hawkins and his team had found much beyond their earliest expectations: to a mean accuracy of $1°$ they claimed they had found twelve Sun correlations; and to a mean accuracy of $1°5$, twelve Moon correlations (also *see* Fig. 50). Hawkins related that following up the initial idea which had occurred to him during a visit to Stonehenge as an ordinary tourist (echoing Newham's own visit) the research was accomplished over the course of a single year; ten hours were spent on measuring charts; twenty hours preparing the computer program; and one minute of computer time with the IBM 7090! Checking out his results, using Bernouilli's well-known statistical theorem, Hawkins believed that there was less than one chance in a hundred million that the alignments were the result of a fortuitous design.

Hawkins assumed that the Station stones belonged to the Stonehenge I building phase. But this alignment included within the Stonehenge I chronology did not meet with wide acceptance among archaeologists. In reckoning his alignments, Hawkins had rather surprisingly missed 94—stone hole C, detected by Newham, which is most certainly a Sun equinoctial line (due east). A fundamental difference between Hawkins' alignments and Newham's concerned the old fundamental problem: what part of the disc (orb) of the Sun and Moon does

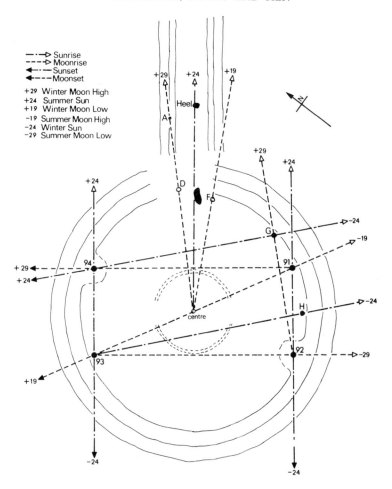

Key:
- —·—▷ Sunrise
- ———▷ Moonrise
- ◀—·— Sunset
- ◀——— Moonset

+29 Winter Moon High
+24 Summer Sun
+19 Winter Moon Low
-19 Summer Moon High
-24 Winter Sun
-29 Summer Moon Low

50 Solar and lunar alignments for Stonehenge Phase I (after Hawkins).

an azimuth refer to? Hawkins believed his computer studies showed that the critical point of sighting was when the full orb of the Sun and Moon was tangent to an artificial horizon, while Newham based his alignments on the first and last gleams, as seen on the actual horizon at time of rising or setting. Acceptance of one idea in preference to the other has the effect of suggesting some alignments in a reverse direction.

Where Hawkins went beyond what Newham and others had

proposed was in his ideas which involved the use of the sarsen-and-bluestone architecture of Stonehenge III to indicate significant astronomical alignments. Fundamentally it is this which the various archaeologist critics of Hawkins' theories found most difficult to accept. Nevertheless, Hawkins' computer studies had shown alignments of this kind to be a possibility. He believed that the five great trilithons, forming the central horseshoe, were likely intended to frame the rising or setting of the Sun and the Moon at the winter and/or summer solstices. Indeed, he recalled that when he first visited the monument as a tourist with his wife in June 1961, he was struck by the fact that it was impossible to see through all three of the narrow openings of the surviving trilithons from any single point. Since this violated what he supposed to be traditional customary architectural design, it immediately suggested that the trilithons were intended primarily to fix viewing lines. It was this which had been the root of Hawkins' own motivation to attempt to unlock the monument's long-hidden secrets.

Although the whole of the monument had now been given an astronomical basis, archaeologists such as Atkinson and Jacquetta Hawkes were not the least bit convinced by the evidence put forward—believing that the whole idea advanced by Hawkins seemed much too fanciful and totally beyond the intellectual capabilities of the so-called barbarian races who had inhabited the British Isles during the prehistoric period. The conflict of ideas between archaeologists and astronomers—the unfinished argument which had been smouldering dormantly like some quiescent volcano since Lockyer's day—suddenly boiled over in print.

Hawkins' article in *Nature* kindled response from all quarters. Most archaeologists who knew anything about Stonehenge were hostile, but some were sympathetic. Newall, although not totally convinced about many of the ideas, nevertheless now felt that Hawkins (and Newham) were on the right track. Hawkins had missed several important references in the older writings concerning Stonehenge, and Newall now took opportunity to draw Hawkins' attention to the long-familiar Greek legend about the mysterious island of Hyperborea. . . .

This legend has now unfortunately become a much hackneyed theme in Stonehenge literature. It surrounds a so-called lost *History of the Hyperboreans* and is quoted by that apparently inexhaustible font of ancient scientific *and* pseduo-scientific history, Diodorus Siculus, in his own *History* (*V*). The Hyperboreans are portrayed as a race living in the north, viz. 'beyond the north wind' who worshipped the Sun god Apollo. In brief, Diodorus tells us that their country was fertile and productive and produced two harvests each year (certainly possible even as far north as Norway with certain crops).

Supposedly Leto, mother of Apollo, was born on the mysterious island, and for this reason Apollo was honoured above all other gods. On their island, the Hyperboreans erected a sacred precinct to Apollo and a temple, spherical in shape. From the astronomical point of view, Diodorus' remarks significantly refer to the Moon as viewed from the island of the Hyperboreans where it appeared to be only a short distance from the Earth and to have upon it prominences. But the truly significant gleaning from Diodorus is that the god visited the island every nineteen years. This was a direct reference to the period well known to the ancient Greeks (and Babylonians) as the 'year of Meton', alluding to the Greek astronomer Meton who, in the fifth century BC, noted that 235 lunar months equal nineteen solar years, so that after nineteen years the phases of the Moon (e.g. First Quarter, Full Moon, etc.) repeat themselves (within a few hours) on the same calendar date.

Supposedly at the time of his appearance, the god played on an instrument known as the cithara (like a lyre) and danced continuously through from vernal equinox until the rising of the Pleiades. The supervisors (astronomer-priests) of the sacred precinct were called Boreales, and succession of position was maintained by hierarchical nepotism.

For a long time the piece about 'the god dancing continuously' had been recognized by astronomical mythologists as a significant allusion to a definite celestial event. But no one could be sure what was implied. George C. Lewis, the classical Greek scholar, in his *Astronomy of The Ancients* (1862) makes reference to ancient ideas which speak of the 'dances of the stars', and he believed it alluded to the circular dance of the circumpolar stars.

Newham had included the Hyperborean story at some length in his booklet *The Enigma of Stonehenge*. This reference had been supplied to Newham by Newall—whose commentary on its possible significance to Stonehenge Newham had also included.

Among several items, Newall drew attention to the point that many authors in writing on Stonehenge refer to Diodorus because of the story's supposed allusion to Stonehenge: namely that the mysterious northern island of Hyperborea was no other than Britain. But, as usual, much of Diodorus' information was quoted second-hand, this time via Hecataeus probably writing about −500 (or about 550 years before the time of Diodorus). Except for the reference to the spherical temple, no other evidence points to a possible connection of the story with Britain.

Newall had an interesting suggestion of his own about references to the Moon appearing only a short distance from the Earth from the island of the Hyperboreans. This he considered might be due to the illusion of the suggested largeness of a Harvest Full Moon at the time of its rising—when the familiar Moon illusion is certainly obvious, and this is a plausible suggestion. However, I believe it might also be construed to allude to the time when the Moon appears to hover for long periods near the horizon especially in high latitudes. Newall also called attention (as others before him had done) to the possibility that the nineteen bluestones may be associated with the nineteen solar years of the Metonic cycle. In addition it was suggested that it might be fruitful for someone to work out the position of the Pleiades for the years − 2000 to − 1000 so that a positive check against the Diodorus reference might be made.

F. Addey followed up this suggestion but found that neither this nor a number of alternative suggestions—with the exception of the Moon—coincided with any stone alignment when seen from the centre of the monument. But the Full Moon *would* appear once every nineteen years over the Heel Stone at the winter solstice about eight minutes after sunset when viewed through the Great Trilithon (55—56). But the Pleiades were certainly unobservable at the time of vernal equinox because they were then in conjunction with the Sun and would rise *unseen* shortly *after* sunrise.

Newall was not the first to refer the nineteen bluestones to a possible connection with the Metonic cycle. Godfrey Higgins in his *Celtic Druids* (1829) wrote: 'The most extraordinary peculiarity which the Druidical circles possess is that of their agreement in the number of the stones of which they consist with the ancient Astronomical Cycles. The outer circle of Stonehenge consists of 60 stones, the base number of the most famous of all the cycles of antiquity. The next circle consists of 40 [sic], but one on each side of the entrance is advanced out of the line, so as to leave 19 stones, a Metonic cycle on each side, and the inner of one Metonic cycle or 19 stones. . . .'

This quote from Higgins is also cited in an early volume of the *Leeds Astronomical Society Journal* (No. 7, *c*. 1900) as part of an article entitled 'Astronomical Theories Relative to Stonehenge' by Washington Teasdale. In this article the author described several interesting theories and discussed a new one just presented at the 1899 meeting of the British Association, which that year had met in Dover. This was a novel paper by a Dr Eddowes who suggested that one of the grooved stones situated near the leaning upright of the central trilithon had been used to support a pole 'in a permanent manner' to serve as the gnomon of a gigantic sun-dial.

In the same article Washington Teasdale also includes another of the more bizarre nineteenth-century astronomical ideas, attributed to a Mr Waltire, who considered 'that the Barrows and Tumuli surrounding the Temple accurately represented the situation and magnitude of the Fixed stars, forming a complete planisphere . . . other barrows registered eclipses which had taken place within a certain number of years and the Trilithons are the registers of the transits of Mercury and Venus'. This idea was to trigger several later ones in similar vein. *

However, perhaps the most interesting aside of Washington Teasdale was when he wrote: '. . . it is a regret that the late James Fergusson was prevented from rounding off his life's work by publication of his projected supplementary volume on Rude Stone Monuments, also that Professor Petrie is now similarly hindered from publishing the vast number of plans and notes on the same subject, which his industry, patience, and intelligence have accumulated. Unhappily we have as yet no Smithsonian Institute in England. . . .' Washington Teasdale could not possibly have imagined that just over half a century later Gerald Hawkins—an astronomer employed by the Smithsonian Institution—was to utilize the self-same resources of this institution in decoding the secrets of Stonehenge!

* In particular one known as the 'Glastonbury Temple of the Stars' (*c.*

CHAPTER VI

Stonehenge and Eclipses

When the equinox alignment and the reference to the Metonic nineteen-year cycle were pointed out to him, Hawkins immediately saw them as additional vehicles with which to probe further into the mysteries of Stonehenge. Already he had a feeling that the title of his own first contribution to *Nature* might have been 'presumptuous and premature'. Newham and Newall had provided the clues, and Newall, in particular, when later he posed the intriguing question: 'Could the Full Moon do something spectacular once every nineteen years at Stonehenge?'

But Hawkins first looked into the question of the rising of the Pleiades. The Pleiades had been cited frequently in connection with several monuments by Lockyer and Penrose; they were one of the most observed and discussed groups of stars in the ancient world. The Sumerians knew the 'Seven Sisters' as Seven Gods, and the Greeks at one time had reckoned them as a separate constellation. The Greek farmers in Hesiod's day reaped their corn when the Pleiades rose at sunrise in May and ploughed their fields when they set at sunrise in November. In the Bible, Job even refers to them in the passage: 'Canst thou bind the sweet influences of the Pleiades or loose the bands of Orion.' One tribe of Australian Aborigines even believed them more important than the Sun and attributed the cause of summer heat to the Pleiades. Every civilization had recorded their presence in the sky, and there is no reason to doubt that they were also well known to the Neolithic peoples of Britain.

Nevertheless, Hawkins, being a practical astronomer, realized that this cluster of 4th-magnitude stars would not constitute a bright object as it rose above the horizon or the Heel Stone; even

1935) which proposed that a series of great designs, mostly zodiacal, were sprawled across the hills round Glastonbury, represented by outlines of natural features such as old boundaries, woods, roads and ditches, etc.

in the unpolluted atmosphere of Britain c. − 2000 they would be invisible until they had risen several degrees above the skyline owing to the effect of atmospheric absorption which is very significant near or just above the horizon.

Returning to the alignments, Hawkins now included those represented by stoneholes B, C and E—taking his cue from Newham's significant equinoctial alignment 94 to C. Stone-holes B, C and E had been omitted from Hawkins' first calculations because he assumed them to be non-unique. As the stoneholes were positioned very close to the Heel Stone centre line, they had simply been dismissed as clumsy marker points to midsummer sunrise.

Hawkins related he went back to the computer in January 1964—two years after the first calculations. The machine was fed with new data, and again the answers forthcoming were truly astonishing. The stoneholes B, C, E and F, when aligned with 93 and 94, showed four almost zero declinations close to two of the Moon's four recognized midway points (Fig. 56). All the new alignments were found within the accuracy limits of the previous Sun and Moon alignments.

The lower midway points were highly significant for these mark the halfway position—the extremes of north and south. From these Hawkins confirmed some of Lockyer's earlier midway points—between the solstices and the equinoxes—which Lockyer had interpreted as solar calendar divisions of the year, but which Hawkins himself now felt indicated instead the Moon at its maximum declination ± 19°.

It was now time for Hawkins to cast his thoughts back to the Metonic cycle and the haunting question of a possible spectacular event performed by 'something' at Stonehenge once every nineteen years. In the literature of Stonehenge there are several references to eclipses. In 1796 a Wiltshire clothier, Henry Wansey, wrote an early piece about the possible astronomical nature of Stonehenge and among other remarks observed significantly:'Stonehenge stands in the best situation possible for observing the heavenly bodies, as there is an horizon nearly three miles distant on all sides. But till we know the methods by which the ancient druids calculated eclipses with so much accuracy, as Caesar mentions, we cannot explain the theoretical use of Stonehenge.' Washington Teasdale had also remarked on the nineteenth-century ideas of a Mr Waltire in reference to eclipses (*see* above). In his first *Nature* article Hawkins himself had already commented that the monument might prove to be a reliable calendar and perhaps function to signal the danger periods for eclipses of the Sun and Moon. The tentative evidence then was that eclipses were possibly involved in phenomena observed by the ancients at Stonehenge. Hawkins now posed the question: Might the big event at Stonehenge be an eclipse of the Moon over the Heel Stone—or alternatively in the gap of the Great Trilithon?

Hawkins adopted what Radcliffe Brown,* the volatile Cambridge anthropologist, had once defined as the 'If-I-were-a-horse' comparative method practised by his mentor, J. G. Frazer. This referred to the apocryphal story that when a certain American farmer found a horse was missing from his paddock, he went there himself to chew some grass and then ruminated about the problem of how he would behave and where he would go in the circumstances if he were the horse! Hawkins, applying this theory to Stonehenge, tried to put himself back into the minds of the Megalithic priests whose status in the community depended on accurate eclipse predicition. . . .

Eclipses, comets and meteorites were astronomical phenomena widely observed by the ancients. But probably only eclipses were predictable (this disregards some very doubtful evidence via old friend Diodorus Siculus that the Chaldeans could predict the returns of comets). It is generally believed that the Chaldeans were first to discover the art of eclipse prediction via the so-called Saros method (*see* below) but did not succeed in doing so before *c.* −750. The Saros method is often cited as the probable method used to predict one of the most famous eclipses in history—the eclipse of Thales now dated 28 May − 585, but it is more likely this whole story of Thales' prediction is some ancient hoax long perpetuated. Indeed if the Stonehenge astronomer-priests did succeed in predicting eclipses, it would predate claims made for any other ancient society.

Hawkins' thoughts turned to the famous but apocryphal astronomical story about the two Chinese astronomers Ho and Hi, and he wondered if the lives of the Stonehenge astronomer-priests might also have depended on successful

---

* 'Anarchy Brown' or 'Andaman Brown' as he was affectionately known to his colleagues.

eclipse predictions. In legend Ho and Hi were supposedly put to death by the emperor Hsia Chung-K'ang for not predicting a total eclipse of the Sun in −2136, and the pair are remembered by one of the best known astronomical verses:

> *Here lie the bodies of Ho and Hi,*
> *Whose fate though sad was visible —*
> *Being hanged because they could not spy*
> *Th' eclipse which was invisible.*

But it was not only in the ancient world that the over-looking of an eclipse could cause repercussions. A dispute occurred in the 1880s between the British War Office and the Admiralty. On this occasion the War Office had requested from the Admiralty—then responsible for such matters—details of important celestial phenomena which would occur over a given period in Africa relevant, and of interest, to the officers in charge of the Nile Campaign. An important strategic night march across difficult country was planned for the night of the Full Moon. On the day the weather was clear and, under the illumination of the brightly lit Full Moon, the order was given to start the march, but no sooner had they moved off than it was noticed that the Moon had begun to enter the Earth's shadow. As the landscape was blacked out, the march had to be hurriedly abandoned, and because the officers in charge had received no prior warning of the eclipse, the Admiralty were later accused by the War Office of wilful negligence.

Eclipses are of such fundamental importance in the under-standing of many problems in astro-archaeology—and particularly Stonehenge—that it is necessary to have a firm grasp of the basic factors surrounding the occurrence of these remarkable celestial events.

Eclipses are of two kinds: solar and lunar. Solar eclipses occur at the time of New Moon; lunar eclipses at the time of Full Moon. At these times the Sun, Moon and Earth are aligned in the same plane perpendicular to the ecliptic (called syzygy = three astronomical bodies in a straight line).

The Moon moves in an orbit which is inclined at an angle of about $5°15$ to the ecliptic; eclipses occur when it is close to the nodes—the positions in its orbit where it intersects the ecliptic (Fig. 51). It is the inclined orbit of the Moon that brings about large changes in the Moon's declination which is the prime

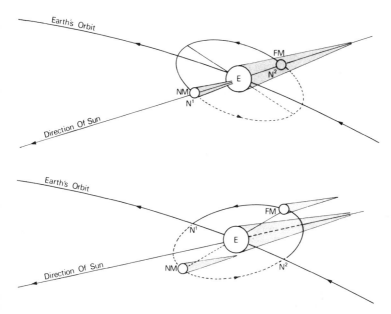

51 Eclipse occurrences. Owing to the Moon's orbit being inclined a little over 5°, eclipses can only occur at New Moon (NM) and Full Moon (FM) when the line of nodes (N^1 —N^2) of the Moon's orbit coincide with the direction of the Sun.

reason for the horizon swings at Stonehenge.

A complication in the occurrences of eclipses is introduced because the nodes of the Moon's orbit do not occupy a fixed position in space but instead have an annual retrograde motion of about 19¼°; this brings about a complete revolution of the nodes round the ecliptic in 18 years 218⅞ days (= 18·61 years) (Fig. 52).

Several ancient races noted that eclipses of the Sun and Moon are linked together in a certain chain, or sequence, which takes rather longer than eighteen years to run out when the sequence repeats itself *ad infinitum*. The eighteen-year period is known by the name Saros. It is widely—but mistakenly—believed that this was the name given it long ago by the Chaldean Babylonians. However, in Old Babylonian the word *Saros* has an ambiguous interpretation and probably is best described as meaning 'a measure'. As a number it also equalled 3,600. It was Halley, the English astronomer best remembered for the

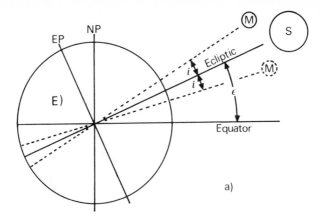

52 (a) The Moon's orbital inclination (i) in relation to the ecliptic (ϵ). The inclination of the ecliptic (obliquity of the ecliptic) changes between values of 21° 39′ and 24° 36′ over a period of about 40,000 years; present-day value = c. 23° 27′ 08″. (b) The celestial sphere showing the movements of the Sun (S) and Moon (M) as seen from the Earth. For an observer on the Earth, the Moon (ignoring the Earth's rotation) travels round the celestial sphere in one month, and the Sun travels round in one year. Since the Moon's orbit is inclined to the ecliptic at about 5°, its position in relation to the ecliptic 'above' or 'below' governs the Moon's declination values ($\epsilon + i$) and ($\epsilon - i$) shown as horizon azimuths at Megalithic sites. The Moon's nodes N_1—N_2 (the crossing points of the Moon's orbit to the ecliptic) regress slowly round the ecliptic in a period of 18·61 years. This period is also very important in tracing out horizon azimuths at Megalithic sites. The position of the lunar nodes are very important in relation to the occurrence of eclipses as these can only occur within the ecliptic limits.

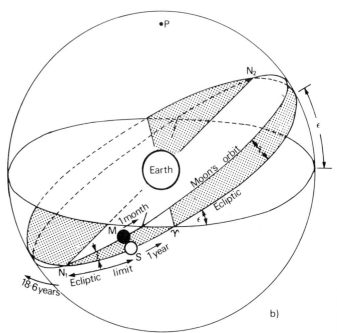

periodic comet which now bears his name, who made the false assumption that it was a word associated with the eclipse cycles; the usage has unfortunately persisted into modern times in spite of repeated protests.

To bring about an eclipse of the Sun, two things must combine: (*a*) the Moon must be at or near one of its nodes, (*b*) this must be a time when the Moon is also in conjunction with the Sun, twelve or thirteen times a year (the time of New Moon). The Sun only passes through the nodes of the Moon's orbit twice a year. Hence an eclipse of the Sun does not and cannot occur at every New Moon.

A regression of the Moon's nodes in combination with the apparent motion of the Sun in the ecliptic causes the Moon in its monthly course round the Earth to complete a revolution in respect to its nodes in less time (27·2 days) than it takes to get back to conjunction with the Sun (29·5 days).

As a consequence of these motions, the Sun starting exactly coincidental with one of the Moon's nodes, returns on the ecliptic to the *same* node in 346·6 days. The first named period of 27·2 days is referred to as the *draconic month* (nodical month), a name given for reasons which we shall refer to later. The other period of 29·5 days is called the *synodical month*. From this it is found that 242 draconic months, 223 complete lunations of the Moon, and 19 returns of the Sun (19 eclipse years) to the same node of the Moon's orbit, all occur in the *same time* within about 11 hours.

Thus (approximately):

Days			*Days*		*Years*	*Days*	*Hours*
242 ×	27·2	=	6585·36	=	18	10	8·5
223 ×	29·5	=	6585·32	=	18	10	7·75
19 ×	346·6	=	6585·78	=	18	10	18·75

From this it follows that if we suppose the Sun and Moon to start together from a node, after a lapse of 6,585 days and part of a day they will be found together very near the same node. During the interval that has passed there will have occurred 223 New and Full Moons. And the final fact is that eclipses recur in about, *but not quite*, the same regular order every 6,585⅓ days (18 years 10 days 7 hrs 42 mins) = the Chaldean 'Saros'.

Because of the time difference amounting to about 11 hours,

this has some appreciable effect. For example, if a solar eclipse occurred at noon today (time of New Moon), then after 18 years and 10 ⅓ days, the phase of the Moon will again be new, but the Sun will not be exactly at the node because the Saros period is about ½ day shorter than 19 eclipse years. The Sun will therefore be close enough to the node for the eclipse to occur. However, the eclipse will not occur at our locality at noon, but at 8 hours longitude (120°) west of our meridian because of the third of a day in the Saros period. For more accuracy it is best to combine 3 Saros periods making 54 years 31 days; but to secure almost a perfect repetition of a series of eclipses, 48 Saroses are combined.

In lunar eclipses, the Earth's shadow (the cause of lunar eclipses) travels across the path of the ecliptic limit at a rate of 1° per day (which is the same apparent eastward motion of the Sun). There is a 24-day period (12 days before the node passage, and 12 days after the node passage) during which a lunar eclipse can occur. Nevertheless, a node passage can occur without a lunar eclipse taking place by the fact that the shadow takes 24 days to pass across the ecliptic limit, whereas 29 ½ days (the Moon's synodical period) must elapse before the Moon's disc overtakes the Earth's shadow again.

The Metonic cycle, cited by Diodorus, refers to another very interesting cycle. In the fifth century BC, Meton found that after a lapse of 19 years, the phases of the Moon recurred on the same days of the same months (within about 2 hours). The number 19 is the smallest number of years that is a multiple of the synodical month = one complete lunation period, and there are very nearly 235 synodical months in 19 Julian years (365·25 mean solar days). The 19-year cycle is quite an accurate one, it is only after 310 Julian years that the computed mean New Moons fall one day earlier than they should. It was this simple Metonic cycle which formed the basis of the calendar of the Seleucid Babylonian empire in antiquity and also the later Jewish and Christian religious calendars, particularly in the computation of Easter. The same cycle also found its way into India where it masqueraded in a different guise. In Europe, during the Middle Ages, this cycle solved all the problems of establishing the dates of the New Moon. It was of great significance to all calendar makers, and the lunar phases shown in the *Book of Hours*, made by the brothers Limbourg for the

Duc de Berry (*c.* 1400) to help while away his time in church, were all obtained by reference to the Metonic cycle. The significant number 19 became known in the Middle Ages as the Golden Number, for the significant dates were inscribed in gold upon public monuments, and as one contemporary quoted: 'This number excels all other lunar ratios as gold excels all other metals.' The Golden Number is simply the number denoting the position of any year in the lunar (Metonic) 19-year cycle. It is found by adding 1 to a given year and then dividing by 19; the remainder then = the Golden Number unless the remainder is = to 0 (zero) in which case the Golden Number is 19 (e.g. the Golden Number of 1972 = 16).

The Metonic cycle of 19 years is *not* in itself an eclipse cycle, neither is the nodal period of 18·61 years. Unfortunately, Hawkins and others confuse their readers by implying that both are eclipse cycles. But, of course, we can see that the number 19 *is* important in eclipses in the Eclipse year = 346·62 days = the interval between successive passages of the Sun through the nodes of the Moon's orbit. And approximately 242 draconic months = 223 lunations = 19 eclipse years.

It is likely that the much maligned Celtic Druids of the Iron Age themselves possessed a 19-year Metonic-cycle-style calendar in the period immediately before the arrival of the Roman legions in Britain. This might well have been inherited from a much earlier North European society (*see* note 11).

Hawkins utilized the cycle of 18·61 years of the nodal period because he felt that this was very close to the 19-year Metonic cycle. During the nodal period of 18·61 years, the midwinter Full Moon moved from north maximum declination of +29° at stone D across the Heel Stone to a north minimum declination of +19° at stone F, and then back again (Fig. 53). In a similar fashion Hawkins noted that the midsummer Full Moon switched back and forth across the viewing line reckoned through the archway of the great central trilithon.

It was now Hawkins tells us that he consulted the standard work on eclipses, *Eclipses in the Second Millennium* by Van den Bergh, for those which had occurred in the period −2000 to −1000 in order to find the month in which eclipses of the Sun and Moon had actually resulted. Utilizing the computer to indicate where the lunar eclipses had been, he noted that an

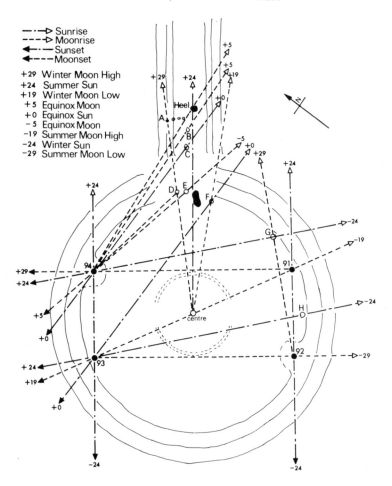

53 Composite solar and lunar alignments for Stonehenge (after Hawkins).

eclipse of the Moon or the Sun always occurred when the winter Full Moon nearest the time of the winter solstice rose above the Heel Stone. But not more than about half of these eclipses were actually visible from Stonehenge. Nevertheless, Hawkins suspected that the possibility that an eclipse might be visible would have been incentive enough for the astronomer-priests to mark the occasion of the winter moonrise above the Heel Stone as an eclipse-warning danger signal. Hawkins read into this idea the possibility that the astronomer-priests would claim for themselves that their skilled intervention had averted disaster (both in the ancient and medieval worlds eclipses were frequently cited as a cause of disasters).

Following his intuition, Hawkins showed that when the swing of the winter Moon carried it over D or F, the Harvest Moon was eclipsed that year. He reckoned that one of the key numbers was the interval between the nights of the winter moonrise over D which was 18·61 years. The other key number was the Metonic cycle number of 19 years. The interval he sought was *almost* 19 but not quite. If he chose 18·61, this clearly would not fit with a Metonic cycle series of 19 years. An extended series would mean there was a jumble of 19s and 18s, with an average of two 19s to one 18. Hawkins realized that a simple 19-year interval looked all right for two successive intervals, but a third interval would be in error by a full year. Soon after any extended series based on a whole number 19-year cycle would lead to considerable and unacceptable errors. The best fit was provided by a triple-time measure of alternate whole numbers, viz. 19 + 19 + 18 = 56 years. From his graphs Hawkins supposed that the Stonehenge Moon phenomenon was repeated every 56 years, and that the triple interval giving a sum of 56 years accurately reflected winter moonrise over Stone D for centuries. Thus the number 56 seemed positively connected with the Stonehenge Moon-rising cycle; but 56 was a strange astronomical number and did not immediately call to Hawkins' mind any known astronomical cycle.

But as a Stonehenge number, the number 56 sounded familiar enough. And indeed it was: the 56 Aubrey holes!

There had never been put forward a satisfactory account to explain the presence of these holes—except as receptacles for human cremation, but why the number 56? The archaeologists had noted they were carefully spaced. Only about half had been excavated, and the rest were found by probing and bumping ('bosing') the surface. Newall had rediscovered and named them the Aubrey holes during the era of Colonel Hawley's excavations in the 1920s. Those that had been excavated contained the remains of cremated bones and other prehistoric objects. Atkinson believed that the holes had been dug about 200 years after the construction of the Bank feature; apparently they were filled again shortly after this. Most of the holes showed signs of disturbance or re-excavation at a later date—some of them several times probably for interment.

In his Stonehenge book Atkinson expressed a belief that the holes had never been intended to hold any kind of upright, neither wooden post nor bluestone. If any worthwhile theory might be forwarded, they perhaps reflected some kind of ritual significance for cremated remains or even perhaps incinerated human sacrifices.

Hawkins published his second paper in *Nature* on 27 June 1964 under the intriguing title: 'A Neolithic Computer'. In this he explained how in his opinion the 56 Aubrey holes served as an eclipse computer—a built-in feature of the monument by which the Stonehenge astronomer-priests kept track of the Moon and perhaps even other celestial events. But how could such a crude computer work? Easy: if one tally (maybe a pebble or stone) was shifted round the circle, one Aubrey hole each year, the extreme positions of the Moon and eclipses of the Sun and Moon might readily be foreseen. The best *modus operandi* Hawkins reckoned was if six tally pebbles, or stones, were spaced at intervals of 9; 9; 10; 9; 9; 10, and each moved one hole counterclockwise each year; in this way 'astonishing' powers of prediction could be achieved. By using six stones, of which three were white and three black, every important Moon event was within reach of the operators for hundreds of years (Fig. 54).

But the new implication that Neolithic man had the intellectual capabilities to conceive and then operate such a computer-like device raised further serious doubts among archaeologists. When Hawkins published the popular account of his work as *Stonehenge Decoded* (1965), it was attacked in several learned reviews by archaeologist dissidents. It was not only in the scientific press that Hawkins' Stonehenge theories attracted wide attention. Newspapers throughout the world carried the story in various degrees of accuracy—some even as front page news. The popular newspapers, especially, drew freely on quasi-Druid Lockyer-inspired material—certainly never contained in Hawkins' work—to provide the necessary dramatic overtones and give the story even more readership appeal. Hawkins' personal mailbag was full for several months afterwards, and years later the letters still flowed in. The public was impressed: this was the kind of science journalism they found interesting, but it strongly reinforced the opinion later

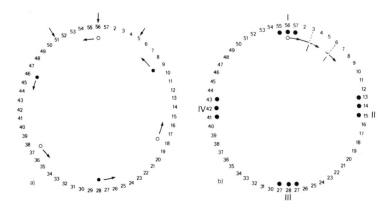

54 Methods cited by G. Hawkins for using the Aubrey holes as a computer for predicting eclipse seasons and swings of the Moon. (a) Hawkins' *modus operandi c.* 1964 using 3 black and 3 white tallies moving round one hole every year. A black or white stone arrives at hole 56 at intervals of 9; 9; 10; 9; 9; 10 years and predicts the Heel Stone Moon events. A white stone arrives at hole 51 at intervals of 18; 19; 19 years and predicts conditions of the + 29° dec (high) Moon. A white stone arrives at hole 5 at intervals of 19; 19; 18 years and predicts events associated with the + 19° dec (low) Moon. (b) An alternative *modus operandi* later cited by Hawkins for the operation of the Aubrey computer using a marker that is moved three holes each year to follow the regression of the nodes of the lunar orbit. Key: I Moon over Heel Stone (solstice eclipse). II December Moon over F. III Moon over Heel Stone (solstice eclipse). IV December Moon over A.

voiced by Jacquetta Hawkes: *the public had been given the kind of Stonehenge they had always wished for!*

Most archaeologists were not entirely negative to the idea of seeing certain astronomical alignments built into Stonehenge— especially in the way cited in the exemplary cautious ideas of Newham. This approach—with reservations—was generally acceptable. Newham's ideas were acceptable as a working hypothesis from which one might take the next cautious step. But the evoking of the Aubrey holes at Stonehenge as a prehistoric eclipse predictor was totally unacceptable to all but a tiny minority of archaeologists no matter how favourably swayed towards the idea some astronomers and the general public following appeared to be.

There can be little doubt that eclipses *per se* held a remarkable fascination for the peoples of the ancient world, and they played an influential role in all affairs. We have, of course, no way of knowing what the Stonehenge builders thought about eclipses or whether they guessed their true cause, and we have no clue to what they believed were the consequences which followed the occurrence of an eclipse. But there is nothing to make one doubt that they held similar views to later ancient peoples who left written accounts. The very term *draconic month* of 27·5 days owes its origin to the eclipse cycle. Many believe the very name and idea originated in ancient China (although perhaps via India) and alluded directly to the battle of the dragon and the Moon which supposedly occurred at the time of a lunar eclipse. On Oriental Zodiacs the dragon's head was depicted as the ascending node and the dragon's tail the descending node. It is in ancient China we can read that when a lunar eclipse took place, the Emperor and his Mandarins devotedly prayed to the gods that the Moon might not be eaten up by the great dragon which hovered about her. After the event, when the Moon had escaped the dragon's influence, a great pantomine was staged when sometimes 200 or 300 priests, bearing lanterns at the end of a long walk, would dance and caper about during a re-enactment of the event. In the same way we can read in the Mayan chronicle, *The Book of Chilam Balam of Chumayel*, a description of a solar eclipse: '. . . the face of the Sun was eaten' and 'a monster plunged head down towards the earth during darkness'. In Babylon the omen tablets and astronomical 'diaries' tell a story of general and widespread belief of fatal and unfavourable consequences following eclipses (*see* note 12). Similar astro-mythological legends abound in the very oldest sources, and Sumerian texts express much the same story in literature going back to *c.* −3000.

During total lunar eclipses the umbral shadow of the Earth assumes a coppery red tinge as it creeps across the face of the Full Moon. This is due to the refraction and absorption effects which occurs when sunlight passes through the Earth's atmosphere. The colour is often highly variable in intensity, and in some eclipses it is of a very deep red. This phenomenon frequently invited dramatic comment and interpretation by ancient writers. The *Anglo-Saxon Chronicle* in +734 is typical and records: 'The Moon was if it had been sprinkled with blood, and Archbishop Tatwine and Beda the Venerable died and Ecgberht was hallowed bishop.' In 1044 Raoul Glaber, a French chronicler, recorded the partial lunar eclipse of 8 November that year and wrote: 'In what manner it happened whether a prodigy brought to pass by the Deity or by the intervention of some heavenly body remains known to the author of knowledge. For the Moon herself became like dark blood, only getting clear of it a little before dawn.'

On more rare occasions the Moon may be blotted out completely by the Earth's shadow. This usually happens following a violent volcanic eruption on Earth when the Earth's atmosphere is choked with suspended dust, and sunlight normally refracted 'round' through the upper atmospheric layers is almost totally absorbed. These are the so-called 'black' lunar eclipses. Such an eclipse occurred on the night of 23 January +753 when according to one writer 'the Moon was covered with a horrid black shield'. A more contemporary 'black' eclipse occurred in December 1964 shortly after intense volcanic activity in the East Indies.

Many neoprimitives still live in fear of eclipses, and members of eclipse expeditions to remote geographical areas have witnessed—first hand—hysterical behaviour wrought by the unexpected disappearance of the Sun or Moon. One of the most famous eclipse stories in history involved Christopher Columbus. When he and his party were threatened with starvation in Jamaica because the locals refused him provisions, he decided to try a ruse. Forewarned of the arrival of the lunar eclipse by his almanac for 1 March 1504, he threatened to deprive them of the light of the Moon and of course he kept his word. When the eclipse began, the terrified natives flung themselves at his mercy and subsequently brought to him all the provisions he required.

These examples serve to underline the point that Hawkins was well justified in believing that lunar eclipses might be the truly significant events which the Stonehenge astronomer-priests wished to register. But this is not sufficient evidence in itself to support a contention that the fifty-six Aubrey hole complex was actually utilized as a Neolithic computer. One principal objection to this idea was that—as a computer—it could be operated several ways. Hawkins himself was keenly aware of this, but tended not to overemphasize the point lest it provide ammunition for the archaeologists to disprove this idea for the fifty-six-hole complex (*see* also below for alternative ideas).

Then on 30 July 1966 Fred Hoyle, the British cosmologist, published in *Nature* his own paper on Stonehenge entitled 'Stonehenge—A Neolithic Observatory'. Indeed, according to Hoyle, no matter what the archaeologists felt about the matter, there could be no doubts that the fifty-six Aubrey holes operated as an ingenious eclipse cycle computer. Hoyle had reworked the alignments of Hawkins, and in his opinion (an opinion which carried great weight in the scientific world because of Hoyle's high academic standing) the arrangements were not random. However, he believed Hawkins' assumption that the Aubrey holes served simply to count cycles of fifty-six years to be a weak idea. He considered that there was no necessity to set out fifty-six holes at regular intervals on the circumference of a circle of such a great radius in order to count cycles of fifty-six. In addition he found it difficult to imagine how the astronomer-priests would have calibrated the counting system proposed by Hawkins and cited the instance that Hawkins himself had used tables of known eclipses in order to discover this. But Hoyle's most telling argument was the inescapable fact that the Aubrey-hole predictor provided only a small proportion of all eclipses that occur. The questions arose: What merit could have accrued to the builders in predictions which may have intervals as far apart as ten years?—a consequence of Hawkins' reasoning. And following this: what about the eclipses that were observed but the astronomer-priests had failed to predict?

Hoyle now suggested, in place of Hawkins' ideas, that the Aubrey circle represented the ecliptic itself (the imaginary circle round the heavens along which the Sun and the planets appear to move, and at the angle to which (5 ¼ °) the Moon circles the Earth). This was a very novel idea and very much in character with Hoyle's sometimes unconventional approach to cosmological problems. But how would such a model operate in practice?

Beginning via Fig. 55—which depicts schematically the circle of the Aubrey holes—Hoyle assumed a time configuration when the Moon is Full. The first point in Aries (♈) is at Aubrey hole 14; S represents the position of the Sun; the angle ⊙ is the solar longitude; M denotes the position of the Moon projected on the

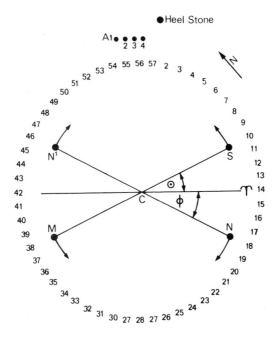

55 Hoyle's Aubrey-hole eclipse predictor.

ecliptic; N^1 the descending node; C, at centre, is the position of the observer. . . .

As time proceeds, the points S, M, N and N^1 move in the direction indicated (by Fig. 55). It follows that S (Sun) makes one circuit per year, but M (Moon) moves in one circuit per lunar month. When the Moon is at N (ascending node), a solar eclipse occurs when the Sun is within roughly ± 15° of N, and a lunar eclipse if the Sun is within ± 10° of N^1. Conversely, if the Moon is at N^1, a solar eclipse will occur if the Sun is within ± 15° of coincidence with the Moon, and a lunar eclipse if it is within roughly ± 10° of the opposite end of the line of lunar nodes.

Hoyle's idea was to represent S, M, N and N^1 by markers, and if the operator knows how to move the markers so as to represent the actual motions of the Sun and Moon, with reasonable accuracy, he can predict almost every eclipse; this he can do in spite of the fact that only roughly half of them will be visible from the position of the observer.

Hoyle believed that this achieved a great improvement on the widely scattered eclipses predictable under the system advocated by Hawkins.

Hoyle's *modus operandi* for moving the markers was as follows:

(1) Move S counterclockwise two Aubrey holes every thirteen days.
(2) Move M counterclockwise two Aubrey holes each day.
(3) Move N and N^{1}clockwise three holes each day.

Hoyle considered it to be a reasonable assumption to allow for the Stonehenge builders to have possessed knowledge of the approximate number of days in the year, the number of days in the month, and the period of regression of the nodes (18·6 years). The last parameter would follow by observing the azimuth at which the Moon rose above the horizon (the Moon swings).

Hoyle noted that with the periods of S, M and N known with reasonable accuracy these would provide an approximate 'prescription' to enable the observer, via Stonehenge alignments, to predict ahead what the position of M, N and S are going to be and therefore to foresee any coming event. Nevertheless, this would only work for a limited period because inherent prescription inaccuracies cause the markers to differ increasingly more from the true positions (in the ecliptic) of the actual Moon, Sun, and the ascending node.

The lunar marker is the first to deviate, for the prescription provides for an orbital period of 28 days (instead of 27·32 days). However, a correcting adjustment to the lunar marker (M) is made twice every month by resort to the simple (practical) expedient of aligning M opposite S at the time of Full Moon, and by placing it coincidental with S at New Moon. The prescription for S gives an orbital period of 364 days, which Hoyle believed was near enough to the actual true period, because it is possible to correct the position of S on four occasions every year. This could be done by practical observation checks along the actual midsummer, midwinter, and equinoctial alignments at Stonehenge.

Hoyle made the point that Stonehenge is also constructed to determine the instant when the ascending node (N) sets at ♈. By placing N at ♈ when the Moon rises at the farthest northern point of its swing (Fig. 56), the N marker can be calibrated once every 18·61 years. Since the error in one revolution is small, the N marker, if started correctly, would only be 1° + out of true position at the end of the first cycle. Now, since the tolerance for eclipse prediction is about 5°, an adjustment to N, every cycle, would enable the predictor to continue to operate indefinitely without appreciable inaccuracy.

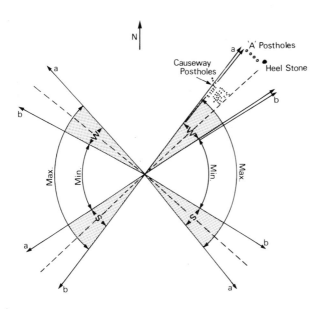

56 Maximum and minimum Full Moon rising and setting azimuths traced out at Stonehenge. The shaded sectors (a—b) show the maximum limits of Full Moon risings and settings in winter and summer, i.e. winter (W) Full Moon rising (north-east); winter (W) Full Moon setting (north-west); summer (S) Full Moon rising (south-east); summer (S) Full Moon setting (south-west).

When the winter moonrise begins at 'a', in about nine years, it will have shifted to 'b'; about nine years later it will be back at 'a', completing the 18·61 year nodal cycle. Note that the corresponding summer moonrise would also trace out analogous 'a' to 'b' and 'b' to 'a' movements. When the Moon is at the 'a' or 'b' position, these represent the major and minor standstill positions respectively which are analogous to the Sun's solstitial standstills (see also Fig. 77). The double line shown in the Heel Stone sector takes into account the difference in choice of azimuth between using first gleam and full orb, plus minor lunar perturbations. Note also that the pecked line marking the mid-point position in the sectors very nearly coincides with the Sun rising and setting alignments at the time of the solstices.

Hoyle, however, recognized that in practice the minimum azimuth of moonrise is difficult to determine and found it could not be determined in the method he first described in showing the working of his Aubrey-hole model. Hoyle demonstrated this graphically via a representation of the shallow slope involved in minimum azimuth swing changes (Fig. 57). This is a point where Hoyle introduced an interesting idea about the arrangement of the Stonehenge alignment markers, postholes A1, 2, 3, 4 (Fig. 56) which he considered have a regular and apparently exact and appropriate placing. What Hawkins in his ideas had supposed should be reckoned as errors in azimuth marker alignments, Hoyle believed were deliberate efforts to obtain more accurate northern and southern extremes at the azimuths where the Sun and Moon appear to 'stand still' (the solstitial standstills). In ten out of twelve values which Hawkins cited as errors (because Hawkins assumed that the Stonehenge builders intended to sight *exactly* to the extremes of azimuth), Hoyle believed he could show that such apparent errors could be cancelled out because the builders had *not* intended to mark azimuth exactly for reason of the practical difficulties in doing so. One of the outstanding cases was the alignment: centre to Heel Stone, where the azimuth error was zero; this suggested to Hoyle a special case, an exception to the general rule, and it may be here, for aesthetic and ritualistic reasons, the builders kept to the direction of midsummer sunrise. The other outstanding example was for alignment 91—94 which Hoyle again (but somewhat arbitrarily and glibly) felt constituted a case where true alignment was all important.

Hoyle had also explored other methods by which the N marker might be calibrated. One method which suggested itself was the special situation at the time when Full Moon coincides exactly at an equinox. The evidence that this method may have been tried by Stonehenge astronomer-priests is contained in several alignments. But Hoyle noted that the method is really unworkable because of the unavoidable errors in judging by practical observation the exact moment of Full Moon which can introduce large errors in the positioning of N, and because of the low inclination of the lunar orbit. Hoyle speculated that this method, if ever attempted at Stonehenge, might well have caused a furore in its day due to the significant emphasis it places to the Full Moon *and* the equinox, and this indeed might well have been responsible for the traditional Easter dating.

Hoyle made out a case that eclipse calibration can be operated successfully *almost* by complete numerology. In operation, S and N move in opposite directions. The Sun moves through N in 346·6 days; nineteen such revolutions = 6585·8 days, whereas 223 lunations is equal to 6585·3 days. Therefore after 223 lunations the N marker must bear almost the same relationship to S as it did previously. Now, if the correct relation of N to S is known by the operator at any one time, N can be reset every 223 lunations (or once every 18 years 11 days). This near-miss commensurability is suffciently accurate to provide satisfactory predictions for 500 years or more. But S needs to be set as before, but an advantage is that in the case of N it needs no practical observation to control it, although *without* observation the correction initial configuration cannot be determined unless the problem is turned round. Hoyle felt that the calibration might be set by practical trial and error—citing that this was probably the method used to determine the Chaldean Saros; nevertheless, he reluctantly admitted that there was no evidence that this method was used at Stonehenge.

To conclude his ideas Hoyle had some philosophical speculations to provide humanistic overtones to the abstract numerical arguments. He believed that from his own studies of

57 Graphical plot showing minimum azimuth Moon-swing changes at Stonehenge (after Hoyle *c.* 1966).

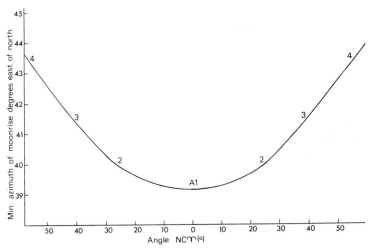

the Stonehenge problem, several cultural features presented themselves. Assuming that Stonehenge gave the Sun and Moon god-like qualities, he asked: what about N? At the time of eclipse S and M are eliminated, and perhaps N must then be a still more powerful god. But N is unseen. Hoyle asked: could this be the origin of the concept of an invisible all-powerful god, the god of Isaiah? Hoyle then wondered if M, N and S might be the origin of the doctrine of the Trinity: three-in-one and one-in-three? He believed it would be ironic if the very roots of our contemporary culture were determined by the god-like quality exercised by the lunar node. Indeed Hoyle in restating this idea had himself been very forgetful of his astronomical history, for, as more than one commentator noted: had not the ancient Chinese utilized this very idea with their concept of the draconic month?

CHAPTER VII

Stonehenge:
The Voices of Dissent

Fred Hoyle's ideas in *Nature* made almost as much public impact as did Hawkins' original contributions. In the same issue, *Nature's* own editorial described Hoyle's new ideas as 'breathtaking' not simply for their ingenuity but for their sheer practicality.

To every astronomer—whether amateurs observing with backyard telescopes or professionals observing with the 200-inch Palomar giant—Hoyle's ideas indeed were stimulating, pragmatic stuff. He had shown in a convincing manner that Stonehenge could function as a Neolithic observatory—an idea strongly reinforced by Newham's paper 'Stonehenge: A Neolithic Observatory' that followed Hoyle's in the same *Nature* issue (below). Hoyle's and Newham's ideas might even be constructed as a sophisticated development of the earlier simplistic lunar notations cited by Marshack. These had perhaps over a long period given Upper Paleolithic and Mesolithic man insights into lunar motion and then in Neolithic times had enabled the Megalithic builders to finally crack the secrets of the solar/lunar eclipse cycle. Thus Stonehenge may have represented a synthesis of some thousands of years of accumulated astronomical knowledge in the same symbolic way that the 200-inch glass giant at Palomar does today. . . .

Hoyle's theories, although they modified Hawkins' earlier theories, seemed to clinch the basic eclipse prediction ideas. With Hoyle's more pragmatic approach, contemporary astronomers could themselves enact the methods of the Stonehenge astronomer-priests and in doing so recognize the simplistic beauty of the numerical methods involved. Not everyone, however, agreed that the ideas were truly pragmatic ones, for the concept of node-stones has the implication of abstraction from practical observational theory and credits the

MEGALITHS, MYTHS AND MEN

Stonehenge astronomer-priests with intellectual abilities much on a par with their twentieth-century interpreters. And yet why not?

Nature's own editorial emphasized that it was the very cleverness of the ideas which Hoyle attributed to the designers of Stonehenge that was going to be the most difficult part of his theory to accept. The editorial rightly asked whether it was likely that people who had not yet invented enduring houses as domestic abodes could possibly have been clever enough to build an instrument of such intricacy at Stonehenge as implied by astronomers. This was the doubt to be frequently echoed by archaeologists.

But the editorial also stressed the significant point that archaeology can usually only describe the mundane, lower limits of the degrees of sophistication of any society, and if the archaeologists knew more than they did about life in Britain around – 2500, they might be in a position to show that Hoyle's ideas were implausible.

The lack of other supporting archaeological evidence for numeracy among the Stonehenge peoples is not conclusive proof that they could not predict eclipses. Indeed it is my own belief that Hoyle, when he embarked on the Stonehenge problem, had firmly in focus the methods practised by the nineteenth-century Tamil astronomers of southern India who, although lacking profound mathematical knowledge, could predict eclipses in a pragmatic fashion by manipulating groups of shells placed on the ground before them.

Both Hawkins and Hoyle admitted there were several possible methods of using the fifty-six-hole Aubrey circle. Hawkins later published an account of a simplified method in which one stone is moved three holes each year. In this method the Aubrey-hole circle performs as an analogue computer that follows exactly the regression of the nodes of the Moon's orbit.

Newham's own paper in the same issue of *Nature* was somewhat overshadowed by the more breath-taking ideas encompassed by Hoyle. Nevertheless, Newham had several ideas in common with Hoyle: Both were concerned to show how the postholes grouped at the north end of the monument—not included in Hawkins' earlier ideas—were somehow significantly connected with the Megalith builders' experiments to obtain refined measurements at Stonehenge.

Newham questioned the validity of Hawkins' so-called fifty-six-year eclipse cycle and the use of the Aubrey holes as a computer; although he did not dismiss the ideas out of hand, he stressed that in his opinion there were features in the monument that *unquestionably* had some astronomical inferences. He felt that the postholes, particularly those grouped round the Causeway Entrance, appeared to be very significant alignment features. These holes seemed to radiate from the centre of the Aubrey circle and to lie within a 10° arc north of the Heel Stone, or solstice line, and arranged roughly into six ranks crossing the line of the Causeway (Fig. 58).

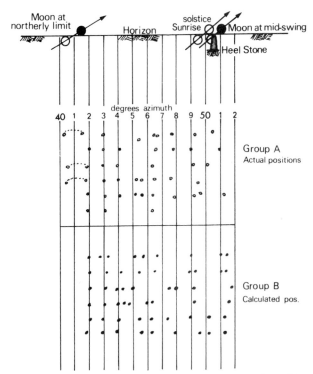

58 Causeway postholes in relation to the horizon limits of moonrise (maximum northerly to mid-swing) and the summer solstice sunrise near the Heel Stone. The group B holes are calculated positions for the full orb of the Moon *c*. – 1700. Actual positions suggest that the postholes are earlier than – 1700, and in some cases 'first gleam' may have been used (after C. A. Newham).

Newham suggested that a fairly reliable record of the Moon's azimuth swings could be found by siting a temporary marker, say a wooden stake, to align each time where the winter Full Moon appeared above the horizon each year. Indeed the postholes were a strong indication that this procedure had been carried out over a large number of years extending through several 18·61 nodal cycles. This, Newham believed, was a long enough period to discover a 19-year phase, or Metonic, cycle and possibly the approximate supposed 56-year eclipse cycle (viz. 3 × 18·61 = 55·83). Here Newham too, like Hawkins and Hoyle, tended to confuse his readers by the supposed correlation between the 19-year Metonic (lunar phase) cycle, the 18·61 nodal cycle, and the 19-Julian year eclipse cycle—a point already made in connection with Hawkins' ideas. But no matter, for this did not materially spoil his line of argument.

The crux of Newham's contribution was an analysis of the azimuths of the Causeway postholes which he compared with the computed winter moonrises covering the period − 2000 to − 1000. He expressed his results graphically with a diagram which he believed showed a remarkable close relationship between moonrise sequences and hole patterns. To Newham the resulting correlation was beyond what he considered the chances of simple coincidence (Fig. 58).

Newham believed that the position and spacing of the four large postholes near the Heel Stone (also cited by Hoyle, *see* above) indicates a relationship with the Causeway holes—especially in conjunction with stone D and the Heel Stone. The A-sequence postholes were strongly indicative of holes once containing 'posts' much larger than the Causeway posts, and this Newham presumed implied greater permanence. If stone B were also included, this represented seven markers which might function as a crude observational 'vernier'. Correlated with the setting Sun in the reverse direction, this provided a means of defining the time when an eclipse of the Moon was probable.

Newham felt that although the 56-year cycle was conjectural, there were certainly grounds for supposing that the builders of Stonehenge possessed ability to define the time of a probable eclipse.

Summarizing his ideas, he concluded there were excellent reasons for inferring 'strong lunar influences' in Stonehenge. He believed: (*a*) That the small stone 11 (Figs. 20 and 44) in the large sarsen circle was intentional to the builders' scheme (and represented a half-day count), and thus the sarsen circle represented the 29·5 days of the lunar month. (*b*) That the double circle or spiral of the Y and Z holes were the 59 days of two lunar months (the double lunation); there was also the strong possibility of a 59-stone complex of bluestones inside the sarsen circle which provided another (more suitable) means of representing the same idea. (*c*) The 19-year phase, or Metonic, cycle was indicated by the 19 bluestones located inside the trilithon horseshoe. All things considered, the evidence pointed directly to a 'Soluna' site where observations of the Sun and Moon were carried out by Megalithic peoples.

. . . In addition, independently, Newham and the French architect G. Charriere—who had also made a study of Stonehenge—had noted that the 'rectangle' formed by the four Stations corresponds *almost* to the latitude (within a few km) required for azimuths of the Sun and Moon to be separated by 90° at their extreme declinations. Therefore it seems that the Stonehenge latitude (51°2) was a deliberate choice by the builders. Thus its location had been dictated by astronomical requirements rather than by availability of stones or other factors favoured to suggest the choice of Salisbury Plain. The evidence provided by the geometry of the four Stations is perhaps some of the most convincing of all to bolster the astronomical ideas for Stonehenge.

In September 1966, Atkinson's long-awaited critique of Hawkins' book appeared in the pages of *Antiquity* under the provocative title 'Moonshine on Stonehenge'. He had already criticized it in a *Nature* review, 'Decoder Misled', when he had used the now infamous epithets 'tendentious, arrogant, slipshod and unconvincing'. In the editorial of the same issue of *Antiquity*, Glyn Daniel, with unrepressed glee, commented: '. . . The *double entendre* of the title will be lost on no one, least of all Professor Hawkins . . . We all feel disinclined to listen to a man who has not bothered to listen carefully to archaeologists and learn what they have to say. . . .'

In a preamble to Atkinson's review article the reader was told it might be subtitled: 'An archaeologist examines that astronomer'. Indeed it was clear that Hawkins had now been identified by some archaeologists as a fully materialized *persona non grata* reincarnate Lockyer. . . .

Atkinson began his 2,000-odd-word broadside with a brief survey of the astronomical speculations. Then he referred obliquely to Hawkins' arrogance and presumption for the evidence showed it was clear enough 'that neither Professor Hawkins nor his collaborator John B. White [who had helped Hawkins write his book] are archaeologists'. Atkinson stressed to his readers that the use of a computer had no bearing on the validity, or otherwise, of the results obtained. This was a valid point to make, since, surprising as it may appear, several general readers of Hawkins' book had believed it was the very use of a computer to study Stonehenge that validated Hawkins' ideas—an ingenuous view which is still widely current.

Atkinson's supposition was that the plans of Stonehenge used by Hawkins had been inappropriate for the task, and one cited by Atkinson was 'a now-obsolete Ministry of Works plan'. He complained that Hawkins had arbitrarily accepted as significant any sight line within $\pm 2°$ of the direction of an azimuth rising; this was quite unrealistic and represented an error about twenty-four times larger than errors found by practical experiments in sighting a pair of sticks. As illustration of what this error could amount to in practice, Atkinson cited the instance that if applied to the position of the Heel Stone, it would be perfectly admissible for this stone to be moved 3·6m (12 feet) towards the north-east without affecting the claim about the summer solstice sunrise alignment. . . .

The argument that the Heel-Stone lean would affect the rising point if corrected (a point often emphasized by Hawkins) was misleading. It ignored the effects of thirty-five centuries of weathering of the chalk surface which had lowered the line of sight to the horizon by about 45cm (18 inches). In the context of the Stonehenge I alignments, the statistical probability that Hawkins had used was wrong. The eight alignments for Stonehenge III were equally inadmissible. . . .

Atkinson, in commenting about the Aubrey-hole theory, did not doubt that the fifty-six holes could be used the way that Hawkins had cited, but whether they were actually used this way was another matter. He criticized the use of holes F, G and H, regarding that they had been formed by 'natural phenomena' such as trees. He believed Hawkins' remarks in the preface of his book unfortunate when he claimed: 'If I can see any alignment, general relationship or use for the various parts of Stonehenge then these facts were known to the builders. Such a hypothesis has carried me along over many incredible steps. . . . '

In retrospect, Hawkins indeed must often have regretted this unfortunate choice of phraseology which provided permanent and substantial ammunition in the hands of his critics.

Atkinson, however, was not entirely negative in his review, in spite of 'the major shortcomings of this book', he made it plain that it contained some excellent suggestions. The idea of the Full Moon rising over the Heel Stone at the time of winter solstice provided 'the best explanation for the Heel Stone so far put forward . . . If it is substantiated . . .'. He agreed with the suggestion that the latitude choice for Stonehenge was no coincidence (first cited by Newham and Charriere). It appeared to be a deliberate choice so that the extreme northerly and southerly risings and settings of the Sun and Moon at the solstices were approximately at right angles to one another. It was in accord with the nearly rectangular layout of the four Station stones.

Concluding, Atkinson admonished Hawkins, almost in the vein of the wise old master and the bright but hasty pupil, believing he had overreached himself because of 'his undoubted enthusiasm for his subject'. Nevertheless, Atkinson felt that one should be grateful to him for guiding the interests of prehistory into the early development of observational science and metrology. In his ultimate paragraph he cites as contrast Thom's work in the same field 'as the meticulous work of Professor Thom'. This latter tone of phrase reflected the widespread acceptance by Atkinson and other archaeologists of Thom's thesis regarding Megalithic structures (see below).

Following these major contributions to the Stonehenge saga, the magazine *Antiquity*, which from its very first issue in 1927 had been closely involved with the Stonehenge debate, invited Hoyle to contribute to a discussion of Hawkins' theories in the light of his own.

In this article entitled 'Speculations on Stonehenge' he pondered: How would *we* do it if landed on a planet with a similar situation and we were only equipped with crude ropes, stone boulders and wooden posts?

Hoyle considered that if landed on a new planet, the first thoughts of man would be to use the apparent motion of the Sun as a measure of time and also as a way of defining a north-south alignment. Hoyle believed that the builders of Stonehenge were not concerned with the north-south direction, and this he supposed indicated too that the twenty-four-hour rotation rate of the Sun—the diurnal rotation—was clearly recognized by the Stonehengers as being irrelevant to the problem of determining the seasons. The shift of the Sun along the horizon would soon be recognized as more significant.

Given only crude material, Hoyle assumed that *we* could expect to measure angles to within $\pm 0°3$ if the foresight marker is some 60m (200 feet) from the backsight. Hoyle then conducted an exercise to determine the seasons, believing that a $\pm 0°3$ accuracy is good enough to determine the date in the year within a day or so except near the solstice points. Then clarifying the geometry involved in sunrise and sunset directions, Hoyle immersed his *Antiquity* readers in what was obviously hard going for some of them, for it necessitated the understanding of spherical trigonometry. Hoyle also explained the methods for finding directions of moonrise and moonset. Again, although the trigonometry involved is relatively elementary, it was difficult going for many—as was later strongly hinted by Jacquetta Hawkes (*see* below).

Returning to the problems at Stonehenge, he reckoned a skyline tilt of $0°6$ above the true horizontal plane. He assumed that the meaning of sunrise and moonrise is when the full orb stood on the horizon and accepted the suggestion by Hawkins that moonrise and sunrise was at the instant these respective bodies stood tangent to the horizon. In addition it was necessary to reckon a negative correction of $30'$ for the effects of atmospheric refraction. This has a significant effect on the moment of sun or moonrise, for when the Sun or Moon is seen, it is actually depressed below the horizon by $14'$ (assuming the diameter of $32'$ for the average subtended angle of the Sun or Moon). Taking into account an horizon elevation of $0°6$ gives a $22'$ elevation; this is Hoyle's value h used in his tables (*see* Tables A and B). Newham had actually measured the true horizon elevations at Stonehenge, and Hoyle's assumptions later required Newham's corrections.

The nub of Hoyle's thesis was whether the alignments given by Hawkins were significant. These had already been much criticized by Atkinson (*see* above). Hoyle told his readers that he too had always been suspicious of a statistical argument based on data which retains an element of subjective judgement: 'If one plays a hunch on the data one might just as well play a hunch on the final result. . . .'

Bearing in mind the accuracy of about $\pm 0°3$ attainable by modern crude sighting methods, Hoyle wondered how this compared with the table of Hawkins' alignments. To show how they did, Hoyle provided tables (Tables A and B) of Hawkins' alignments and inserted alongside Hawkins' measured azimuths an equivalent calculated azimuth taking into account the various corrections (using $h = 0°5$).

TABLE A

Position	Seen from	Measured azimuth(°)	Calculated azimuth(°)	
G	92	40·7	$41·1 + 1·96h_m$	moonrise
A	Centre	43·7	$41·1 + 1·96h_m$	moonrise
91	92	49·1	$49·7 + 1·63h_s$	sunrise
Heel	Centre	51·3	$49·7 + 1·63h_s$	sunrise
94	93	51·5	$49·7 + 1·63h_s$	sunrise
F	Centre	61·5	$60·5 + 1·45h_m$	moonrise
91	Centre	117·4	$122·2 + 1·45h_m$	moonrise
H	93	128·2	$130·2 + 1·63h_s$	sunrise
G	94	129·4	$130·2 + 1·63h_s$	sunrise
92	93	140·7	$142·6 + 1·96h_m$	moonrise
92	91	229·1	$229·8 - 1·63h_s$	sunset
93	94	231·5	$229·8 - 1·63h_s$	sunset
93	Centre	297·4	$229·5 - 1·45h_m$	moonset
94	G	309·4	$310·3 - 1·63h_s$	sunset
94	91	319·6	$318·9 - 1·96h_m$	moonset

Table A: Hawkins' cited (measured) alignments compared with Hoyle's table of calculated (and corrected) azimuths. Hoyle assumed the horizon elevation to be uniformly equal to 0·70°, the appropriate value for h is about 0·50°. The result was that Hoyle derived the following pairs of values: (40·7, 42·1), (43·7, 42·1), (49·1, 50·5), (51·3, 50·5), (51·5, 50·5), (61·5, 61·2), (117·4, 122·9), (128·2, 131·0), (129·4, 131·0), (140·7, 143·6), (229·1, 229·0), (231·5, 229·0), (297·4, 298·8), (309·4, 309·5), (319·6, 317·9). In each bracket the measured azimuth appears first. Although Hoyle supposed there are detailed variations of h from one azimuth to another, so that discrepancies of the order $\pm 0·5°$ would be expected, it was readily apparent that the differences between numbers within the brackets are far outside the suggested margin of error, $\pm 0·3°$. Larger discrepancies still occur in Hawkins' citations of sarsen circle alignments (Table B, below).

TABLE B

Position	Seen from	Measured azimuth(°)	Calculated azimuth(°)	
Heel	30—1	51·2	$49·7 + 1·63h_s$	sunrise
8—9	53—54	120·6	$122·2 + 1·45h_m$	moonrise
6—7	51—52	131·6	$130·2 + 1·63h_s$	sunrise
9—10	53—54	139·4	$142·6 + 1·96h_m$	moonrise
16—15*	55—56	231·4	$229·8 - 1·63h_s$	sunset
20*—21	57—58	292·0	$299·5 - 1·45h_m$	moonset
23—24*	59—60	304·7	$310·3 - 1·63h_s$	sunset
21—22	57—58	315·2	$318·9 - 1·96h_m$	moonset

(Starred numbers refer to missing stones whose positions have been estimated from neighbouring stones.)

Discrepancies between measured azimuth and calculated azimuth in Table A showed them to lie outside the suggested margin of error of ± 0°·3. Errors for Stonehenge III (sarsen circles and trilithons) were even larger (Table B). In two the error was very large and in excess of 5°. Some larger errors were to be expected here owing to difficulties in placing stones in exact alignments, but generally Hoyle's analysis seemed to bear out Atkinson's earlier criticism.

Leaving the question of discrepancies for the moment, Hoyle now felt it was time to pose the question: What were the builders trying to do? or rather what would *we* do ourselves? Would *we* attempt to fix sighting lines to agree precisely with calculated values? This Hoyle believed depended on motives. If the motive served to provide useful information, viz. for dating of the seasons and predicting eclipses, it would be unwise to set the alignments exactly at the extreme directions of swing because of the apparent 'standing still' of the Moon and Sun at extreme (solstice) positions. Hoyle likened the problem to trying to judge by eye the exact lowest spot of a very flat valley. He had now reached the point made in his earlier paper in *Nature* (*see* above), i.e. that it is more practical to erect the sighting line a degree or two inside the extreme positions so that the Sun and Moon can be seen before and immediately after the extreme azimuth; the extreme azimuth would best be judged half-way between the two observations.

Hoyle showed that the discrepancies could be accounted for

by assuming that this indeed was the *modus operandi*; he believed it was demonstrated conclusively by the fact that in twelve cases out of fifteen in Table A and in seven cases out of eight in Table B the argument was valid, for the 'error' had the same sign and this could not be expected from a random effect. It implied that it was similar to obtaining nineteen heads in twenty-three tosses of a coin. Yet on a random basis the chances would be rated even. The statistical chance of nineteen in twenty-three was 1 in 1,000.

The upshot of it all, Hoyle conjectured, was far-reaching. It not only required Stonehenge to be designed and built to operate as an astronomical device, but the consequences of this idea demanded a level of intellectual attainment for its builders much above that believed standard among a community of primitive farmers. 'A veritable Newton or Einstein must have been at work—but then why not?' wrote Hoyle.

Over the question of determining equinoxes and eclipses he supposed that the inherent geometrical difficulties of defining the time of equinoxes was why equinoctial sighting lines do not appear to play a significant part in Stonehenge structures. In respect to eclipses he referred back to his *Nature* article and reiterated his own ideas that the Aubrey circle was a kind of protractor 'to judge angles within a degree or so' and not a counting device as Hawkins would have it. Atkinson had asked him whether a circle of such large radius was necessary and why not a wooden peg-board and switch M, N and S round the board? Hoyle himself believed it would be interesting to know how large a peg-board one would need to attain the same accuracy as the Aubrey circle. But a peg-board was a vulnerable device in terms of usage, especially over a time scale as long as twenty years. Several peg-boards might have led to confusion. A more definitive system would be the use of large, heavy stones to represent M, N and S; stones which could not be moved out of place by an accidental knock.

In his final remarks entitled 'Speculations', Hoyle summed up his general beliefs in the matter. He wrote that it was not until he read Neugebauer's account of Babylonian methods *c.* − 600 that he understood how eclipse predictions were made, until then—'It seemed no more than obscure numerology'. Hoyle's remarks further reinforce the view that he had been much influenced by the old pragmatic methods practised by the

148 MEGALITHS, MYTHS AND MEN

Tamil astronomers which had been cited by Neugebauer. Hoyle was certainly not alone in admitting his lack of knowledge about eclipse predicting methods, and until the Stonehenge controversies of the mid-1960s, the subject was considered rather esoteric and best left to the few interested specialists.

Hoyle had formed several cultural hypotheses about the builders of Stonehenge. He believed that there were three universal essentials for high intellectual achievement: Food, leisure and social stability, and good communication. He could not see why conditions for these were not present in Southern England society c. − 2000. He wondered—in view of the African tribes' use of drums for disseminating information at high speed—could not a similar system have been in vogue c. − 2000? It was a mistake, he thought, to equate intellectual achievement and technological advance. Perhaps before the 'human gene pool' had been diluted in modern times, there existed in prehistoric times groups whose intellectual norm was considerably higher than that of the present day. Following the period c. − 2000, widespread population movement might well have diluted these groups and produced a sharp genetic decline leading to a cultural inversion. . . .

Hoyle may indeed be right in this assumption. The Megalith builders seemed to have been in sharp decline before − 1000. When Caesar arrived, he was greeted by the woad-covered barbarian hordes vividly described by him and classical propagandist writers. But even so there *was* a scientific Celtic-Druid calendar whose origin remains obscure.

In the interim period between Hoyle's article appearing in *Antiquity* and the awaited replies of other contributors, a new paper was published in *Nature* (4 February 1967) entitled 'Eclipse Cycles and Eclipses at Stonehenge' by R. Colton and R. L. Martin. These two contributors had been following the arguments of the Stonehenge debate and had decided to look into the whole question of eclipses and check whether Hawkins' assumptions about the role of the Aubrey holes held true.

They first took opportunity to point out the false reasoning relating to the 19-year Metonic cycle being a hitherto unrecognized eclipse cycle as Hawkins claimed. Several writers had already referred to the fact that there is no true commensurability between the 18·61-year nodal swing and the 19-year (235 lunations) phase cycle. Damningly, Colton and

Martin found that Hawkins had overlooked the fact that the Moon is not in direct opposition (180°) to the Sun after successive periods of his alleged cycle.

Colton and Martin decided to take a start from lunar eclipses which had occurred rather than use computed eclipses, and as the Moon's orbit had not changed appreciably since −1500, they arbitrarily chose a period 1855 to 1958. When these were plotted graphically, they noted it formed what they believed to be an original analytical eclipse-ephemeris. From the plot they were able to recognize several eclipse cycles: 135 lunations, 804 lunations, the 223 Saros cycle, 311 lunations, 88 lunations and 41 lunations. The 135 lunation cycle had been well known to the Chinese as an eclipse predictor; the two authors commented that the Chinese had also been aware of the 235 lunation Metonic cycle which they knew as the *chang*. The 804 lunation cycle showed a repeating unit of 65 years 2 days made up of two 19-year intervals and one of 27 years 2 days. This they noted was a true eclipse cycle because the incommensurability in the two 19-year periods of −16° is almost balanced by an error of +15°09 in the 27-year 2-day period (334 lunations). Even after the full period has elapsed, it causes a relative movement of the nodes and the Earth-Sun line amounting to only 0°91, and the cycle can repeat many times.

Colton and Martin noted that the 19-, 19-, 18-year (= 56) sequence suggested by Hawkins is actually 19, 19, 18 years plus 11 days. As an eclipse 'cycle' it is very short indeed because there is no way to compensate for the error in the two 19-year periods. They considered that a 47(-year) sequence of 19, 19 and 9 years minus 9 days, which gives a good 581 lunations cycle, would be more logical.

Colton and Martin believed it safe to assume from their analyses that the Aubrey holes at Stonehenge were not constructed to predict eclipses on a 56-year cycle. Hoyle's alternative hypothesis was 'elegant and ingenious', but they emphasized that the success of his method was not confined to the use of a complex of fifty-six holes. Hoyle's method, viewed within the context of the limited astronomical knowledge of the period, appeared unlikely. Although it predicted every lunar and solar eclipse, it gave no information what eclipses could be seen at Stonehenge; they believed that only the exclusion of an eclipse could be reckoned its only safe prediction. But Colton and Martin did not make it clear that there is no simple eclipse cycle known which can predict total solar eclipses for any one locale on the Earth. *All solar eclipse cycles relate to the Earth as a whole.*

In place of the Hawkins or Hoyle hypotheses, the two authors suggested that a simple method of prediction known from the third millennium BC would serve better, since it predicted only lunar eclipses visible at Stonehenge. This method relied on noting when the Sun and Full Moon were diametrically opposed. In this condition if the Moon rises a short time, say 15 to 30 minutes, before the Sun sets, an eclipse of the Moon will occur that night which will be visible; but if the interval is longer, an eclipse will not be visible. If the Full Moon rises *after* the Sun has set, the eclipse is already past. It was possible, they believed, that the Aubrey hole circle *might* well have served as a protractor to judge when the setting Sun and rising Full Moon were exactly opposite each other—but they rather suspected the fifty-six holes were there for quite a different purpose.

Actually an eclipse of the Moon can be visible when paradoxically *both* the Moon and Sun are above the horizon and apparently not quite opposite. This unique situation, however, was not cited by Colton and Martin. This is one of the strangest natural events which can occur and at first glance may seem impossible bearing in mind that for an eclipse to take place, three bodies must be in line (syzygy). The anomaly is brought about by refraction in the atmosphere. The setting Sun has actually already set but appears not to have done so because its position below the horizon is displaced upwards by refraction. By the same token, the rising Moon has not yet actually risen, but its image is displaced upwards by refraction and becomes visible prematurely. Geometrically this brings the two bodies closer by more than 1° of a great circle—the net result of double displacement due to refraction. The same situation can also occur at sunrise and moonset. Pliny the Elder was witness to an interesting morning eclipse of this kind on 22 February +72.

Colton and Martin speculated that the numerous stone circles found scattered round Britain might well have been used as protractors, since no other convincing explanation as to their purpose had yet been generally accepted. However, they noted that the use of such stone circles for their suggested method of predicting solar eclipses was a poor one because of the great difficulty in observing the Moon near conjunction.

Following Hoyle's contribution, *Antiquity* threw the discussion open by inviting comments on Hoyle's articles. The journal subsequently printed replies received from Hawkins, Atkinson, Thom, Newham, Sadler (then Superintendent of the British National Almanac Office who had drawn attention to some inaccuracies in the eclipse-cycle reasoning of Hawkins and Hoyle) and Newall, the archaeologist, whose first article on Stonehenge had been written for *Antiquity* thirty-eight years previously.

Archaeologists, at first decidedly cool to the astronomical theories, had become much more interested in the whole problem now that the astronomers apparently could not agree amongst themselves.

Hawkins was given first opportunity to reply to Hoyle and did so by setting out the outline-thesis of his own belief to clarify the position. He believed: (*a*) Stonehenge was a Moon and Sun observatory; (*b*) it provided a counting device (the Aubrey holes) for predicting the extremes of the Moon on the horizon and for eclipses; (*c*) Stonehenge may have represented a particular example of a general culture.

He noted the fact that Hoyle supported the first two hypotheses and agreed with his conclusions, but with regard to (*c*) he felt Hoyle's extension to the philosophical interpretation 'extremely provocative'. He begged to disagree with Hoyle over the question of the so-called builders' errors—believing these to be the results of observational difficulties; it was likely that the Stonehengers would probably not see the theoretical extreme azimuth because the full lunar phase would not occur very often at the moment of moonrise, and cloudy nights at the time of Full Moon would introduce a similar systematic effect.

Hoyle, he believed, went beyond what he called his own 'guarded' conclusions that the Stonehengers were more intelligent than previously thought. This Hawkins referred to as a 'fascinating speculation', yet not even one as gifted as Hoyle was qualified to explore the far regions of archaeology and anthropology. . . .

Atkinson's contribution provided a much weightier and more aggressive general critique. After reiterating some of the familiar salient points which entered into the arguments, he used the opportunity for another attack on Hawkins' theories, drawing upon the new evaluation of the basic data such as the value of the obliquity of the ecliptic and new figures provided for a number of site alignments—noting that some of these differed by more than 2°5 from the earlier figures. These were important since Newham had determined the actual horizon elevations for Stonehenge which varied between $+0°33$ and $+0°62$ while Hoyle had assumed a uniform value of $0°7$.

Atkinson (recognized as one of the few archaeologists competent to tackle the mathematical inferences) had recalculated azimuths for full orb and for the first and last light (viz. the 2' of the Sun's and Moon's disc showing above the horizon). For both cases the mean error turned out to be six times greater than the maximum error of 0°3 Hoyle had assumed for the builders' capabilities. Taking into account the direction of the sign of the error, Atkinson found that first and last light azimuths provided slightly better fit to Hawkins' alignments, but that the difference was insufficient to justify a choice assumption in one mode of observation over another except to illustrate that the full orb condition is not necessarily a correct one—suggested by Hoyle for its advantage. However, Atkinson remarked that his calculations were only to be reckoned as 'an interim exercise' owing to their being based on alignments derived from a mixture of plans and air photographs whose reliability was uncertain. For this reason he refrained from publishing revised tables at this stage.

Atkinson then opened the question about the height of the Stonehenge Bank feature—a key factor, he believed, in the arguments and one long neglected. The Bank was now a very inconspicuous feature and went unnoticed by many visitors to the monument. Atkinson's calculations showed that at one time it must have stood at a height of nearly 2m (6 feet). This taken into account with an observer's eye-height of 1·53m (5·1 feet)— based on the average height of males in the West Kennet Long Barrow—suggested to him that for *risings* of the Sun and Moon, the crest of the Bank would have been lower than the horizon line. However, for settings, the Bank feature would have intercepted the horizon line by up to $+1°$ and therefore would have formed a local artificial horizon, unless of course the Bank had been deliberately lowered at these points. But Atkinson's calculation indicated that only the size of error and not its direction sign in Hoyle's table (Table A) would be affected.

He noted that one of the sunset alignments 91—92 significantly passes through a marked gap in the Bank adjacent to Aubrey hole 20, corresponding to a solid causeway across the ditch. Atkinson argued that it could not be established for certain that this bridged gap was an original feature, but its true purpose might well have been to provide a clear sight line to the horizon beyond.

With respect to the Aubrey circle, Atkinson believed it of only modest accuracy: the margin of errors inherent in its layout prevented the successful prediction of total eclipses, but possibly it was good enough for partial eclipses. . . .

Nevertheless, in consideration of the data he had raised he admitted that none of it appeared to affect Hoyle's ideas substantially. He liked Hoyle's ideas better than those of Hawkins. With Hoyle's method it could be seen to offer an explanation how Stonehenge might be used to predict eclipses, but added this did not prove Stonehenge *was* used in this way. Yet in the prehistoric context Hoyle's interpretation was more difficult to accept owing to the degree of 'conceptual abstraction'. He admitted that the position of the Heel Stone and Station stones, and particularly the latitude choice by the Megalith builders, were 'astronomically determined'. However, for several reasons he was unable 'to go all the way' either with Hawkins or Hoyle. . . .

His principal reasons were summarized as follows:

The Aubrey holes are very ill-adapted to serve as permanent marks. The digging and the refilling of the holes he described as 'redundant for either purpose'. He believed Sadler's critique that eclipses could be predicted more simply, and Colton's and Martin's rejection of the fifty-six-year eclipse cycle, damaged the case for the Aubrey hole usage. . . .

Coming to the problem of alignments, it was his opinion that in practice Stonehenge alignments were only likely in *one* direction owing to the positive horizon-line elevation (which does not allow for an accurate 180° reversal), and this indeed is a telling criticism. A reverse direction he believed was a matter of coincidence owing to the inherent geometry of the celestial sphere, and for this reason he was doubtful of the validity of reciprocal alignments.

In the instance of the alignments using holes F, G and H, these were also doubtful owing to the lack of evidence that they constituted man-made holes. He was wholly sceptical of any alignments involving the architectural features of Stonehenge III, supposing that they rested on 'subjective estimates' of original positions of dislodged or missing stones; even if these were known, one would still be faced with the problem that a sight line could only be defined by centring one gap between stones upon another gap. . . .

Thom's contribution to the discussion was confined to so-called evidence found elsewhere in Britain—for up to then he had done very little field-work at Stonehenge. He cited the evidence of lunar lines at Callanish first found by Boyle Somerville in 1912 and the numerous discoveries of his own up and down the length of Britain. On the evidence so far presented, he himself was prepared to accept that Stonehenge was a solar and lunar observatory. But then he asked the pertinent question: Why was it necessary to have so many solar and lunar sites? Thom's own suggestion was that Stonehenge might have been intended as the main centre to control others. In his final speculations, Thom (a Scotsman) might well be echoing (tongue-in-cheek?) the sentiments of the contemporary Scottish nationalists when he considered that a central bureaucracy in the south of England was unlikely to have been influenced by a plea from the north that mountainous terrain (where Thom himself cited many alignments) provided much more opportunity for accurate determination of lunar and solar cycles. . . .

Newham's contribution also reiterated much he had said before. He stressed that Hawkins' eclipse cycle ideas now appeared untenable if one believed Hoyle's better theory—and he had been persuaded so by the telling critique of Colton and Martin. The concept of the Aubrey circle as a digital computer was little more than an 'ingenious flight of imagination'. Nevertheless, the idea of eclipses was possible, and the Aubrey holes might instead be some kind of protractor. While agreeing with Hoyle's suggestion to account for the so-called errors, i.e. the alignments indicated a little short of extreme azimuth, he maintained that the principle was not new and instanced that there was evidence that several early peoples had adopted the same method, but it was used via the first or last gleam of sunrise or setting and *not* the full orb as favoured by Hawkins and Hoyle. He criticized Hoyle's method of reverse alignments (as did Atkinson) and generally believed that Hoyle was not really aware of several practical factors involved in the monument. . . .

Sadler, who earlier had shown that a better eclipse predictor was one using forty-seven holes, had not been able to make a further and more thorough appreciation, and there was little probability of him being able to do so in the future. However, he suggested that in principle it was possible to do an analysis utilizing different levels of intelligence in order to discover how long it might take at each particular level of intelligence to determine empirically the rules which—'according to Hoyle'— were built into Stonehenge. (Indeed Sadler's suggestion would provide a splendid, original and worth-while doctoral thesis for a graduate-student equipped with the necessary background and insights.)

Newall, as veteran Stonehenge archaeologist and forever watchful of astro-archaeological inferences in the monument, provided the concluding remarks to the discussion. He believed that Hawkins and Hoyle would have done better by leaving out mention of holes F, G and H. He had written to both *before* they wrote their papers with the information that F was an unfinished excavation and that no one could say what it was, and G and H were not man-made.

By removing them from Table A it implied that one-third of the alignments are coincidences. He also criticized Hoyle for using E. He agreed about the axial alignment (Table B) in each direction with emphasis on the winter solstice (always a keen preference of his), but he was *very, very* doubtful about all the others. The inference from this was that six out of eight were doubtful, and this as a whole made eleven doubtful out of twenty-three. Ending on a note of query to the reader, Newall remarked: 'That seems a lot. What do you think?'

All the principals involved had now had opportunity to air their views, and it fell to Jacquetta Hawkes, a declared and vigorous critic of the astronomical ideas, to provide a summary and comment on the views which had been expressed.

Jacquetta Hawkes—in the role of impartial reviewer—had indeed been a surprising choice on the part of the Editor of *Antiquity*. Wife of the English man-of-letters J. B. Priestley—

whose novels and plays are obsessed by time themes—she herself had earned a reputation as a popular writer and reviewer on archaeological subjects. Apart from her hypercritical attitude to astro-archaeological ideas involved in Stonehenge, she was also against acceptance of Marshack's lunar notation theories. She herself had frequently flirted with proto-astronomical ideas in some of her own writings, particularly in *Man and the Sun* (1962) in which she traced out, often in fine speculative style, the influence of the Sun in man's cultural past. In this book she appeared to subscribe to the ideas for the Stonehenge orientation and observatory theories, writing: 'The whole temple with its many openings upon the sky may well have been used for measuring the rising and setting of moon, planets, stars and constellations, but the orientation of the mighty trilithons must prove that here at Stonehenge, as elsewhere, the supreme deity was the Sun God himself. . . .' But in matters relating directly to practical observational or mathematical astronomy her views were those of a layman.

Her review entitled 'God in the Machine' (1967) set off in a splendid uncompromising manner with the hard-hitting theme that every age had the Stonehenge it deserved—or desired. This point was indeed fair comment, and her words were echoed again—albeit unwittingly—when the chosen Chief of Stonehenge neo-Druids was asked on a TV programme why nothing much had been heard of the Druids from the fourth to the seventeenth centuries AD. He replied: 'The Druid is always present: he only emerges when society requires and demands him!'

In her critique, Jacquetta Hawkes briefly cited those who had advocated astronomical orientation and referred to Lockyer as the 'then Astronomer Royal'. This particular *faux pas* was a slip first apparently committed by Atkinson in his Stonehenge book and since oft repeated by those using this work as a definitive reference source. Lockyer in fact was never Astronomer Royal. At the period in question he was a member of the Board of Visitors of the Greenwich Observatory; William Christie was then Astronomer Royal, a position he vacated to Frank Dyson in 1910.

Coming to the modern astronomical period, beginning June 1961, she was unimpressed by Gerald Hawkins' motivations which had led him to investigate Stonehenge. She laid emphasis on the weaknesses of his ideas, first citing Sadler's then Colton's and Martin's commentaries on the so-called fifty-six-year eclipse cycle. These criticisms, she related, were also endorsed 'by an eminent correspondent whose name had to be withheld'.

Hawkins for his pains was to be in receipt of almost all Jacquetta Hawkes' brickbats. It was obvious he had not yet been forgiven by some archaeologists for his presumptious, Lockyer-like, excursions into archaeology. However, it was soon apparent from the tone of her arguments she was neither game nor inclined to take on the additional burden of a David-and-Goliath attack on Hoyle, for she admitted 'few of us were confident that we were capable of following his reasoning'.

The rest of the review was simply a reiteration of views expressed earlier. It was Jacquetta Hawkes' concluding remarks, along with her opening comments, that carried the strongest and most telling punches: She could see no argument to change her previous belief that Stonehenge was intended primarily as a sanctuary—its purpose was mainly ritualistic and not intellectual. Its solar orientation was intended as some religious symbolism in the way Christian churches expressed this symbolism. She believed we should show that this was indeed the scientific age by refusing to give way to our own wishful thinking.

Last word in this particular round of argument went to Newham, but this did not grace the pages of *Antiquity*. In 1970 he published his second booklet *Supplement To The Enigma of Stonehenge*, and in Part I he took opportunity to reply to Jacquetta Hawkes—declaring that part of her summation of the Stonehenge debate had been unfortunate. In particular he criticized one of her remarks that referred to the long established *knowledge* of Stonehenge, maintaining what she should have referred to was the long accepted *belief*—for, as Newham commented, the two meanings are not the same. Coming to the nub of the problem, Newham alluded to the human attitude 'with its sheep-like tendency to follow-my-leader' and admitted that he too was no exception. 'Anyone being introduced to a subject such as Stonehenge, inevitably acquires ideas which are biased in a direction dependent on the way the subject was introduced. Once a particular idea has been accepted, especially one of long standing, few people take the trouble to analyse all the relevant factors. . . . '

Jacquetta Hawkes herself is certainly not always free of the wishful-thinking syndrome, for this has cropped up in her books. In her *Man and the Sun*, where she argued vigorously for acceptance of the idea that Stonehenge is a unique temple of a Sun-God cult in Britain (which perhaps it was), she referred to the famous bronze and gold sun chariot recovered from a Danish bog and then wrote wistfully: '. . . if only something like it could have been found at Stonehenge!'

The remaining section of Newham's *Supplement* was a reasoned recapitulation of the whole question of Stonehenge alignment-theory. In part 2 he related the circumstances of the 1966 discovery of three significant postholes during the construction of a new extension to the visitors' car park. This was an exciting new find, the significance of which was at first over-looked. Newham had long expressed the opinion that the Stonehenge astronomer-priests had made use of outlying markers, and he had previously spent many hours in searching the area round the monument for remaining traces of these. The holes were found as three disturbances in the chalk bed-rock immediately below ground level at the lower end of the park where they are now marked by three concrete circles set in the carriageway (Fig. 59).

These holes are 9 to 12m (30 to 40 feet) apart, set in low ground about 250m (275 yards) north-west of the sarsen circle in roughly an east-west alignment (Fig. 60). Newham related that at first none of the alignments appeared to be of significance, but a further examination showed otherwise, for all three proved to be aligned to important setting phenomena involving the Sun and Moon when observed from the four Stations (91—4) and Heel Stone positions. A more detailed site survey revealed that the holes had once contained posts to align on the distant horizon; to do this their height above ground level must have been of the order of 9m (30 feet).

Newham believed that this implied the use of tall, straight tree trunks. He was delighted when this was confirmed by excavations showing the holes with unmistakable signs of decayed bark rings from trees *c*. 75cm (30 inches) in diameter. In addition the holes showed signs of the wedges that would have been necessary to support and permanently maintain such tall trunks in a vertical position.

59 The car-park postholes, Stonehenge.

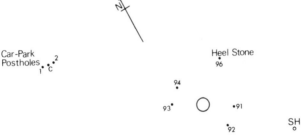

60 The three car-park postholes at Stonehenge (1; C; 2) in relation to the Heel Stone and Stations. SH represents a depression (possibly a stonehole) which may be significant to a lunar alignment.

Newham's contention was that these three postholes were the most positive astronomical discovery made at Stonehenge. Not only did these positions align on Sun and Moon settings with extreme accuracy, but they represented unambiguously non-reversible alignments as seen from the Heel Stone and the four Stations. Thus they indicate:

(1) Midquarter sunset   dec. +16°
    Winter moonset   dec. +18°76 (Minor position)
(2) Summer sunset   dec. +23°92
(3) Midwinter moonset   dec. +29°03 (Major position)
(4) Midwinter moonset at observed mean extremes
(5) Summer solstice sunset

Newham also noted that the centre post bears the same relation to Sun and Moon settings as the Heel Stone does to the mean winter moonrise and summer solstice sunrise when seen from the centre of the sarsen circle.

Summarizing his arguments Newham believed that the following use was made of individual posts:

(a) No 1 served only as a solar alignment, viz. the last light of the summer solstice sunset seen from Station 91, and midquarter sunsets seen from the Heel Stone (the same as 91—93).

(b) No 2 served only as the marker for the moonset, when at the minor extreme of Moon swing, as seen from the Heel Stone. Both poles would therefore have to be shorter than the centre pole to align on the horizon, owing to the distance and ground elevations of these observation positions.

(c) The centre hole position was aligned on the extreme northerly or major moonset position when seen from 92.

(d) The centre hole as seen from 94 also aligned on moonset when midway between the other two extremes. Its position is just short of the summer solstice sunset line, so that a pole bears a similar relation to Sun and Moon settings as the Heel Stone does to their rising when seen from the centre of the sarsen circle.

(e) Although from 93, none of the holes appear to align exactly on either Sun or Moon phenomena, the centre hole is less than a fifth of a degree short of the extreme major Moon alignment at full orb. Newham believed it possible that some of the Station positions were also used in connection with summer moonrise or winter sunrise. If a post or stone were to be found in the south-easterly direction, a more final assessment would be possible. Newham considered that the remarkable geometrical layout of the car park postholes to other main features indicated there were other such alignments still to be found.

Newham also discussed the problem of the fifty-six Aubrey holes. While he admitted that both Hawkins' and Hoyle's ideas were ingenious, he cast doubt on both of them. Hawkins' ideas, he believed, were more easy to dismiss simply on numerical grounds, for the fifty-six-year eclipse cycle did not appear to exist in practice. Hoyle's ideas could not be dismissed for numerical reasons; but, echoing the sentiments of more sober minds, Newham felt that they implied knowledge to a degree far beyond that indicated by the prehistorical evidence for the period. Newham expressed his opinion that while various ritualistic solar purposes ascribed to Stonehenge may well be justified, it seemed illogical to deny (as some archaeologists continued to do) the even stronger possibilites of lunar connections, but he concluded: 'Implicit faith cannot be placed in all the interpretations given to the findings of astronomers and archaeologists alike. Perhaps the truth lies somewhere between the two extremes.'

CHAPTER VIII

Metrics and Moonstones

Although Stonehenge is the most important Megalithic monument in Britain which shows indications of some kind of astronomical alignment, it is not the only one as we have seen. Lockyer's own investigations were far-reaching and took him and his friends to remote sites scattered through the length of Britain, including Ireland.

One of the sites mentioned by Lockyer—although he did not appear to have visited it himself—is at Callanish on the Isle of Lewis (lat. 58° 12′ N). In 1912 Vice-Admiral Boyle Somerville followed up Lockyer's earlier reference to a possible stellar orientation (the Pleiades), and subsequently believed in addition he had found strong evidence for solar and lunar alignments (*see* note 13).

Boyle Somerville was an active worker in the investigation of field monuments and at different times made accurate large-scale plans of twenty-seven stone circles. Unfortunately he also made some rather ingenuous assumptions concerning the general nature of topographical alignments (*see* Chapter 10). In turn, long before the Stonehenge investigations of the 1960s, Alexander Thom was utilizing the clues left by Lockyer, Somerville and others (*see* note 14), and he had been busily surveying many of the less impressive stone circles—particularly those in the remoter parts of Scotland.

Although Thom's work was known to interested parties, it generated little publicity and was generally ignored by archaeologists who, subsequent to Lockyer's ill-fated ventures, were highly sceptical of *all* supposed alignments relating to field monuments. However, those interested in astronomical interpretations began to follow Thom's work more closely after 1954 when he published a paper in the *Journal of the British Astronomical Association* entitled: 'The solar observatories of

Megalithic man'. This was followed in the next few years by contributions to other journals with papers entitled: 'A statistical examination of the Megalithic sites in Britain' and 'The geometry of Megalithic man'. Thom's work was now associated with the term 'Megalithic astronomy', and the usage of this term is now generally preferred in references to British and French Megalithic sites rather than the term astro-archaeology which now has a more cosmospolitan inference and covers a much broader prehistoric and historic chronology.

By the early 1960s, Thom had drawn attention to many of the less impressive-looking Megalithic remains, several of these were undoubtedly of great importance. Thom was by now convinced that Megalithic man in Britain knew a great deal more about geometrical constructions than prehistorians had given him credit for—including the properties of eclipses and the means of designing compound circles. From the evidence that Thom had accumulated it also seemed likely that ancient man in Britain had a standard unit of length which had influenced the geometrical constructions and the dimensions and shapes of stone 'circles'. Although many circles are indeed round, others are egg-shaped, elliptical or distorted in some way.

Atkinson, a severe critic of Hawkins' Stonehenge theories, was the first archaeologist to declare openly his welcome of Thom's Megalithic theories. It is often repeated that Atkinson was the only field archaeologist who could understand the mathematics involved. Atkinson himself went on record as saying that the great majority of archaeologists are not as numerate as an educated person should be, and as a consequence are unable to appreciate, or use, the new (numerate) methods in a critical way; but he added in the same breath (and rightly so!) that one could tell lies with numbers just as easily as one could with words. . . .

Thom's ideas became better known to the public after the wide publicity afforded Hawkins' discoveries at Stonehenge which had kindled a widespread interest in Megalithic monuments. It was now generally recognized that Thom had gone beyond the ideas of his predecessors and even contemporary fellow astro-archaeologists. Perhaps he had completely answered the challenge put out by Fergusson *c.* 1872 in his *Rude Stone Monuments*, subsequently only partly answered by Lockyer,

Somerville, Newham and Hawkins. . . . In his book Fergusson wrote: 'Till some practical astronomer will come forward and tell us in intelligible language what observations could be performed with the aid of the circles of Stonehenge, we may be at least allowed to pause. Even, however, in that case, unless his theory will apply to Avebury, Stanton Drew, and other circles so irregular to be almost unmeasurable, it will add little to our knowledge. . . .'

The outcome of Thom's persevering Megalithic surveys, up to the late 1960s, is contained in two slim hard-cover volumes, *Megalithic Sites in Britain* (1967) and *Megalithic Lunar Observatories* (1971). Neither volume sets out to be overtly technical, but neither is a popular treatment in the sense that Hawkins' Stonehenge books were geared to the popular market with an eye to later paperback sales.

Thom tells us that his method was to visit Megalithic sites and, via theodolite and tape, measure the positions of the remaining stones as accurately as possible; fallen and buried stones were located sometimes by prodding with a bayonet. Since many of the British Megalithic sites are situated in remote spots amid boggy moorland away from roads and even rough cart tracks, Thom's journeyings to the 450 sites he claims to have visited often involved long solitary walks with the awkward theodolite and tripod slung over his back. His earliest surveys began in the 1930s, and by the late 1960s he had made over 300 accurate plots and in addition had visited many more sites.

The crux of Thom's theories concerns his concept of the so-called Megalithic yard of 2·72 Imperial feet and the double yard, or Megalithic fathom (5·44 feet). Much of Thom's subsequent reasoning hinges on *a priori* assumptions that such a standard unit of measurement was in usage in North-West Europe *c*. – 2000. The unit was discovered by Thom's analysis of his own surveys; and only by supposing that such a unit existed was it possible for him to make geometric sense of the schemes of ancient man.

Thom argued that this measure is very close to the old Spanish *vara* (meaning 'rod', 'stick' or 'yard measure'). This unit was taken to the New World by the Conquistadors where its usage can be traced through the old Spanish territories of Middle and South America. However, its interpretations soon varied between different locales, and in Mexico it represented a measure of 32·87 inches, while in Uruguay it was 33·828 inches. Even in Spain, before metric measurements were introduced, the *vara* had several interpretations: the Valencia *vara* equalled 35·55183 inches while the Castile *vara* equalled 32·94 inches. The *vara* is also closely related to the old Bavarian ell of 32·766 inches and the Austrian ell of 30·78 inches.

Thom speculated that the *vara* probably came to Britain via the migrations of Megalithic peoples from Iberia. Whether such large-scale migrations ever took place to Britain now appears unlikely when judged in the framework of the New Archaeology (*see* below). Much more convincing evidence of the great antiquity of the measure is that the Megalithic yard is very close to the human pace and the Megalithic fathom to the double pace. The double pace, at least, can be traced back to Roman times in the *passus* (= 5 Roman feet; 1 Roman foot = 11·6 inches (296mm) = 16 digitus; 1 digitus = one thumb width = 18·5mm). The passus is likely to have had long antecedents before being adopted by the Romans.

Thom's investigations into prehistoric and ancient measures was by no means the first. Some of the great controversies of the past, which would now fall into the province of astro-archaeology, were involved in so-called standard unit lengths. Stukeley will always be remembered for his ill-fated 'Druid cubit', and Piazzi Smyth—the one-time Astronomer Royal for Scotland—for his infatuation with Pyramid inchology and his 'Bible-in-Stone' ideas that still have loud echoes in contemporary pseudo-scientific journalism.

Measures used in the ancient world are widely recognized to have been based on simple, easily remembered units such as the finger 'digit', palm or span, foot, arm length, pace, and arm-stretch. A study of ancient civilization shows this to be true—in part. There is the well-documented Roman digitus, or thumb nail, the Roman foot and related pace; earlier there was the Egyptian cubit—a measure of the length from elbow to fingertip; later there is also the apocryphal standard foot of Charlemagne, the standard arm-length yard of Henry I, and the archaic barleycorn measure still retained in modern shoe lengths. One of the earliest linear units of Middle Eastern civilization and known unambiguously from the archaeological record is the Babylonian cubit. An example of this is found inscribed as a standard measure on the basalt statue of Gudea of Lagash now a prize exhibit in the Paris Louvre. This cubit is dated around −2130 and depicts a measure of 19·5 inches (495mm) and a 'foot' measure of ⅔ cubit equal to 13 inches (330mm). Nevertheless, several ancient measures seem unrelated to natural sizes. One example is the old English measure, the ell, a unit also derived from an elbow measurement; later, however, it came to represent a much longer measurement than the natural 'cubit'.

Even in ancient Egypt, measurements were complicated by the use of two different cubits. There was the everyday 'short' cubit of 17·72 inches (0·454m) and the royal cubit of 20·62 inches (0·528m). The royal cubit was used in the setting out of the pyramids; some even believe that this cubit measure of 7 palms (1 palm = 4 digits (jeba) = 28 digits) may be related to an early twenty-eight-day lunar cycle. The royal cubit was also used in Egyptian land measurement, and the basic unit, the 'double remen' was the diagonal of a square having sides of one cubit length. For field measurement the Egyptians certainly recognized that in a triangle with sides in the ratio 3:4:5, the angle opposite the longest side was always a right angle. This knowledge was the result of experience rather than ability to work out a formal mathematical proof in a manner known later to have been accomplished by Pythagoras. However, the Pythagorean theorem was certainly known thousands of years before Pythagoras; this is confirmed by many Babylonian texts and it can without any doubt be acknowledged as genuine, widespread geo-mathematical knowledge possessed by several prehistoric peoples.

After realizing that an ancient quantum measure was involved in the design and layout of Megalithic circles, Thom arrived at the figure of 2·72 feet for his 'Megalithic yard' (MY). Applying the unit to constructions and sizes of the variously shaped 'circles', he was sure that such a basic unit existed. He believed an analysis of his results showed three things: (*a*) The precision of the measurements did not increase with the length of a measurement; (*b*) the results were the same whether the unit was derived from English or Scottish circles; (*c*) the builders of the circles appeared to have measured to the centres (or centre lines) of the stones in a ring.

Thom supposed that the key to the problem of distorted or oval circles was that Megalithic man was not prepared to accept the incommensurability of the value of π (3½) and searched for a whole round number. By accepting that Megalithic man abhorred the acceptance of 'something more than 3' and had decided that an integral number 'about 3' would suit him better, the apparently distorted, irregular-figured circles gained a new meaning. Thom noted that many of the smaller circles had a diameter of about 22 feet. These circles are 8 Megalithic yards in diameter; if π (= 3·142) had been used, the perimeter would have been adjusted. Thom believed that for large circles and longer distances it was likely that Megalithic man had used a measuring rod of 2½ MY (6·80 feet) and 10 MY (27·2 feet). After analyzing different categories of circle, he noted that the ratio of circumference to diameter was 3·059 for some, while for others 2·957. Thus it appeared that Thom had found a significant clue to the long puzzled-over, irregular circles which—by general opinion—were supposed to have been the result of crude or sloppy setting out by the Megalith builders.

Boyle Somerville, writing in 1927 about the large-scale plans he had drawn up of twenty-seven stone circles, remarked: 'In not one case are the stones composing the ring placed in a true circle; that is to say, it is not possible to draw a line joining all the stones which is mathematically circular. The best that can be done is to draw two consecutive circles, forming a band, wide or narrow within which the stones forming the ring may fall.' At Stonehenge he noted particularly: 'The eight stones (inner bluestones) remaining *in situ* do not stand on the arc of a circle, but lie between the limits of two concentric circles, 4 feet apart . . . Strictly speaking, the figure formed by the stones has no single central point and consequently no ''axis''.'

It is likely that Thom, as direct heir to Lockyer, A. Lewis (*see* note 12) and Boyle Somerville, had been strongly motivated by all their writings, and these latter remarks of Boyle Somerville may likely have been *the* very stimulus to solve the mystery of the irregular circles. . . .

As a result of his work carried out over several decades, Thom was able to classify stone rings into different categories: flattened circles, types A, B and D; egg-shaped, types I and II; ellipses; and compound and concentric circles (*see* Fig. 61). The egg-shaped rings in particular provided Thom with the insight that, in addition to using a standard quantum, the builders in the process had discovered the principle of Pythagorean triangles. He proposed that circle dimensions were often adjusted slightly to conform to integral numbers, thus making the circumference as near as possible to a multiple of the larger unit.

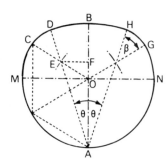

Type A   Flattened circle.

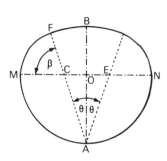

Type B   Flattened circle.

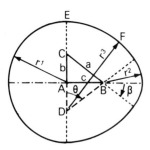

Type I   Egg-shaped circle.

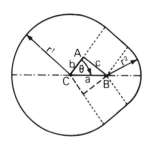

Type II   Egg-shaped circle.

61 Thom's geometry relating to flattened and egg-shaped circles. In Type A flattened circles AB/MN = 0·9114. In Type B circles AB/MN = 0·8604. Type D represents a modified Type A circle where AB/MN = 0·9343. In Type I egg-shaped circles the reconstruction is based on two Pythagorean triangles placed base to base. In Type II the triangles are placed together with a common hypotenuse. (For a detailed geometric analysis *see* Thom's *Megalithic Sites in Britain* (1967).)

Although Thom did not publish any data on Stonehenge until 1974 (*see* below), his earlier work included a comprehensive study of neighbouring Avebury, 25km (16 miles) to the north. Avebury is the greatest and most remarkable (compound) circle in Britain, if not in the whole world. Thom suggested it was not only the size which contributes to its greatness. Avebury is remarkable because of the exceedingly high precision apparent in the setting out and the distinctive manner in which its arcs were built up from a basic Pythagorean triangle so that each triangle of the construction retains integral units. Today he believed this was only surpassed in carefully executed, high class surveying. He claimed that Avebury has a much more complicated basic geometry than Stonehenge, and that it includes the largest complex of Megalithic circles known.

Thom said that the clues which led him to unravel the geometry of Avebury did not spark from Stonehenge and other large circles, but from some small unimpressive circles on remote Scottish moors and the hills of Wales. He believed that the results of his work at Avebury were the most conclusive and 'the final proof' of the exact size of the Megalithic yard, and the construction of the monument demonstrated unambiguously the use of even larger linear units of 2 ½ and 10 MYs. . . .

Avebury, like Stonehenge, greatly attracted the attentions of the older antiquarians. In an early reference John Aubrey noted that Avebury far surpassed Stonehenge 'as a cathedral doth a parish church'. Its area is five times as great as that of St Peter's in Rome, and it was once estimated that upwards of a quarter of a million people could stand within the boundaries defined by its inner ditch. Its sheer size, 11·5 hectares (28 ½ acres), and complexity, gives it a status of being one of the most puzzling Megalithic monuments yet studied.

Sir R. Colt Hoare was also much impressed and wrote in his *Ancient Wiltshire* (1812): 'With awe and diffidence I enter the sacred precincts of this once hallowed sanctuary, the supposed parent of Stonehenge, the wonder of Britain and the most ancient, as well as the most interesting relict which our island can produce.' Earlier Stukeley, in his book *Abury*, had also described it in fine style, writing that it showed 'a notorious grandeur of taste, a justness of plan, an apparent symmetry, and a sufficient niceness in the execution: in compass very extensive,

62 Avebury: oblique aerial view.

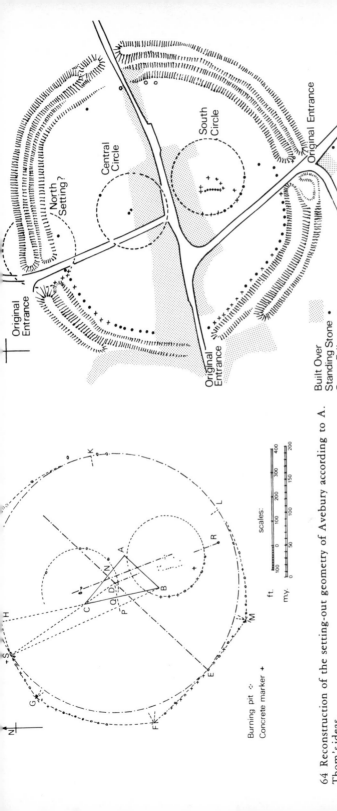

64 Reconstruction of the setting-out geometry of Avebury according to A. Thom's ideas.

Diameter of inner circles = 125 MY = 340·0 feet.

Distance between circle centres = 145 MY.

The basic design is set on a 3:4:5 triangle in units of 25 MY.

Thus AB = 75; AC = 100; and BC = 125.

BS = 260; CS = 140; CD = 60; DE = DS = DK = DL = 200.

ED is parallel to BA and H is on BC produced.

For Thom's construction arguments refer to his *Megalithic sites in Britain* (pp. 89—91).

scales:

ft. [100 50 0   100   200   300   400]

my. [0   50   100   150   200]

Burning pit ∴

Concrete marker +

Built Over

Standing Stone •

Stone Fallen o

Stone Hole +

[100 0 100 200 300 400 500 feet]

63 Plan of the stone circles at Avebury.

Original Entrance

Original Entrance

Original Entrance

Central Circle

North Setting?

South Circle

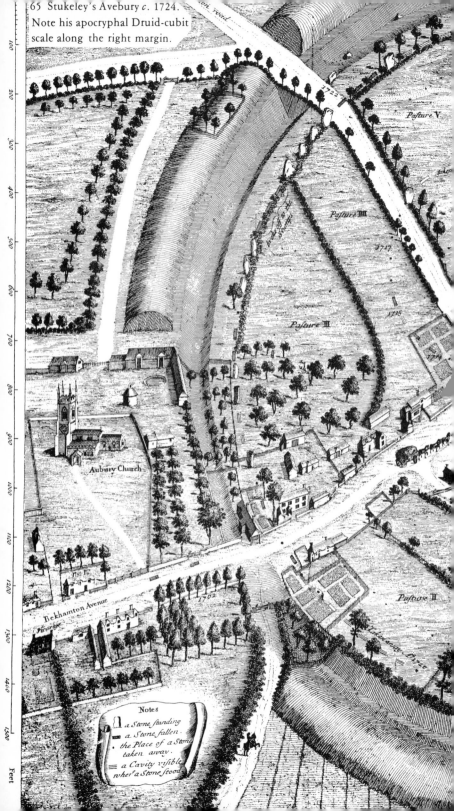

65 Stukeley's Avebury *c.* 1724.
Note his apocryphal Druid-cubit
scale along the right margin.

Pasture V

Pasture IIII

Pasture III

Aubury Church

Beckhamton Avenue

Notes
▍ a Stone standing.
◗ a Stone fallen.
● the Place of a Stone
    taken away.
▤ a Cavity visible
    where a Stone stood

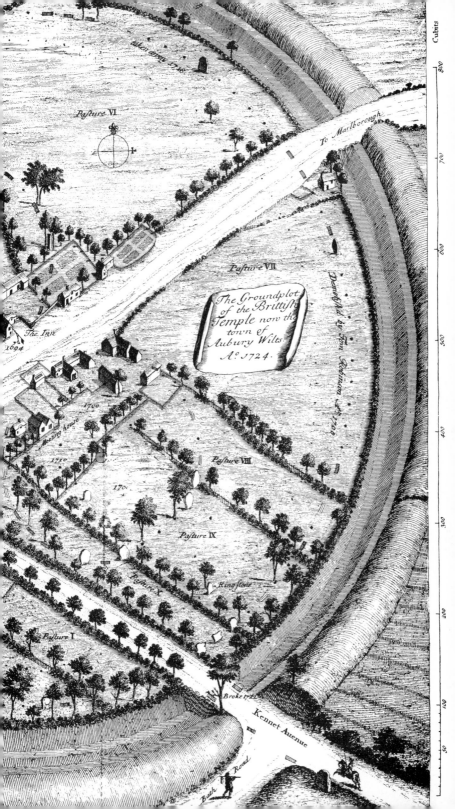

Cubits

800

To Marlborough

700

Pasture VI

600

Pasture VII

The Groundplot of the Brittish Temple now the town of Aubury Wilts Aᵒ 1724.

500

Drawn by Tom Robinson Aᵒ 1724

The Inn
1694

400

1700

The Dighous

1710

Pasture VIII

300

1700

Pasture IX

Ringstone

200

Pasture X

Pasture I

100

Broke 1724

Kennet Avenue

50

Bath Road

in effect magnificent and agreeable. The boldness of the imagination we cannot sufficiently admire'.

It was from Stukeley's researches at Avebury that we know a great deal about the monument before modern development obliterated much of it. William Stukeley (1687—1765) was born at Holbeach in Lincolnshire and later became one of those colourful and romantic eighteenth-century characters. By profession he was a doctor and studied at Cambridge and St Thomas' hospital in London, after giving up a law apprentice-ship at his father's office. Personal recognition and his wide range of scientific interests secured him a Fellowship of the Royal Society at the age of thirty. He became the first secretary of the Society of Antiquaries, and between 1718 and 1725 he carried out a monumental series of field observations at Avebury, Stonehenge and elsewhere. This finally resulted in his books *Stonehenge* (1740) and *Abury* (1743). In 1729 he took orders and in 1747 became a rector in London.

Stukeley is now best remembered for his romantic notions about the Druids and was long known himself as the 'Arch-Druid'. In particular he is remembered for his ideas about the so-called serpent worship at Stonehenge and Avebury; these he believed had been serpent temples of 'Dracontia'. He appears to have based his ideas on a mythical story, via Pliny, which told of the Druids of Gaul having used as a charm a certain magic egg made by a snake. In this way he conceived the Druids to be serpent worshippers. At Avebury the stone circle on Overton Hill (the Hakpen) was assumed to be the head of a snake and the sinuous West Kennet Avenue the neck. The sarsen circles represented coils in the snake's body, and the rest of the serpent was made up of other megaliths and avenues (the lost 'Beckhampton Avenue'—*see* below). He even went so far as to alter the circles of his original survey of the Sanctuary on Overton Hill to egg-shaped structures so as to fit the snake theories better! Nevertheless, without Stukeley and his dedication to serpent worship we should know a great deal less. His work in the earlier period from *c*. 1718 to 1730 shows him at this time to have been the finest field-archaeologist in all England, and this great reputation was maintained until the end of the eighteenth century.

Like many romantic characters of the period he possessed a strong underlying vein of mysticism in his make-up which

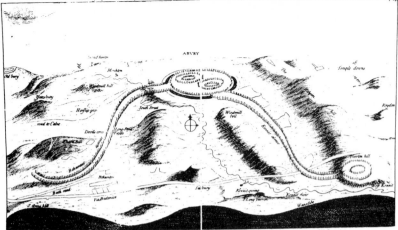

ABVRY

Prohonoratli Dno Dno Philippo Dno Hardwick summo magnæ Brittanniæ Cancellario tabulam. i.m.d. W.Stukeley.

66 Avebury and the West Kennet and Beckhampton Avenues restored according to Stukeley's ideas.

66b Avebury in prehistoric times, looking north, according to a reconstruction by Alan Sorrell (c. 1958). Note the West Kennet Avenue feature leading to the south entrance.

became even more manifest as he grew older. He joined the Freemasons in 1721, and in the garden of his house in Grantham he laid out a Druidical grove and temple where in 1728 he sadly buried a still-born child.

He lived to the age of seventy-eight, perpetrating his pseudo-Druidical and other archaeological atrocities to the very end. He was strongly religious—if unorthodox. He claimed that all pagan religions, particularly that of the Druids, had in many of their concepts foreshadowed the tenets of Christianity, including the doctrine of the Trinity. One of his prize romantic notions was his belief that on the site now occupied by Piccadilly Circus in London's West End had once stood the very barrow where the king of the Trinobantes was buried.

In plan Avebury consists of a rampart of earth roughly circular in form, and whose outline has a diameter of c. 360m (1,200 feet). Inside this rampart and situated close to the inner foot of it is a ditch, and close again to the inner side of the ditch is the Great 'circle' that once consisted of about a hundred upright stones.

Within the large outer circle lie the remains of two (possibly three) smaller circles, both measuring, in accordance to Thom's survey, 340 feet (125 MY) (Fig. 64). At the centre of the northernmost circle (known as the central circle) are the remains of a tomb chamber (dolmen)—known in Lockyer's day as the 'Devil's Den'; in the centre of the south circle is a single upright stone (menhir). All the stones incorporated in the monument are local sarsen and highly typical of those which can still be seen strewn about the district.

Nowadays, as can be seen from any photograph, a very large part of the village of Avebury lies straddled within the area defined by the bank and ditch, and it obscures many of the ancient features of the monument. So obscured was the monument even in medieval times that features which could be recognized were attributed to true works of nature. One reference to Avebury in the tenth century supposed it to be a burial place—as its name implies. According to an old charter of King Athelstan dated +939 that describes the local boundaries of the Manor of Overton (in which Avebury lies) one can glean a direct reference to Avebury: 'Then to Collas barrow, as far as the broad road to Hackpen; thence northward up along the Stone row (the great avenue); thence to the burying places. . . .'

67 Some pioneer investigators of Megalithic monuments: *Top left*, Sir Norman Lockyer (*c.* 1904); *top right*, Sir Flinders Petrie (*c.* 1895); *bottom left*, John Aubrey (*c.* 1666); *bottom right*, 'Arch-Druid' William Stukeley and his wife Frances (*c.* 1730).

The first serious excavation was made by H. St. G. Gray, in the period 1908—22. He investigated some sections of the bank and ditch, but it was not until 1934—9 that the true nature of Avebury was resolved by the work of the wealthy amateur Alexander Keiller.

In places the ditch is over 9m (30 feet) deep but is now filled to about 5m (17 feet). Straddling the encompassing ditch, there are three, possibly four, original causeway entrances; proven are those to the north, south, and west while the one now to the east is still doubtful.

The great outlying bank rises to about 4·5m (15 feet), and its perimeter measures 1,200m (¾ mile). Excavations have shown it to be composed of chalk rubble dressed with a revetment of blocks excavated from the beds of Lower Chalk in the ditch bottom. Material at higher level on the bank has been shown to be formed from material gleaned only from Middle Chalk beds. The labour involved for the construction of these massive earthworks in terms of man-days puts it on a par with the Megalithic pyramid engineering of Egypt. The immensity of this prehistoric public works undertaking becomes even more apparent when it is realized that the only excavation tools available to its builders were antler picks and oxen bones. The British archaeologist Geoffrey Wainwright estimated that the earthworks at Avebury involved more than 1·5 million man-hours, yet Avebury was only one among several henges of similar bank and ditch construction. It was not until the great surge of canal, road and rail building, which accompanied the Industrial Revolution four millenniums later, that native 'pick-and-shovel' British workmen were again to be engaged in such large public works undertakings.

But one of the grandest ancient features of the monument was the Great Stone Circle whose outer circumference, formed by its one hundred uprights, lies about 9m (30 feet) inside the ditch. The central inner circle once comprised about thirty upright stones of which only four remain. These were set, according to Thom's survey, to a diameter of 340 feet (125 MY); in the middle of this circle was a setting of closely spaced upright stones named by Stukeley the 'Cove', similar to a setting of stones at Stanton Drew in Somerset. Of the southern circle only five perimeter stones remain in position out of an original total of thirty-two, and these were also, according to Thom, set to the

diameter of 125 MY. Thom gives the distance between the two
inner circles as 145 MY. In the rather doubtful so-called
northern circle, only three stoneholes have been found.

Rivalling the Great Stone Circle is the West Kennet Avenue
(the 'Stone row' of older citations). The remains of this double
row of sarsen monoliths is the first part of the monument to be
seen by a visitor approaching from the south (Fig. 69).
Originally it consisted of about 200 uprights set in pairs spaced
24m (80 feet) apart in the direction of the Avenue and 15m (50
feet) across the width of the Avenue. The Avenue was the
connecting link between the Great Stone Circle and a feature a
mile away on Overton Hill, known as the Sanctuary (Stukeley's
Hakpen or Snake's Head Temple); this began as a circular
Megaxylic structure and was later rebuilt with stone (Fig. 66).

When Aubrey first visited Avebury in 1648, all the stones
forming the Avenue seem to have been in existence either
standing in their original holes, or fallen lying near by. It was
about this time, or shortly after, that deliberate destruction
began. Many of the sarsens were broken and then split into
smaller, more manageable fragments by hammering, or they
were fragmented by a more subtle method that involved first
heating the stone by fires built around it and then striking it
along a line marked out by cold water.

In 1934, when Alexander Keiller excavated Avebury, there
was ample evidence remaining which showed this highly
effective method of fire destruction. Pits dug beneath prostrate
stones were found blackened and charred by fire, and burnt
fragments of sarsen were all that were left of the once massive
megaliths. Stukeley, whose work at Avebury is particularly
significant in documenting the history of the monument, left to
posterity a drawing which vividly depicts the fire-and-water
method (Fig. 71). It is also from Stukeley's drawings that we can
picture the Sanctuary on Overton Hill as it was. The year after
his visit, the stones were removed to clear the field for
ploughing, and the exact position of the site was only
rediscovered from Stukeley's notes. Nowadays, as is also the
case with the stones missing from the Avenue, concrete markers
fill the old subsurface stoneholes found by modern excavation
and thus provide the visitor with a realistic impression of some
the monument's former Megalithic grandeur. Stukeley's own

69a The bank-and-ditch feature (south-west quadrant) at Avebury.

69b The West Kennet Avenue leading to Avebury from the south.

description of the magnificent Avenue is still worth reading—
'... The Kennet Avenue consisted originally of one hundred
stones on each side, reaching from the vallum of Abury town
to the circular work on Overton Hill. Mr Smith, living here,
informed me that when he was a schoolboy the Kennet Avenue
was entire from end to end. The stones composing it were of all
shapes, sizes, and heights that happened, altogether rude.
Some measured six feet thick, sixteen in circumference. If the
stones of a flattish make, the broadest dimension was set in the
line of the avenue, and the most sightly side of the stone inward.
The founders were sensible that all the effect desired in the case
was their bulk and regular station. When I abode here for some
time on purpose, for several summers together, I was very careful
in tracing it out, knew the distinct number of each stone
remaining, and where every one stood that was wanting; which
often surprized the country people, who remembered them left
on the ground or standing, and told me who carried them away.
Many of the farmers made deep holes and buried them in the
ground they knew where they lay. Lord Winchilsea with me
counted the number of the stones left, 72, anno 1722. I laid it all
down in the nature of a survey, on large imperial sheets of paper,
and wrote a detail of every stone present or absent; but it would
be very irksome to load the press with it.'

The stones found buried beneath the overburden of soil
between 1925 and 1939 were restored to their former positions
whenever possible. One stone buried was dated by its modern
excavators to the early fourteenth century. This stone had
evidently prematurely slipped into the burial pit prepared for it
and in doing so had crushed a barber who had joined in the
destruction without appreciating the hazards of stone tippling.
His skeleton was found beneath the stone. His trade was
indicated by his scissors, and his date of death by the coins intact
in his purse. But it was later during Stukeley's time that the
much more damaging phase of destruction began via the
fire-and-water method. The earliest deliberate destruction was
no doubt motivated by the attacks of the early Church on the use
of pagan sanctuaries way back in Anglo-Saxon times. Later
destruction was motivated by economic factors. The fields were
cleared of obstacles in the way of more effective husbandry, and
the menhirs were found to be a convenient source of building
stone. Stukeley had counted seventy-two sarsens in the Avenue,

70 Cup and ring marks inscribed on an Avenue megalith at Avebury.

71 Stukeley's contemporary sketch of 'the fire-and-water' method of destroying sarsens at Avebury c. 1724.

but by the 1920s only nineteen remained in position.

A second avenue known as the Beckhampton Avenue was claimed by Stukeley to have extended to the sarsen circles from the south-west marked by two stones (known as Adam and Eve). It is now believed that the Beckhampton standing stones represent the remains of an independent stone circle with an avenue. Stukeley was sure it once existed and provided a description: 'The Beckhampton Avenue goes out of Abury town at the west point, and proceeds by the south side of the churchyard. Two stones lie by the parsonage gate on the right hand. Those opposite to them on the left hand, in a pasture, were taken away in 1702, as marked in the ground-plan of Abury. Reuben Horsal remembers three standing in the pasture. One now lies in the floor of the house in the churchyard. A little farther one lies at the corner of the next house on the right hand, by the lane turning off to the right to the bridge. Another was broke in pieces, to build that house with in 1714. Two more lie on the left hand opposite. It [the Avenue] then passes the south of the bridge. Most of the stones hereabouts have been made use of about the bridge, and the causeway leading to it. . . . '

Smith in his *British and Roman Antiquities of North Wiltshire* (1884) completes the Beckhampton description, writing: 'Moreover, we have some evidence of the existence of the avenue in this direction, in the fragments of sarsen stones which may still be seen there, as the Rev. Bryan King has pointed out in his note on this subject (*Wiltshire Magazine* vol 26 pp. 377—383).' King himself wrote: 'Beginning with the walls of the churchyard and of the church and of the manor-house, with its enclosures, in an entire length of full half-a-mile from the earthwork on the west side of Avebury to the corner of the large field in which the two large stones near Beckhampton now stand, there are very few lineal yards which are not occupied by causeway, walls or cottages, all formed of sarsen stone, sufficient and more than sufficient, to absorb all the stones of the Beckhampton Avenue.'

Lockyer after his own visit to Avebury claimed that the so-called Beckhampton Avenue and the cove feature (the 'Devil's Den' inside the central, inner sarsen circle) were both orientated to the May sunrise and May ceremonials; while the West Kennet Avenue was once used to observe the rise of Alpha

72 Avebury. Massive sarsen marking the west side of the North Entrance.

Many of the massive sarsens round Avebury (*see* also 72b, 73b, 107) have distinctive shapes which may have been very significant in Megalithic science or in the Megalithic cultus.

72b The 'Adam and Eve' sarsens ('The Longstones') near Avebury—possibly the sole surviving remnants of the lost Beckhampton Avenue.

73 Avebury: view looking south-east from Stukeley's 'Pasture II' (*see also* Fig. 65). The remains of the barber (*see* text) were found under the sarsen stone, seventh from the left. 73b (*See* caption 72 opposite.)

Centauri (Rigel Kent) as the morning star warning of the November sunrise.

It was during the period of modern restoration that Keiller corrected an earlier and erroneous belief that the sarsens which formed the West Kennet Avenue were simply crude unhewn blocks of stone. Keiller showed that the Megaliths had been deliberately dressed to conform to certain required shapes. Some of the sarsens showed the now familiar Bronze Age ornamental features known as 'cup and ring' (*see* Fig. 70). These consist of irregular double concentric circles surrounding a pair of depressions; the earliest examples appear to be fashioned from natural holes that occur in sarsen stones, while the later ones suggest a completely artificial origin.

Keiller's excavation of the Avenue has revealed that its course was traversed by field boundaries belonging to a complex of Early Iron Age and Roman fields, thus indicating in an unmistakeable way that the significance of the Avebury Sanctuary and the route to or from it had been forgotten by the time of the Early Iron Age. As Keiller himself noted: '. . . the contemporaries of the Druids so far from watching stately processions of mistletoe-bedizened, white-robed priests winding along the avenue, were ploughing cornfields across its line and chipping flints in the lee of its unconsidered fallen stones. . . .'

The results of Thom's survey at Avebury was to persuade him that it had been set out to an accuracy approaching 1 in 1,000. This on the face of it may appear to be an ambitious claim for Megalithic man. Thom himself claimed that this kind of accuracy is only achieved today by experienced surveyors with good optical equipment. But in the author's own experience a modern survey team—even without an optical theodolite—can achieve the same metrical accuracy in a closed traverse by using a metal chain only.

Such a claim made by Thom for Megalithic man is not extravagant in the context of history, and the case of the pyramids immediately comes to mind. Flinders Petrie's definitive survey of the Great Pyramid built by Khufu (Cheops) *c*. − 2500 showed it to be orientated to about the same degree of accuracy that Thom claims for the builders of Avebury. No one can be quite certain about the precise method used by the

Egyptian surveyors in this period of the Old Kingdom. It is known that in a later period temples were orientated by using stars to obtain a true azimuth. Egyptian texts cite the use of stars in the constellation of the Bull's (or Ox's) Foreleg (Ursa Major) in conjunction with a plumb-line device known as a *merket*. Nevertheless, methods before the New Kingdom Dynasties may very well have been more refined, but nowhere can we find a reference to the actual technique used in setting out the Great Pyramid.

In the determination of a true azimuth by astronomical means the *unassisted* eye can achieve an accuracy of 1 to 2' of arc even with only a moderately long sight line. As the surveyor responsible for setting out true azimuths—using astronomical techniques—for US military Interglobal Communication Stations on Yorkshire and Scottish moors, this author frequently experimented with very long sight lines, finding that in these instances the unassisted eye could determine an azimuth to within 1' of arc (checked by astro-theodolite readings). The only limitations to greater accuracy is the resolving power of the human eye, and those with exceptional vision might certainly achieve even better results.

Thom's British site explorations led him to suppose that three compound rings in particular show designs which lead up to the compound Avebury construction. He believed that the geometrical constructions of these rings showed what he referred to as mastery of the technique for finding designs that incorporate 'an elegance of symmetry and proportion' but which at the same time incorporated 'a hidden significance' in respect to their integral parameters being governed by multiples of 2½ MY. His occasional choice of words such as 'a hidden significance' causes some unease to those familiar with Piazzi Smyth's metrical obsessions with 'hidden' significances in pyramid dimensions and proportions.

Thom cites as example the Welsh circle of Moel ty Ucha (Fig. 74) and thought that here the builders had attempted something very different from what they had attempted previously elsewhere. According to Thom, they began with a circle 14 MY in diameter and therefore 3½ × 14 = 44 MY in circumference. This he infers did not suit their purpose, for they desired a multiple of 2½ MY for the perimeter. It was now Thom assumes that they invented a method of constructing flattened sections on the ring which, with minimum distortion, reduced it to a circumference of 42 ½. To do this required a minimum of two radii, each of which had to be integral; in addition, the finished ring, in order to conform to others, required an axis of symmetry. But this was not all. Thom believed another external condition had to be satisfied in order to accommodate the azimuth rising point of the star Deneb (Alpha Cygni). Round about the time of the associated epoch, Deneb rose at azimuth 17°3. Thom assumed that the builders wanted this shown in the construction so that the cross axis indicating the rising star would also indicate true north. However, instead of an azimuth of 17°3 the builders got 18°. He argued that this angle is the complement of 72°, one-fifth of 360°. Although the Greek geometers later showed how to construct an angle of 72°, this could only be done by the Megalith builders as a trial-and-error process. Thom showed this is possible by scribing arcs on the ground.

74 Moel ty Ucha. At 'B' there are two outlying stones fallen (after A. Thom).

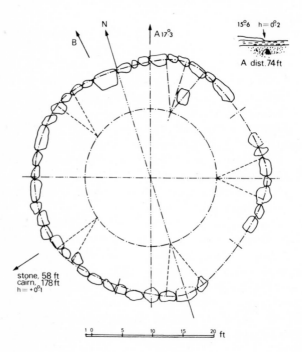

The next circle treated by Thom is at Easter Delfour in Scotland. Here the outer stone ring is partly buried in rubble; he considered that the original form of the monument was a hollow cairn. He said that this is borne out by the dimensions of the inner ring which = 8 MY in diameter. He claimed this ring to have much in common with Moel ty Ucha, but it consists of four parts instead of five. Using geometrical constructions Thom again argued a case for a circle with an outer diameter of 22 MY, and in addition a small inner circle of 6½ MY. He was certain that he had unlocked the geometry of the site by assuming *a priori* construction modules for it (Fig. 75).

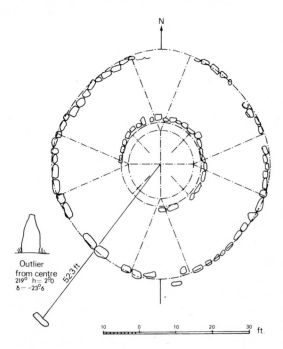

N

Outlier
from centre
219° h= 2°0
δ= -23°6

52.3 ft

10   0   10   20   30 ft.

75 Easter Delfour (after A. Thom).

The third ring, and member of the group, is at Kerry Pole in Wales. Thom began his arguments by stating that this example was 'a very unimpressive site'. The reconstruction of the geometry was based on circles whose diameters are 32 MY and 16 MY. His geometrical arguments are again very persuasive and presented in immaculate style. He found all the radii integral: 16, 8 and 30 MY, and the perimeter differed only by a value of 0·12 from a multiple of his larger 2½ MY quantum (Fig. 76).

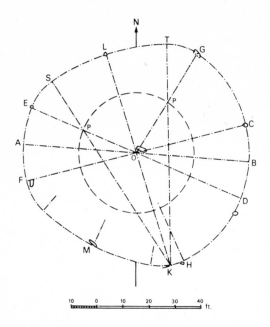

76 Kerry Pole (after A. Thom): AB = 32; CD = 10; EF = 10; GH = 28; OP = 8; KS = 29·98; perimeter = 97·38. (All units in MY.)

Thom's ideas concerning geometrical reconstructions of Megalithic circles reached full development with his explanation of the Avebury ring and its lesser, inner rings. Avebury is of course a much larger site and therefore technically more difficult to set out using primitive 'chaining' methods. The traverse of Thom's own survey was 900m (3,000 feet) long and at three points was controlled by astronomical determinations of azimuth. He tells us that his own closing error was 18cm (0·6 feet).

Thom related that without knowledge of the exact length of the Megalithic yard in the case of Avebury he believed it doubtful that its planned construction could have been rediscovered. He showed the Great Circle to comprise of several arcs of different radii; two of them measuring 750 MY (Fig. 64).

Thom admitted that since only half the ring has been excavated, the remaining part is less certain. In one section, only a single stone remains upright. He drew his constructions on tracing paper assuming the module Megalithic yard to be 2·720 feet. He related that had the value adopted been 2·730 feet, the large ring would have been too large by some 1·5m (5 feet) and would have passed outside the remaining stones. Thus in this demonstration he had gained 'a striking proof' that the MY was a real quantity and the very unit adopted by the Avebury builders to set the size of the ring.

Thom's method of interpreting compound Megalithic circles that led to his personal solution of the Avebury construction is typical of the metrical method in all the circles he studied. He maintained he could show that his assumptions of the MY and its preferred integrals used in circle constructions had a sound statistical basis. However, in respect to the astronomical inter-pretations which follow as a consequence of his reconstructions and *a priori* assumptions, this was a more difficult problem to handle by rigorous statistical methods. Nevertheless he cited a list of over 250 observed lines indicated by his surveys (*Megalithic Sites in Britain*, pp. 97—101). Most of the cited stellar alignments are the same as Lockyer's stars: first magnitude, or brighter, stars such as Capella, Rigel, Castor and Pollux, Deneb, Antares, Bellatrix, Spica, Altair, Arcturus and Procyon. All these stars are reduced to azimuths for dates falling between − 2000 to − 1500, since the archaeological evidence indicated this to be the period when the circles and associated structures were built. The list contains many supposed Sun alignments. Where it differs most radically from Lockyer's work is in the inclusion of numerous Moon alignments.

Thom cites astronomical azimuths being provided by:

(1) a slab;
(2) two or more stones not separated too far away;
(3) a circle and a closer outlier;
(4) two circles;

But for the Sun and Moon the minimum requirements are:

(1) an extended alignment;
(2) two well separated stones;
(3) a circle which has an outline some hundreds of feet distant; or

(4) a natural foresight identified by some simple indicator.

Thom considered that the stars were used as timekeepers. They could be used at times of rising, at culmination on the meridian (the observer's north-south line), or at setting. There is direct textual evidence to show that the Greeks, from Hesiod's time onwards, used stars in this very way (the method probably was derived from a much earlier Upper Paleolithic tradition). For example, in a play by Euripides a character asks: 'What is the star now passing?' To which came the reply: 'The Pleiades show themselves in the east, the Eagle (Aquila) soars in the Summit of the heavens.' During the time of the early Egyptian dynasties beginning c. -2150, star asterisms or constellations (the Decans) were used in a similar fashion. These decanal star clocks are shown on many coffin lids, and this tradition was continued by artists long after the epoch when the decanal rising lists had any scientific meaning for gauging time (Fig. 17). Later during the Rameses period more elaborate star clocks were evolved, but the use of these seems to have been lost long before the influence of Babylonian and Greek ideas on Egyptian astronomy. Star maps printed in Europe as late as the seventeenth century also provided similar information as do modern planispheres.

Thom noted that many of his stellar lines seemed to indicate the use of Capella (Alpha Aurigae). In northern Europe this star always seems to have been important in agriculture and husbandry, and in the Middle Ages it was known more familiarly as the 'Shepherd's star'. Lockyer in his Egyptian studies claimed he had found at least five temples orientated to Capella, and Penrose in similar fashion cited several Greek temples—including one to the goddess Diana Propyla at Eleusis.

At Avebury, Thom cites Deneb. About the epoch in question this star transited the meridian below the north celestial pole about midnight. Thom claimed that Deneb was a particularly useful star in nocturnal Megalithic timekeeping. At Avebury its supposed setting was indicated by the extended line joining the two large inner circles (Fig. 64). Other so-called Deneb alignments are indicated in circles at Seascale, Ballantrae and Nine Maidens.

Sirius, the brightest star in the sky and known to the

Egyptians as Sothis (and related to the Sothic year), had, according to Thom, no indicators on British Megalithic sites. However, he believed that such indicators were not necessary, for the three stars forming Orion's sword belt provided a sure enough guide (Fig. 37). According to Lockyer's ideas the rising of Sirius was indicated by at least seven Egyptian temples.

In addition to his alignment and metrical theories, Thom also forwarded some ideas about the ancient calendar. Lockyer and others claimed evidence for the division of the ancient year into at least eight parts, or divisions, which regulated the ceremonial or the farmer's year. From his study of British (and later French) alignments, Thom claimed that at least sixteen equal divisions of the year were discernible with each of the sixteen 'months' made up of periods of 22/23 days. He also hinted that a thirty-two 'month' division calendar may some time have been used.

CHAPTER IX

More Metrics More Moonstones

Thom's Megalithic studies, inspired by the work of Lewis, Lockyer and then Boyle Somerville, go much beyond any of these pioneers. All three, however, had provided significant clues for Thom to follow up: it was from Lewis he hit upon the idea of classifying circles; it was from Boyle Somerville he found his clues about lunar alignments at Callanish; and it was from Lockyer he inherited stellar alignments and the controversial analytical method of using the long-term changes of the Sun's obliquity as a tool for dating Megalithic monuments. It will be recalled that Lockyer, using the so-called mid-Avenue line at Stonehenge, arrived at a date of − 1680 ±200 years; most believed the method unpractical and Lockyer's result coincidentally fortuitous, for the choice of the mid-Avenue line had been too arbitrary.

Thom, nevertheless, maintained that Lockyer's basic method was valid enough if accurate backsights and foresights could be identified in a monument or in a surrounding region near a Megalithic site. Since Lockyer's time a more accurate value of the variation of obliquity had become available (it is now known to have ranged between 21° 39′ and 24° 36′). Thom adopted values derived from De Sitter's work (1938) which showed it to be decreasing at a rate of about 40 seconds per century in the period − 1800 to − 1600.

Thom devoted much of his second book *Megalithic Lunar Observatories* (1971) to showing that it was possible to date Megalithic monuments via the rate of change of the Sun's obliquity if one had sight lines long enough to derive azimuth accurate of 1′ of arc or less.

To appreciate his work it is necessary to first look again at the factors controlling the apparent movement of the Moon. It will be remembered that in relation to lunar alignments at

Stonehenge it was essential to take into account the 5° inclination to the ecliptic of the Moon's orbit. It will also be remembered that the crossing points of the Moon's orbit—the nodes—appear to regress round the ecliptic in 18·61 years. The 5° inclination of the path described by the Moon causes its rising and setting points (azimuths) to swing back and forth along the horizon with a much greater amplitude and rate of change than that of the Sun. Lastly it will be remembered that an eclipse can only occur when both the Sun and Moon lie approximately in the line of the nodes (Fig. 51).

The mean value of the Moon's orbital inclination is $5° 8' 43''$, but this is only a *mean* value. Tycho Brahe (1546—1601), the famous Danish nobleman-astronomer and the last great pre-telescopic observer, noted that the inclination of the Moon's orbit to the ecliptic was not a constant value as the Greeks had earlier supposed. Tycho found that it ranged through a minor swing of about $9'$ on each side of the approximate mean value of $5° 8'$. This results in a minimum inclination of $4° 58½'$ and a maximum of $5° 17'$ at times of quadrature and syzygy respectively. Although this discovery is attributed to Tycho Brahe, it appears to have been known to the Arabs in the tenth century and then forgotten. Thom, however, believed that from his study of this $9'$ swing, it was a factor familiar to Megalithic man when he built his circle observatories at the beginning of the second millennium BC.

The Sun's annual change in declination shifts from $+ \epsilon$ to $- \epsilon$ (where ϵ represents the value of the obliquity (the actual tilt of the Earth's axis) = $23° 27' 8''29$). If the Moon's orbit lay in the same plane as the Sun's apparent movement, it would follow the same annual declination change over the period of one month. But since it is tilted at about 5°, this is not so, therefore the Moon's limits can be expressed as $\pm (\epsilon + i)$ and $(\epsilon - i)$ where i represents the inclination of the Moon's orbit. At this stage it is also well to remind ourselves about the Moon's nodal swing round the ecliptic in 18·61 years, but it must also be remembered that the Moon's path among the stars (because of its revolution round the Earth) carries it across both nodes (ascending and descending) *every* month.

However, in addition to the above we also have the variation of $9'$ discovered by Tycho Brahe which we now know is due to a perturbation effect. This causes the pole of the lunar orbit to

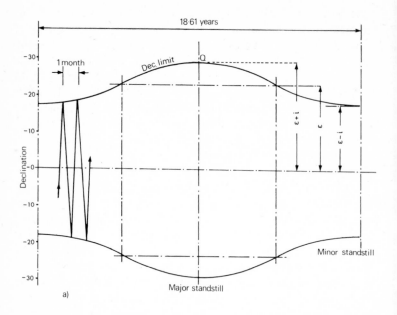

a)

77 (a) The Moon's declination limits traced out during one complete revolution of the line of nodes in 18·61 years from minor standstill through major standstill back to minor standstill. The 9′ perturbation effect (*see* text) is too small to show up on this scale. (b) The Moon's declination changes in one month from nearly − 30° to nearly + 30°. (c) The Moon's monthly declination maxima over several years with the ± 9′ perturbation effect superimposed. Note that the section between the arrows is the period traced out in (b) (after A. Thom).

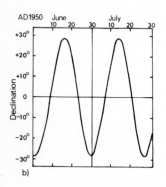

b)

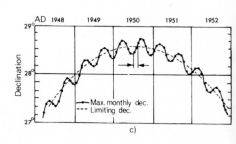

c)

move uniformly on a small circle of a radius of *c*. 9′ over a period of 173 days.

The 9′ variation is a sufficiently large enough quantity to be eclipse-important. Thom has illustrated the effects of this short-term 9′ declination change (Fig. 78) which in the example of November 1968 indicates a declination change of +28° 33′ to − 28° 33′ over a two-week period. This figure also shows in easily assimilated graphical form the ecliptic limits when eclipses can take place. Note that these periods are of about three weeks' duration. Thom's point is that they occur when the perturbation factor is a maximum value. The figure (Fig. 78) illustrates well the underlying factor that eclipses can only occur within the prescribed ecliptic limit. In the example provided by the occurrence of Full Moon on 2 April 1969 it was then just *outside* the limit and therefore missed intercepting the Earth's shadow.

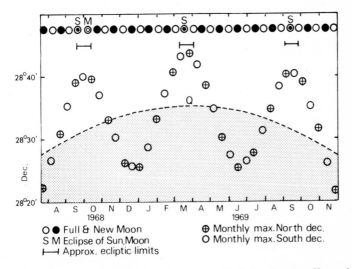

78 Lunar declination maxima for the 1969 standstill showing the effects of the 9′ perturbation factor on the Moon's path and eclipse occurrences. Note the line Q (major standstill) in this figure and in Fig. 77a (after A. Thom).

It was Thom's belief that if the Megalithic observers were able to detect this highly significant perturbation effect via circle and stone alignments, and could gauge its period, they would then be armed with sufficient data to predict eclipses. He has applied his methods to both solar (solstitial) and lunar sites. Two of the most important lunar sites he has described are at Temple Wood in Argyllshire and Mid Clyth in Caithness.

Temple Wood (near Kilmartin) is a small circle with an inner ring and cist (Fig. 79). Near by is a line of five up-right stones (menhirs), one of these has cup marks inscribed on it. Another

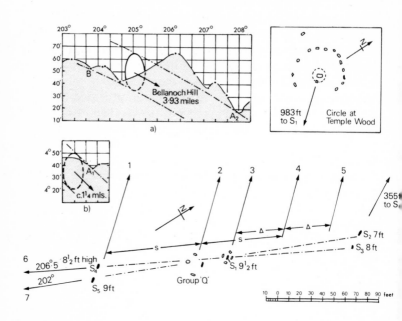

79 Temple Wood, Kilmartin, Scotland, showing A. Thom's configurations for lunar sights $c. -1770$.
Key:

(a) Moon setting dec $= -(\epsilon + i)$.

(b) Notch behind circle, Moon setting with dec $= +(\epsilon + i)$.

(1) Upper limb (of the Moon) setting (b) in notch A_1 when lunar dec $= +(\epsilon + i)$.

(2) Centre setting (b) in notch A_1 when dec $= +(\epsilon + i)$.

(3) Lower limb setting (b) in notch A_1 when dec $= +(\epsilon + i + \Delta)$.

(4) Lower limb setting (b) in notch A_1 when dec $= +(\epsilon + i)$.

(5) Lower limb dec $= (\epsilon + i - \Delta)$.

(6) Moon behind Bellanoch Hill (a).

(7) Moon first touches horizon with dec $= -(\epsilon + i + \Delta)$.

The arrow directions show exact configurations when Thom assumes $\epsilon = 23°54'.3$; $i = 5°8'.7$; $s =$ semi-diameter of Moon $= 15'.5$; $\Delta = 9'.0$.

group of stones is at Q of which three stones are upright. Temple Wood itself is located approximately 295m (980 feet) from S_1 at an azimuth of 315°.

The ground round about is level and in a valley surrounded by hills of varying heights. The position is ideally situated for using a very long sight line whose foresight is indicated as a natural notch in the hill. This indeed is the crux of Thom's reasoning, for he argued the case that Megalithic man was able to obtain azimuths of the Sun and Moon to a very high accuracy by using a distant skyline notch as an azimuth marker. For example, at Temple Wood natural foresights are found at distances of 2km (1·25 miles) and 6·3km (3·93 miles). Observing from the standing stones S_4—S_5 (Fig. 79) one sees a well-defined notch in the distant hills about 2km (1·25 mile) away. This notch Thom proposed represented the principal foresight azimuth for the Moon at its most northerly position during the period of major standstill (declination $\epsilon + i$). At this instance the tangent of the *upper* limb of the Moon in c. -1770 coincided with the southern hill slope forming the notch (Fig. 79b). If one used the centre point setting of the Moon, this gives declinations at position $2 + (\epsilon + i)$, and additionally a *lower* limb setting when the declination at position 3 is $= + (\epsilon + i + \Delta)$ where $\Delta =$ the 9′ perturbation factor, and a lower limb setting for declination at position $4 = + (\epsilon + i)$. A sight line looking along the stone rows towards Bellanoch Hill (Fig. 79a) provides a lower limb azimuth in notch B = declination $(\epsilon + i)$ and upper limb in A_2 when declination $= -(\epsilon + i)$. For all these phenomena Thom assumed values of $\epsilon = 23°54'\!.3$; $i = 5°8'\!.7$; $s = 15'\!.5$; $\Delta = 9'\!.0$.

But in addition to the simple observational data and the assumed values of obliquity (ϵ), lunar orbit inclination (i), semi-diameter of the Moon (s), and the perturbation factor (Δ), it is also necessary to apply several important corrections as follows:

(1) terrestrial refraction;
(2) astronomical refraction;
(3) horizon dip;
(4) parallax;
(5) temperature (which influences refraction values in a variable manner).

Some of these are straightforward quantities which can be gleaned direct from existing tables. In others assumptions need to be made as in (5) where no data is available for nocturnal temperatures in Megalithic times. The parallax correction (4) has a fluctuation through an angle of $\pm 4'$ in a period of about a month. It seems likely that parallax correction in conjunction with refraction would have produced inexplicable anomalies to Megalithic observers. Thom, however, believed that this did not prevent them from determining meaningful results.

Thom's method involves the necessity of *first* making an approximation about the likely epoch in which observations were made. The obliquity of the ecliptic is now assumed to be changing at the rate of $2'$ per 300 years. His method, after making corrections, is to work backward in time. From the foresight position of the Moon's upper or lower limb (or less accurately from the orb centre) and knowing the altitude of the horizon notch one can compute declinations actually observed and then compare them with expected declinations.

The example of Temple Wood serves well to illustrate Thom's method (refer also to Fig. 79).

Obliquity of ecliptic $\quad\quad\quad\quad (\epsilon) = 23°54'3 \ (c. -1770)$

Moon's orbital inclination $\quad (i) = 5°8'7$

Semi-diameter of Moon
(to correct obs. for upper
or lower limbs) $\quad\quad\quad\quad\quad (s) = 15'5$

Perturbation factor $\quad\quad\quad\quad (\Delta) = \ 9'$

Thom claimed that the Megalith builders' intention at Temple Wood was to provide for two observers: one for observing the Moon's *upper* limb, and the other for the *lower* limb. This would then perhaps explain the presence of stones in Group Q (Fig. 79) which gives the position of the Moon's centre in the notch; two observers could average the observations and eradicate errors due to small changes in the Moon's semi-diameter. The position of the larger upright stone S, with cup marks, Thom maintained is significant since it denotes the extreme northern swing position $(\epsilon + i + \Delta)$ for the *lower* limb.

From the methods and working of the above example it can be seen that Thom's ideas had far-reaching implications for the intellectual capacity of Megalithic man much on a par with those cited by Hoyle for the design and operation of his eclipse-pre-

dictor at Stonehenge. If we are to accept uncritically all that
Thom shows to be hidden in the site at Temple Wood and the
other comparable sites included in his survey, it indicates quite
clearly that prehistoric men had a knowledge of the Moon which
was only rediscovered by Europeans in modern times.

Thom's claims for the Megalithic site at Kintraw, in
particular, has been subject to wide publicity. This is an
example of the so-called solstitial sites where he believed that
the Megalithic indicators for rising and setting points of the
Sun, at the time of summer and winter solstices, are so
unambiguously represented it is possible to deduce, with great
precision, the Sun's solstitial declinations for the precise epoch
of its construction. With this piece of work he realized the long
awaited accuracy which Lockyer, a pioneer in this method, had
always strived for at Stonehenge.

Thom suggested that the Kintraw site in Argyll provides the
midwinter sunset $c. -1700$ in a foresight notch formed by two
hill peaks (the Paps) on the island of Jura some 45km (28 miles)
to the south-west. Kintraw is a remarkable site for several
reasons. It provides some of the longest sight lines yet claimed
for Megalithic observatories, but it is the configurations of the
various elements involved in the stone complex which have
attracted most comment and speculation. The site itself (Fig. 80)
is situated on a small plateau on a steep hillside. From ground
level the mountain target area is obscured by a nearby ($c. 1.6$km)
foreground ridge. To enable the observer to see the col notch,
Thom reasoned that it had been necessary to establish an
observation platform on a steep hillside to the north of the
plateau across a deep gorge. This in turn would lead to a cairn
being erected on the observation site in line and at a height so
that the notch could be seen. A 'platform' was actually located
on the steep hillside where two boulders provided a notch
suitable for viewing the col.

This supposed observation platform has been subject to fairly
rigid archaeological scrutiny to determine whether it was indeed
a partly man-fashioned feature of the landscape or whether it
had been formed fortuitously by the accumulation of scree
debris and other natural factors. So far (1975) no signs of human
occupation have been found, but the absence of material such as
charcoal and other material suitable to allow radio-carbon dating
calibrations has not deterred Thom and his co-workers from

claiming that the platform is indeed strong indicative evidence
for its use as an observation point in Megalithic times.

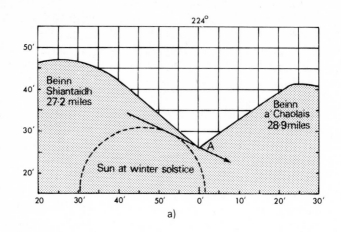

a)

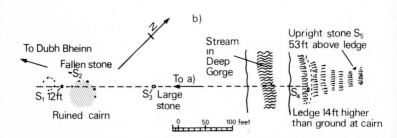

b)

80 Alignments from Kintraw, Argyll, Scotland. (a) Mid-winter sunset from
Kintraw. (b) Plan view of Megalithic remains. (c) Moonset at dec = − (ε − i)
seen from the ruined cairn (see b).

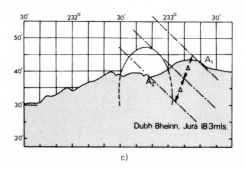

c)

Another of Thom's solstitial sites is at Ballochroy 64km (40 miles) to the south of Kintraw. This provides two positions for sunset: one for *midwinter* sunset (upper limb) over Cara Island as seen from a line projected through standing stones S_1—S_2—S_3 (Fig. 81a); and the second for *midsummer* setting (upper limb) as seen from S_1 over Corra Bheinn (Fig. 81b).

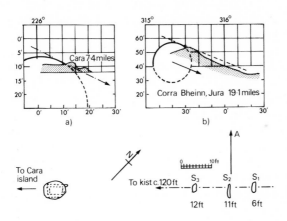

81 The solstitial site at Ballochroy, Scotland. (a) The Sun at midwinter setting over Cara Island as seen from the stones. (b) The Sun setting at midsummer as seen from S_1; from the Kist the azimuths are 5' greater. 'A' indicates (accurately) the direction to Corra Bheinn determined by the flat face of centre stone S_2 (arrangement after A. Thom's ideas).

From his investigations of these so-called solstitial sites in Scotland, Thom has arrived at the result of $\epsilon = 23° 54'.2$ ($\pm0'.7$) which corresponds to the epoch -1750 (±100 years). Since there were insufficient sites to permit a statistical standard error to be calculated, Thom's method was to accept a mean 'guess'. He felt it unlikely that any substantial improvement could be achieved to the method until further sites were found and measured to an accuracy of $\pm20''$.

One of the most remarkable aspects of Thom's Megalithic studies at Scottish sites was his interpretation of the curious fan-shaped stone arrays in Caithness. In several of these arrays the slabs are positioned with their long axes laid parallel to the direction of the row (Fig. 82). These stone rows had been surveyed in 1871, but their curious layout, with the individual stones seldom more than 45cm (18 inches) high, had long provided an even bigger puzzle as to their true purpose than had Megalithic circles. However, according to Thom these rows perhaps represent primitive stone computers used by the astronomer-priests to solve complex problems involving extrapolation which arises as a consequence that the Moon's maximum declination may be reached when it is not at its rising or setting point. Owing to the 27·21-day factor, lunar declination undergoes a relatively fast monthly change (passing through declinations ±23° 51′ 09″). The result is that the Moon may reach a maximum declination and then start to decrease again between two observations which normally would be separated by at least an interval of a full day. Without recourse to some extrapolation method this could lead to an error up to 10′ of arc in an azimuthal fix when the astronomer-priests were attempting to fix an extreme lunar position by two (before-and-after) observations. Thom's interpretation of these fan-arrays perhaps represents the greatest degree of sophistication yet claimed for Megalithic man, and for good reason they have been referred to as 'Megalithic graph paper'.

82 The sector-arrays at Mid-Clyth, Caithness, which Alexander Thom cites as a possible example of a primitive stone computer erected to solve extrapolation problems involving observed Moon-swings (layout geometry after A. Thom).

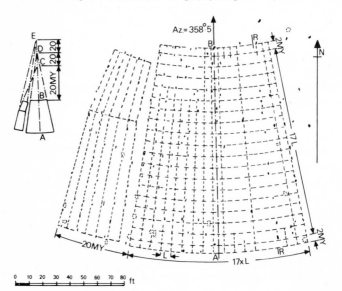

Thom had noted that the British *lunar* sites—rather than solar sites—contained the largest upright stones (menhirs). It was after his investigations of Scottish sites that he turned his attention to the great Megalithic monuments in Brittany, especially to those in the Carnac region. Carnac has been nicknamed: 'the Mecca of the Megalithic World'.

These French monuments, like their British counterparts, have attracted the attentions of antiquarians and would-be decoders for centuries, and the literature is full of fanciful and less fanciful speculations as to what purpose the great single menhirs, laid out in long *alignements*, played in the lives of ancient men.

The most impressive of the single upright stones in Europe is Le Grand Menhir Brisé, Er Grah, or Men-er-Hroeg (Fairy Stone), near the town of Locmariaquer (Fig. 85). It is now recumbent and broken into five pieces, one of which is missing from the site. The stone had certainly fallen before 1727 when M. de Robien, President of the Parlement de Bretagne, made a drawing of it in the position it now occupies. Its weight, calculated in accordance to its volume and density, equals something in excess of 350 metric tons, and when erect it must have stood over 20m (66 feet) high. Some, however, consider the stone may have broken during the course of its erection owing to the top end being overheavy and so may never have functioned in whatever manner intended by its erectors.

In Brittany there are several large menhirs still standing which range in height from 9 to 12m (30 to 40 feet), and menhirs ranging 7 to 8m (23 to 26 feet) are not uncommon. In Brittany twenty-five menhirs over 7m (23 feet) have been counted, but published heights are often unreliable.

A characteristic of the Brittany monuments is the absence of stone circles like those found in Britain. The nearest example to British circles are those on a small islet at the site of Er-Lannic. Here two incomplete circles (cromlechs) of standing stones now form a horseshoe encroached by the sea. Nevertheless, both differ appreciably from British examples. More characteristic of the French Megalithic sites are the gallery graves that reach a maximum concentration in the Carnac area between the gulf of Morbihan and the Etel River. More characteristic still are the vast arrays of stones composed of parallel or slightly converging lines of menhirs—the most important and extensive of which also occur in the Carnac area.

At Carnac—'the cemetery of the bones'—the menhir alignments take an easterly direction for more than 5km (3 miles). They consist of several thousand upright stones and represent the greatest concentration of Megalithic remains in Europe. In the west they begin at the village of Ménec—'the place of the stones'—then extend eastwards through Kermario—'the place of the dead'—to Kerlescan—'the place of the burning' and Petit-Ménec (Ménec-Vihan) and at one time extended as far as the river Crache (*see* Fig. 88).

The alignments fall into three distinct groups:

(1) *The Field of Ménec* starts 960m to the north of the village of Carnac and extends in a direction east by north-east (*c.* 70°) for 1,167m at an average width of 100m. There are eleven lines containing 1,099 menhirs, the tallest of these is 4m and the smallest 60cm. To the north and south of the main rows are several now recumbent menhirs which follow the same direction.

(2) *The Field of Kermario* begins after a gap of 340m. It extends 1,120m with an average width of 101m in which 982 menhirs are placed in ten lines following a north-easterly direction (*c.* 57°). The largest menhir, now fallen, measures in height 6m 42cm, and the smallest is about 50cm.

(3) *The Field of Kerlescan* follows the Kermario field after a break of 393m. Its length is 880m by 139m wide and consists of thirteen lines of stones containing a total of 540 menhirs extending approximately eastwards (95°). The largest menhir measures in height 4m, and the smallest is about 80cm.

Each of the above three fields are quite distinct, and each has a separate orientation. In addition to the vast rows of menhirs there are several large associated 'cromlechs', passage graves, tumuli, and isolated menhirs. The now isolated menhirs probably formed part of a group, the rest of which have now disappeared, and any intended single menhirs might have been less frequent than the present-day scene suggests.

83 The Avenues at Le Ménec: oblique aerial view (*see also* Fig. 89).

Methodical excavation of the monuments in the Carnac region dates back to M. de Robien in the period 1727 to 1737. Many graves appear to have been robbed in prehistoric times, and by Gallo-Roman times several of the *allées couvertes* (covered gallery graves) were occupied and in regular use as domestic quarters, judging from the debris found inside them. This undoubtedly influenced Victorian chroniclers such as Fergusson to be persuaded that the monuments were created at this later period. But the standing stones have been used as landmarks at all periods and are frequently associated with secondary bronze and gold hoards.

Nothing quite like the Carnac alignments occur in Britain. Most of the menhirs forming the rows have been at some time disturbed, particularly those resting on outcrops and without holes. Many are subject to misdirected restoration in the nineteenth century, and it has been frequently noted that not in a single case can one be sure that the present position an upright occupies is exactly the position intended it by its original erectors. Many of the uprights known to have been re-erected or repositioned in recent times are denoted by a little square hole near their base which is filled with reddish cement.

Theories about the purpose of the menhirs have given rise to the same kind of speculative literature as that surrounding Stonehenge and other British monuments. The interpretation of the Carnac menhirs, particularly the single isolated menhirs, has been referred to as 'the archaeologists' nightmare'. In the burial mounds one finds human remains, weapons, pottery, domestic implements, necklaces, bracelets and clasps. Similar remains and artefacts are found in among the rows of menhirs, but near the larger, isolated menhirs no human remains are found—even when the subsoil conditions are suitable for their preservation.

Theories for the isolated Carnac menhirs range from grave memorials or grave indicators, idols for pagan worship, landmarks that serve like the so-called British ley markers (*see* below) to symbols of a prehistoric phallic cult. The latter theory is supported to some degree if related to more contemporary Megalithic remains elsewhere where phallic cults are known to have been practised or still are. The celebrated nineteenth-century folklorist Baring-Gould (*see* note 15) recounted that the Brittany menhirs were closely associated with fertility rites until comparatively recent times and cites the example that childless peasant couples were often persuaded to dance round the local stone when a child was required. According to Baring-Gould, the couple were escorted to the stone by relatives. While the couple stripped naked, the relatives stood guard at a discreet distance to ward off strangers. Completely naked, the couple hand-in-hand circled the stone several times—the exact number of times depending on the local formula—before rejoining their

84 *Alignements* at Carnac, Brittany.

85 Le Grand Menhir Brisé (Mane-er-H'Roech), Brittany, now lying in four pieces.

86b A local antiquarian records a French dolmen c. 1

86 The Marquis de Robien, President of the 'Parlement de Bretagne' and eighteenth-century pioneer archaeologist at Carnac.

86c Stone rows depicted at Carnac c. 1805.

relatives. A similar fertility legend is associated with the British Iron Age hill-figure, the Man of Cerne.

A popular local legend associated with the Carnac stone alignments relates: 'St Cornély was a Pope at Rome from where he was hunted by Pagan soldiers who pursued him. He fled before them, accompanied by a yoke of oxen, which bore his baggage and on which he mounted when weary. One evening he arrived on the outskirts of a village called Le Moustoir where he wished to stop; having, however, heard a young girl insulting her mother he continued his way and arrived shortly at the foot of a mountain where there was another small village. He then saw the sea in front of him and immediately behind him soldiers in battle array and stopped to transform the whole army into stones. As a souvenir of this great miracle the inhabitants of the surrounding country erected on the spot where he stopped a church dedicated to St Cornély. That is the reason why these long lines of stones standing to the north of the village of Carnac are seen, and why so often at night ghosts are observed walking in the alleys called ''Soudardet san Cornély'' or ''Soldats de St Cornély''. Pilgrims from all countries flocked to the place to implore St Cornély to cure their diseased cattle. He cured them all in remembrance of the great service rendered to him by his yoke of oxen during his flight. The pilgrims, coming to the ''Pardon of St Cornély'' passed among the stone soldiers. The men were supposed to bring stones, the women earth, and to drop them on an elevation near to Carnac, where in the due course of time they formed the mount of St Michel.'

This folktale was supposedly the legend told by the first Irish monks who came to preach the gospel in this part of Brittany.

In Brittany folklore the 'Little People', more familiar to Irish landscape, are often cited, for tradition relates that the 'dolmens' were the dwellings of the Kerions—a dwarf people who supposedly inhabited the country in former times. Even today in some parts of Brittany one may still hear the expression 'As strong as a Kerion'.

Lockyer in his Stonehenge book also made reference to the Megalithic monuments of Brittany and in particular referred to the work of the Frenchman M. Gaillard, one of the pioneer orientation-theory enthusiasts. Gaillard had published the results of his investigations into the astronomical nature of

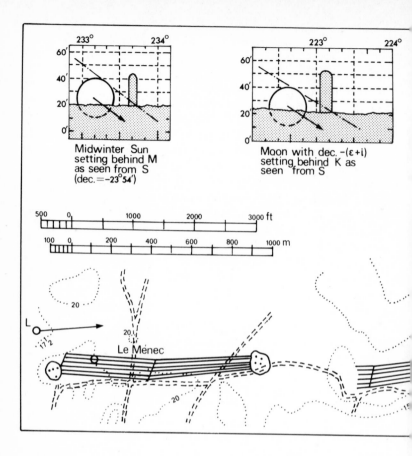

88 Alignments and menhirs near Carnac, Brittany, as interpreted by A. and A. S. Thom *c.* 1971.

Key:

A   Menhir on tumulus—to Er Grah dec = $-(\epsilon - i - s)$.

B   Menhir beside tumulus—to Er Grah dec = $-(\epsilon - i - s - \Delta)$.

C   Stone 2 feet high—to Er Grah dec = $-(\epsilon - i + s - \Delta)$.

D   Fallen stone—to Er Grah dec = $-(\epsilon - i - s)$.

K   Menhir 12 feet high.

L   Menhir 12 feet high—to M, lunar dec = $+18°.00'$

M   Menhir 20 feet high (Le Manio).

S   Menhir 9 feet high.

Contours and heights in metres; ground above 25m is shaded.

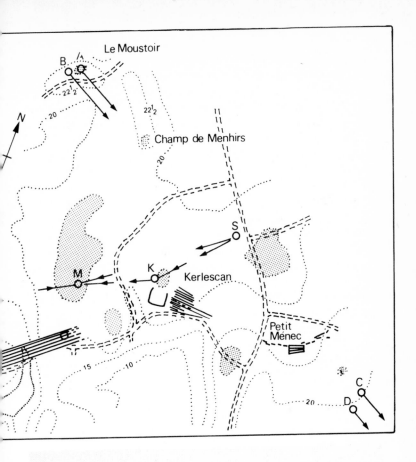

French monuments in his *L'astronomie préhistorique* (1897). He had not been the first Frenchman to be convinced of the astronomical nature of the stone arrays and avenues, but like Lockyer he became known to a wide public through his popular writings.

Gaillard had tried to show that the avenues had a solstitial orientation. However, his work was by no means as precise, or convincing, as that claimed by Lockyer for himself, since Gaillard had only utilized a magnetic compass to determine his bearings and had chosen some rather aribitrary reference markers. Gaillard's method was to use what he called an 'index' menhir. Lockyer commenting on one of Gaillard's solstitial interpretations at Le Ménec (Fig. 89) remarked that there did not appear to be a very good reason for selecting the indicated B menhir—except that it fell into the correct line of the solstitial azimuth from an origin taken on the cromlech.

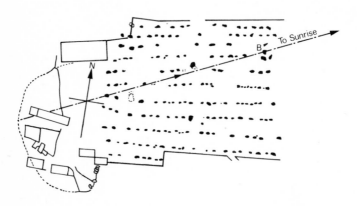

89 A solstitial rising azimuth in the stone rows at Le Menec, Brittany, according to Felix Gaillard *c.* 1890.

Lockyer was more impressed with Devoir's work. Devoir was a lieutenant in the French Navy and had a solid grounding in geometry and surveying which he put to good use in his investigations of the Megalithic monuments in the Finistere region, immediately north-west of Carnac. He devoted several years to the subject, conducting his surveys with a plane-table. His surveys included many parallel arrays of stones, and he soon found they were frequently orientated towards the north-east, lying in a sector defined by N 50°E and N 55°E. Others were even more exact to the local solstitial line, S 54°W → N 54°E, just right for the latitude 48° 30'N.

Following Devoir, several others attempted to formulate more advanced ideas. Baschmakoff in 1930 attributed the Brittany Megaliths to a pre-Aryan culture which possessed a calendar dividing the year into eight astronomically determined parts that indicated the occasions for festivals or feasts. Baschmakoff, as an ethnologist, looked at the monuments with a different eye to that of archaeologists or astronomers; in a flight of speculative fancy he believed that the rows of menhirs and their associated carvings represented clans and their totemic emblems. These grand designs were supposedly laid out by an elite priestly class, echoing Lockyer's and latterly Hoyle's similar speculations, but the construction work needed to be done was carried out by a *fellahin* division of their society. The bull, ram and serpent emblems cited by Baschmakoff have been eagerly pounced upon by those who see in them indications of an early Asian-type Zodiac in vogue in Europe in prehistoric times.

Thom arrived at Carnac already in possession of a fully developed astronomical model to explain Megalithic sites. Following his knowledge acquired on British sites that the tallest stones (menhirs) are usually lunar backsights, he decided to first concentrate on the larger more isolated of the Carnac menhirs. Thom, however, now reasoned that the largest stones need not be restricted to backsights: why not also foresights? It was natural that his attention should be directed towards the recumbent and broken Er Grah. This indeed proved to be a fruitful starting point.

It was necessary for Thom to assume a position in which Er Grah had stood in the position intended by its builders. This of course ignored the possibility that the stone may never have been successfully erected (*see* above). Thom chose the spot to be at the centre of the extreme north-west end of the position where it lies at present.

The outcome of Thom's survey was that he became convinced that the geometrical designs of Le Ménec, Kermario and the Kerlescan stone rows, and the associated outlying menhirs, constituted a huge lunar observatory actually centred on Er Grah itself (*see* Fig. 90). Applying the same values for the rising and setting points of the Moon at the major and minor standstills to Er Grah as a lunar foresight, he derived a table of backsight positions for several stones (some at considerable distance away).

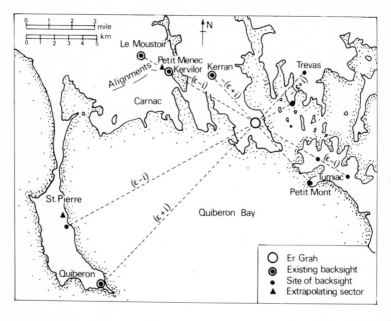

90 Er Grah as a lunar foresight marker (after A. Thom).

Thom believed that to fix the position for Er Grah must have involved careful observations of the Moon over several hundreds of years. These observations would have revealed inexplicable anomalies to the Megalithic observers owing to variations in parallax and refraction. The time span necessary in setting the outlying menhirs must have involved continual vigilance during each period of major and minor standstill. Thom imaginatively conceived parties of observers out at all possible places in attempts to see the Moon rise or set behind high trial marker poles. He assumed that at night the poles would need to be equipped with torches at their tops (shades of Lockyer's earlier ideas), since any other marks would not be seen until actually silhouetted against the Moon's disc. This necessitated working with an earlier proto-observatory so that the astronomer-erectors could be kept informed about the kind of maximum which was being observed and the state of the 9′ perturbation factor. Following this there would be nine years of waiting until the next standstill occurred when the next four lunar stations were being sought. . . .

It is impossible, of course, to summarize all Thom's work without omitting sections which are relevant to the final arguments. Any serious and critical reader or student of Megalithic astronomy needs to consult all his papers so that each idea in turn can be digested, weighed, and then assessed. However, the nub of Thom's Megalithic surveys of the Carnac sites resulted in his finding close parallels with the Megalithic sites in Britain.

He confirmed his Megalithic yard and found what he considered a remarkable uniformity of a measuring unit which he believed must have been a rod equal to 6·802 ±0·002 feet (2½ MY). The sixteen-month Megalithic calendar held true, while rows of stones at Petit Ménec and St Pierre were found likely to have been used as extrapolating sectors in the manner he had first suggested for similar rows of stones at Caithness. Later surveys indicated that the cromlechs at Le Ménec associated with the stone rows conformed to his Type I and II egg-shaped rings of the kind previously studied in Scotland.

It was not until 1974 that Thom published his first Stonehenge contribution which he based on a completely new topographical survey. This survey confirmed that the centre of the monument defined by the bank-and-ditch feature and the Aubrey holes differed from that of the sarsen circle by 50cm. Differences in centre points had been noted previously by others (*see* above).

Using his standard 2½ MY rod (6·803 feet: 2·04m) he measured the Aubrey circle to give a circumference of 131 rods. The sarsen circle he claimed had been laid out with the selfsame MY rod measure; its external circumference gave 48 rods and its internal 45 rods.

Thom reconstructed the sarsen trilithons on two concentric ellipses 30 × 20 and 27 × 7 MY. The inner ellipse showed an integral of Megalithic rods—accurate to 2·5—6·25cm. The layout of the trilithons was also dictated by Megalithic measures; they were 1 rod wide, spaced internally ¼ rod apart and with 4 MY between trilithons. Somewhat glibly, Thom claimed the 'mixture' of measurements he found indicated 'aesthetic' considerations by the builders.

The layout of the Y and Z holes also attracted Thom's attention. He claimed that they were not true circles but rather two spirals composed of two semicircles of different radii spaced half a Megalithic rod apart. He believed they were analogous in design to the well-known 'cup and ring' marks found as petroglyphs on many menhirs.

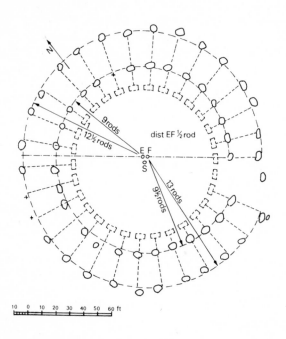

91 Alexander Thom's interpretation of the Y and Z hole geometry at Stonehenge. S represents the centre of the large sarsen circle. E and F are the centres for the semicircles set out to radii 9 and 12½ rods (western half) and 9½ and 13 rods.

In his study of the bluestone rings, he accepted Atkinson's ideas that sixty stones once formed the larger circle, but considered that from his geometric analysis both were less precisely laid out than the sarsen rings. Nevertheless, he suggested that the inner ring was laid out over a conjoint circle and ellipse, with the foci of the ellipse on the perimeter of the circle (Fig. 92).

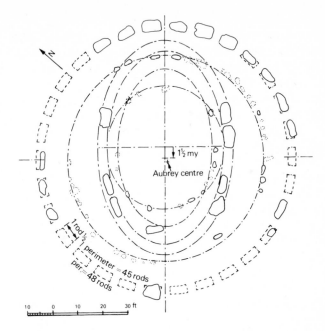

92 A. Thom's reconstruction of sarsen-ring geometry and other interior features at Stonehenge.

Of more significance to the general alignment debate was Thom's discussion of the small mound ('Peter's Mound') 2·7km (1·7 miles) to the north-east first noted by C. A. Newham during his surveys round Stonehenge for signs of possible horizon markers. The mound was included in Thom's new survey, and its azimuth was determined as 49° 47:3 from the Aubrey ring centre and 49° 45:5 from the Heel Stone. For the solstitial line this then gives dates respectively of – 2700 (± 400) and – 3300 (± 400). He noted these dates fell into chronological line with the newer radiocarbon dates for the Aubrey holes.

Coming to the question of lunar alignments, he referred to Newham's pioneer work and agreed that it looked as if Stonehenge may have been the centre of a huge lunar observatory. Thom, however, believed that Stonehenge, instead of providing a lunar foresight, as he had outlined for Le Grand Menhir Brise at Carnac, indicated a universal backsight from which distant markers on the horizon might be observed.

Discussing the question of the postholes near the Heel Stone, he considered they indicated an extrapolation sector similar to those he had found in Caithness and Brittany for observing the Moon in its extreme positions.

Thom noted that other lunar markers may be found round Stonehenge. A stone is shown on the Ordnance Survey map at the north-east corner of Fargo Plantation which could indicate the setting point of the Moon at its maximum declination, but this is a modern boundary stone. However, on the same azimuth, at a distance of 14·7km (9·16 miles) is also Gibbet Knoll near Market Lavington which might have been just visible from Stonehenge—silhouetted against the Moon's disc.

As a general conclusion Thom agreed with earlier ideas (anticipated by Newham) that Stonehenge seemed to indicate several lunar alignments, and it was possibly the centre of a larger area for lunar observations like that he had found at Carnac. Because radiocarbon dates were now pointing to construction work at Stonehenge as beginning in the third millennium—and not in the second millennium as had previously been indicated—some reappraisal of the chronology was required. However, this might be explained by assuming that the study of lunar movements began very early at Stonehenge and had extended over a period of several hundred years. And it was just possible it was as a result of this early, perhaps pioneer, work that observatories were then subsequently set up elsewhere in different parts of Britain.

CHAPTER X

Leys and Ley Hunters

A by-product of Lockyer's study of British Megalithic alignments were the phenomena of the so-called leys and the ley hunters. The name associated with the leys is that of Alfred Watkins (1855—1935), but it was chiefly Lockyer who provided the stimulus and background from which the ley phenomena developed. Lockyer pointed out that two straight lines could be drawn through Stonehenge which, when extended, passed through features that were probably of great antiquity. One line passed through Sidbury, Stonehenge, Grovely Castle, and Castle Ditches (the azimuth Lockyer adopted for the Avenue at Stonehenge); the other passed through Stonehenge, Old Sarum Mound, Salisbury Cathedral, and Clearbury Ring. In addition, the lines were so arranged that Stonehenge, Grovely Castle, and Old Sarum Mound formed a 'perfect' equilateral triangle. It was after noting these curious relationships that Lockyer's interest in other British Megalithic monuments increased.

Watkins related in his book, *The Old Straight Track* (1925), that he knew about these so-called alignments before reading Lockyer's account, but there can be no doubts that Lockyer's widely read Stonehenge book was the unambiguous seminal influence. Lockyer's work triggered similar ideas in Boyle Somerville, later himself a vigorous ley hunter.

Watkins, a keen photographer of the countryside, was born in Herefordshire. It was in his native county that he first developed his ideas which were later extended through the length and breadth of Britain. On his country rambles, to find photographic subjects, Watkins recounted he began to notice that beacon hills, mounds, earthworks, moats, and old churches built upon pagan sites seemed to fall in straight lines. Further investigation convinced him that Britain was covered with a network of straight tracks running from beacon hill to beacon hill with the way clearly marked by a mound or clump of trees on high points, by notches cut in mountain ridges, and in the lowlands by standing stones or pools carefully placed to reflect the light of a beacon and lead the traveller straight on.

Watkins claimed that some of the tracks were proven Sun alignments, others were more mundane traders' tracks, while others still were shown to be paths tracing a particular star at a certain time of year. . . .

Watkins defined the word 'ley' to describe a sighted track—'rightly or wrongly' he told his readers. He admitted that philologists believed the word (or its alternative spellings: lay, lee, lea, or leigh) to mean a meadow or enclosed field of some kind. However, he suggested that its prehistoric (pre-Roman) meaning was certainly not that, but he had little evidence to support his contention. In English place names, ley, and its alternative spellings, is extremely common.

Watkins arrived at his 'ley' theories from experience as a practical countryman, field naturalist and respected country photographer—and (there can be little doubt) from inspiration triggered via the facile pen of Lockyer and others. However, it seemed he had always been deeply affected by the numinous ancient atmosphere of his native Herefordshire—and its half-remembered folklore. Much can be gleaned about the man from his fondness for books like W. H. Hudson's *Hampshire Days*. In the introduction to *The Old Straight Track* (the 'definitive' ley hunters' manual), Watkins quotes Hudson's strangely evocative and moving: 'We sometimes feel a kinship with, and are strongly drawn to the dead, the long long dead, the men who knew not life in towns, and felt no strangeness in Sun and wind and rain. In such a mood on that evening I went to one of these lonely barrows. . . .'

Watkins came from a long-established county family. What imbued him with a curiosity for ancient monuments and ancient ways were his travels in country districts as a brewer's representative. Whatever his failings may have been as a scientific-age field archaeologist, he comes across as an absolutely sincere man—so more is the pity that his life's work has many of the overtones of a mare's nest.

The cult of the leys via Watkins' theories had its genesis one hot summer's day in the early 1920s. On that afternoon, Watkins recalled, he was riding across the Bredwardine hills some 19km (12 miles) west of Hereford and stopped on a crest for a moment in order to take in the sweep of the panorama before him. It was then he noticed something which he believed no one in Britain had seen for thousands of years: it was as if the more recent surface of the great landscape had been stripped away, revealing an unambiguous web of lines linking the ancient sites of antiquity that stretched out before him. Each fell into place in the whole scheme of things; old stones, holy wells, moats, mounds, crossroads, and pagan sites obscured by Christian churches stood in exact alignments that ran on for as far as the eye could trace. In a single all-powerful visionary moment, Watkins, as a self-appointed cult leader, was witness to what one of his later disciples described as 'the magic world of prehistoric Britain', but which Watkins less histrionically described as 'a glimpse of a world almost forgotten when the Roman legions marched across it'. He related that 'like Jim Hawkins in *Treasure Island*, I held in my hand the key plan of a long-lost fact. . .'.

However, it seems likely too that Watkins was affected by the same muse as that which caught Wordsworth when he composed his great nature poem 'Prelude' (1805 version):

> *I had a reverie and saw the past. . .*
> *To have before me on that dreary Plain*
> *Lines, circles, mounts, a mystery of shapes*
> *Such as in many quarters yet survive,*
> *With intricate profusion figuring o'er*
> *The untilled ground, the work, as some divine*
> *Of infant science, initiative forms*
> *By which the Druids covertly expressed*
> *Their knowledge of the heavens, and imaged forth . . .*
> *I saw the bearded Teachers, with white wands*
> *Uplifted, pointing to the starry sky*
> *Alternatively, and Plain below . . .*

Watkins maintained that the so-called old straight tracks which crossed the landscape of prehistoric Britain over mountains, dales, and lowland woods had decided the site of almost every kind of human communal activity. Like astro-archaeological pursuits of today, the pursuit of the old straight tracks brought the investigators into contact with many of the specialist -ologies, for Watkins remarked that one must follow where the line leads '... and, like the ball of thread in the legend of Queen Eleanor and Fair Rosamund, it leads to all kinds of spots...'.

Watkins told his readers that following the old straight track would reveal new facts in other branches of knowledge outside their own ken, but he remarked that he himself resisted following them—especially religion. No doubt he had in mind Lockyer's own painful experience after meddling in others' preserves when he wrote this, but likewise Watkins also believed that human knowledge was not built into watertight compartments, '...it does not help real advance for an investigator to be warned off any reference to the several -ologies with which his subject makes contact'.

Watkins set down his first ideas in a booklet, *Early British Trackways*, which he subsequently admitted was written somewhat breathlessly. In fact it was in print five months after he had received that first visionary clue that sunny afternoon in Herefordshire. *The Old Straight Track*, which followed it, was the result of more mature reflections and was in print a little over three years later under the aegis of Metheun, a highly respected London publishing house. Watkins' book was much influenced by Frazer's *The Golden Bough*, Lockyer's *Stonehenge* and many of Boyle Somerville's scattered writings.

When the Old-Straight-Track cult spread, and a postal club was formed, Boyle Somerville became a member and remained so until 1939 when the club was disbanded on the outbreak of World War II.

Watkins' vision-inspired theories, however, cut no ice with most archaeologists who pointed out—and continue to point out to Watkins' modern disciples—that coincidental alignments are bound to occur in a landscape like Britain's which is scattered with remains left by several thousands of years of human habitation. Crawford, an Antiquaries Society colleague of Boyle Somerville, and editor of *Antiquity*, refused all advertisements for the book, believing, like most of his other influential colleagues, that Watkins' theories were pure nonsense and could rightly be committed to the lunatic fringe of archaeology.

Nevertheless, in spite of its archaeologist detractors, Watkins' *The Old Straight Track* was read by a wide public—particularly the second cheaper edition published in June 1933. After World War II, two new editions were printed, in 1946 and 1948. In the post-war edition it appeared in Metheun's list incongruously alongside giants such as F. E. Zeuner's monumental epic *Dating the Past*, Grahame Clark's *Archaeology and Society* and C. F. C. Hawkes' *The Prehistoric Foundations of Europe*. The book eventually went out of print and was then diplomatically dropped from Metheun's list. In 1972 it was reissued by the Garnstone Press, a publishing house specializing in popular books with strong hypermystical overtones. In this edition it was prefaced by John Michell, a self-confessed flying saucer enthusiast.

To the ingenuous or impressionistic younger reader innocently coming across Watkins' book for the first time on a public shelf, it can indeed be a highly influential experience. Unknown to the new reader is the battery of caustic and damning criticisms by academic reviewers whose contributions are hidden in tomes inaccessible. As a schoolboy, and fresh from Lockyer's message in *The Dawn of Astronomy* and *Stonehenge*, I found Watkins' *The Old Straight Track* lurking one day on a shelf in the public library. In one night's revelatory reading, its pages were devoured eagerly; its message assimilated. I dreamt that night of a long forgotten astronomer-priesthood dominating the ancient British landcape—albeit Watkins himself was never sure whether the purpose of the prehistoric designs was secular or religious. The following weekend, armed with my 1-inch Ordnance maps and a compass, I sallied forth among my native Yorkshire hills, mounting my own first ley-hunting expedition, putting the message of my new mentor into practice. . . .

Watkins' message, with its ever-enquiring schoolboy appeal, told the would-be ley hunter to keep his eyes open when cycling or motoring whenever 'on a bit of straight road' for signs of any marker, hill point, church, mound or earthwork—for such an observation almost certainly led to the discovery of a ley through the point and on the road.

In his appendices, 'Ley Hunting', Watkins provides much information and advice in the vein of Lockyer's 'Astronomical Hints For Archaeologists' contained in his Stonehenge book. Watkins stressed the importance of both indoor map and outdoor field exploration. He was right too when he said that many mounds, ancient stones and earthworks were missing from large-scale maps, such as the 6-inch to 1-mile. He also provides some useful hints concerning compasses, glass-headed pins, maps, drawing boards, T-squares, circular protractors, etc., in fact all the paraphernalia that a would-be ley hunter requires for his field studies.

After equipping oneself with 1-inch maps, Watkins tells his readers to look out for: ancient mounds 'which are called tumulus, tump, barrow, cairn, or other names'; ancient unworked stones [but *not* those marked as boundary stones]; moats; traditional or holy wells; beacon points; crossroads with place-names, and ancient wayside crosses; churches of ancient foundation and hermitages; ancient castles, and old 'castle' names.

When these objects were located, they were to be marked in as a ring on the map. When a mark point was found (or other indication such as a mound or stone), the ley hunter was to place the straight edge against it and then move it to see if *three* with ringed points could be found to align (or alternatively two ringed points and a piece of existing straight road or track). If this proved possible, a pencil line was now required to provisionally designate the potential ley.

In following up Watkins' instructions there are Sherlock Holmesian overtones. He tells his readers that faint traces of an ancient track or earthwork were most easily detected when the Sun is low and on one side, as in late evening. Winter, he maintained, was an ideal time for ley exploration owing to the absence of leaves on the trees, but he provided a cautionary warning when he remarked that a great multiplicity of leys in a small area would 'surprise' and perplex the ley hunter, but added that it was a fact that had to be accepted.

For the wayfarer who likes to keep his eyes open and his senses alert, Watkins-style ley hunting provides an innocent enough pastime for country excursions. But how scientific is it? Even without the help of Crawford and other dissenting archaeologists, I soon began to suspect it was not. Orientation ideas based on sight notches in distant hills, traders' tracks, beacon sites aligned to tracks, *some* Sun alignments, Christian churches erected on pagan mounds or sites rang true, and to some extent still do. But I could never quite swallow the more hyperspeculative ideas, specially those concerning his ancient men of the leys, the so-called Dodman surveyors, who supposedly marked out tracks and alignments in prehistoric times, and Watkins' references to the use of sighting staves and tenuous archaeological links with Babylonia, Josephus, Moses and Tutankhamen. All this conflicted with my rapidly developing, healthy scientific scepticism, and soon I suspected that most of his ancient alignments were nothing more than fortuitous ones.

What puzzled me was that no other contemporary author referred to Watkins' straight-track discoveries. Grahame Clark's *Prehistoric England* (1940)—a brilliant synthesis in its time—made no mention of Watkins' discoveries, although Clark's book itself included chapters on ancient trackways, hill forts and sacred sites. It was finally a better informed reference librarian who cleared up the mystery and confirmed the suspicion that Watkins was *persona non grata* to professional archaeologists.

For aircraft navigators perched aloft over wartime Britain, Watkins' leys, involving chalk hill-figures and crosses etched out in downland turf, provided splendid directional aids. They were appreciated by British and enemy alike until hurriedly camouflaged at Air Ministry orders!

It was in the 1960s, after reading some of Thom's ideas in an article about Megalithic alignments, that I recalled Watkins' similar ideas via Lockyer and Boyle Somerville. Could it be, I wondered, that Thom had also come under the influence—even subconsciously—of Watkins' straight track theories? Watkins had cited hill notches to mark sight lines and ancient trackways. But it was Boyle Somerville rather than Lockyer who developed the orientation ideas based on far distant hill summits. Boyle Somerville searched out numerous alignments that sometimes extended through an alignment marked by a cairn or earthwork which then projected fortuitously through an abrupt gap in the distant hills. He developed these ideas in several long articles on the subject, one of which—and now perhaps a classic of its kind—was printed in the very first issue of *Antiquity* (1927), preceding the review article by A. P. Trotter entitled 'Stonehenge as an Astronomical Instrument' (*see* above).

In 'Orientation' Boyle Somerville discussed the original usage of the word, and how modern usage had changed its meaning. He stressed that the orientation found in monuments of antiquity was no new discovery, but that its existence was still largely doubted. He maintained that the connection between Death and Orientation was well proven—citing the fact that the Christian custom of laying the dead in the ground with the feet towards the east still existed. Or, in other words, these interments were in fact 'orientated'.

Boyle Somerville went on to cite the interesting ideas to account for the believed orientation of long barrows. Nearly all of them are directed to some easterly point, but some markedly northward or southward of east and not following a precise west-east orientation. His opinion of this was that it was done because this was the direction from where the race originally reached Britain. By way of analogy he referred to the examples from Polynesia, where the dead were supposedly taken to the western part of an island facing the direction from which the great Polynesian migration had come. However, an equally plausible idea (not cited by Somerville) is that barrow orientation may indicate a precise calendar date for sunrise or sunset direction when the interment (or death) took place, or alternatively it may indicate a significant cultus date. Choice of direction (east or west) depends on whether emphasis is given to the rising *or* the setting point of the Sun. As Boyle Somerville himself remarked: 'if survival after death was believed in, the idea of resurrection almost logically follows. Orientation to a rising Sun, or star, clearly typifies this idea, while orientation to a setting body (which also occurs in prehistoric monuments) perhaps typifies the belief of some different, and gloomier-minded race, in a final descent to some underworld to the westward....' Recent ideas about the Newgrange Megalithic passage grave (*c.* – 3000), which is orientated to midwinter solstice, lend support to these general conclusions (Fig. 93) (*see* note 16).

Boyle Somerville was under no doubts about the Sun's importance as an 'orientation calendar', and this idea is certainly borne out by similar findings among neoprimtive societies in the modern millennium (*see* note 17). But some of his other examples and views about orientation were clearly not always endorsed by Fellows of the Society of Antiquaries. Like Lockyer before him, Boyle Somerville was too receptive, a little too credulous and uncritical to the whole concept of orientation.

His more sober beliefs were that in a circle, the stones to be employed for the purpose of fixing the alignments were usually

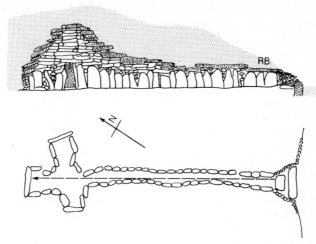

93 The passage-grave at Newgrange, County Meath, Ireland, which has been radiocarbon dated to − 3100 ± 100 years (corrected date). It seems likely that the grave was deliberately orientated by its builders so that precisely at winter solstice rising the Sun's rays (dashed line) shone along the passage through the roof box (RB).

indicated by being considerably larger than other stones of the circle. The chosen foresight, or the stone nearest the Sun in taking the observation, was engraved all over with 'cup' markings. In two cases he noted that additional standing stones were placed at a short distance outside the actual stone circle, to form a third stone on the alignment. This he claimed was intentional so that there could be no doubts as to the line to be followed for the orientation.

From a close study of Boyle Somerville's writings one can, indeed, see the genesis of some of Thom's ideas. It is of interest to note that Thom's later ideas, derivative of one of the old-straight-track club members, has been eagerly pounced upon by neo-straight-trackers such as John Michell. In his *The View Over Atlantis* (1969)—a stable companion to the reissued *The Old Straight Track*—Thom's, Lockyer's and Boyle Somerville's work is represented as providing strong confirmatory proof of many of Watkins' ideas, and included are more recent 'interpretations' of Watkins' basic ideas formulated by John Michell himself.

Michell in his book incorporates an account of pyramidology (endorsing its ideas), and by manipulating Thom's Megalithic yard he equates it with all manner of numerical and metrical puzzles of the ancient world (complete with mystical overtones). In a remarkable chapter entitled 'The Alchemical Wedding' he tells his readers that the Great Pyramid was in fact an instrument of alchemy which could be proved by a study of the pyramids' numbers and the principles which they represented (even up-staging the hyperspeculative fancies of pyramidologists such as Taylor and Smyth—*see* below). The outcome was that the Great Pyramid was constructed to fuse the two elements: celestial and terrestrial. It was in fact the instrument of inspiration. From the union was gestated the spirit of God in men and the establishment of the New Jerusalem on Earth.

Woodhenge, a Megaxylic monument, was supposedly laid out according to a plan derived from the magic square of Mercury. In an exceptional flight of fancy, Michell considered that the proximity of Woodhenge to Stonehenge was in line with sound cosmic reasoning, since Woodhenge was only less than 2 miles from Stonehenge, 'the former solar capital'.

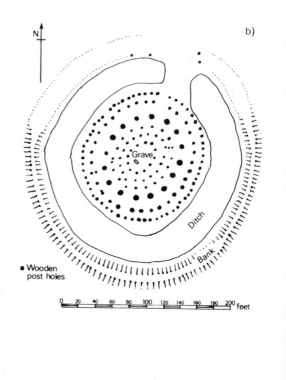

b)

94a Woodhenge, near Stonehenge: oblique aerial view, looking south-east. Concrete blocks now mark the excavated holes. Note other ghost circles of Neolithic age in the adjacent field. The Woodhenge Megaxylic henge site was discovered in 1925 by aerial photography and is probably contemporary with Stonehenge I. When the site was excavated, a shallow grave was found just off-centre (94b) containing a (sacrificial?) infant with a cleft skull. 94b The axis of the elongated circles is orientated towards the midsummer sunrise. Thom claims that the geometry of the site was arranged so that each of the six posthole rings had a perimeter which was a multiple of 20 MY. Thom also cites an alignment for Capella in −1790. Several archaeologists believe that Woodhenge was built as a roofed structure.

Michell's metrical schemings are breathtaking. Even if they were only partially correct, they would be comparable to the realization of the astrophysicist's dream: the finding of the 'Rosetta Stone' to equate the microscopic world of the atomic particle with the macroscopic world of the cosmos. Michell believed the whole of prehistoric science to be succinctly expressed in his so-called Great Pyramid equation $1080 + 666 = 1746$ (a numbers game to beat all numbers games!). In the same vein, Michell tells his readers that the Pyramid was constructed to represent the four principal linear units of antiquity: the foot, yard, cubit and Thom's Megalithic yard; he then proceeds to show, in good old-fashioned Q-E-D-style, how this can be deduced via the construction of two circles each with a diameter of 555 feet and a circumference of 1,746 feet. This excursion into classical metrology makes Taylor's and Smyth's Pyramidinchology sound like nineteenth-century dogma, yet an ever-credulous (nay gullible!) lay-readership laps it up and constantly demands more from its author and publisher.

Michell's Megalithic investigations naturally include Stonehenge, which he calls the 'New Jerusalem', and Glastonbury—also referred to as the 'New Jerusalem'. Utilizing Thom's Megalithic yard in the 'alchemical fusion', he endeavours to upstage Thom in his suggestions for a geometrical layout of Stonehenge by providing a graphical construction of a metrical scheme uniting the British monument with the Great Pyramid. For good measure he throws in the old idea that Salisbury Plain was a giant orrery. Silbury Hill is cited as being erected by a former race of giants. Litchfield Cathedral is related to the magic square of Mars—whatever that may be. Literally and metaphorically, no stone is left unturned in his grand tour. Even Hoyle's earlier speculations concerning possible drum beating at Stonehenge is dragged in to demonstrate that 'stone levitated by sound could become a flying chariot moving along the line of a certain magnetic intensity, whose course was marked out on the ground by alignments of stones and earthworks, linked by raised causeways and rides through the forest...'. Indeed under the aegis of Michell, Watkins' old-straight-track theories were fashionably updated to conform to claptrap space-age cults. In *The View Over Atlantis* and the other of Michell's books written to conform to this *genre*, one is constantly left wondering whether

Michell is in deadly earnest or whether he is simply indulging in a glorious send-up of the whole business. . . .

With the reprinting of Watkins' book and under Michell's stimulus, the neo-straight-trackers have become a very active body. The editor of *Antiquity* again refused a straight-track advertisement; this time not for Watkins' book but for a cult magazine, *The Ley Hunter*, which apart from leys covered topics as diverse as Bats, Wishing Stones, Old Mother Midnight and even included an article evocatively entitled 'Why Flying Saucers followed the Leys'. When a somewhat credulous journalist suddenly 'discovered' the leys for himself and was rash enough to write about it in a leading influential British Sunday newspaper, there followed a phenomenal postbag on the subject. In reply, one sceptical correspondent wrote about fifteen country pubs which followed a straight line; another reader came up with an 'educational' alignment for half a dozen schools. One of the best replies received was from a correspondent who discovered some forty alignments of telephone call-boxes in the Chiltern Hills (a ley-hunter's paradise). Another ingenious ley-hunting experience was sent in by an anonymous Oxford don, who, with tongue firmly in cheek, recounted how he had discovered that all the Roman Catholic churches in inner London formed a perfect logarithmic spiral.

Of course, there were also correspondents whose attitude to leys was not always transparently clear. Someone in Cornwall discovered a global ley which began on an alignment composed of a dozen or more West Cornish churches and prehistoric hill forts and then somehow fell in line with Rome, the Valley of the Kings (Egypt), and a major concentration of Aztec and Maya pyramids!

Even the starchy, but influential, *London Times* has developed a modern predilection for indulging ley hunters and like pseudologists and occasionally carries sympathetic reviews in its book pages—incongruously cheek-by-jowl with the well-informed *Nature-Times* science reports (e.g. *Mysterious Britain*, see *The Times*, 23 November 1972).

An ever-present problem facing the whole of Megalithic speculation is separating the facts from the fancies. There are several well-documented examples where Christian church sites are purposely involved in, or are non-accidentally related to, Megalithic or prehistoric pagan sites. It is also well established that in an earlier period the Church instructed that pagan sites should be obliterated by building over them. A reference in the Venerable Bede's *Ecclesiastical History* tells of a letter from Pope Gregory to Abbot Mellitus in which he sent a message to Augustus that pagan temples ought not to be destroyed but sanctified and converted to churches. Another direct historical reference can be gleaned from Patrick, Bishop of the Hebrides, who desired that a church be built wherever upright stones were found. In Brittany many old churches and crosses are placed near dolmens and menhirs, and the largest country fairs are also held in similar positions. The decrees of Nantes in +658 exhort bishops and their inferiors to dig up, remove and hide stones where they could not be found. There are several other historical passages relating to the same directions; in the Edict of Theodosius, pagan shrines were to be consecrated as Christian churches, and the Edict of Honorious strictly forbad the demolition of heathen temples.

One of the most interesting of British Megalithic/Christian sites is at Knowlton in Dorset where the church is erected inside a henge monument. In Cardiganshire (Wales), at the Church of Yspyytty Cynfyn, three menhirs form a circle and are incorporated in the circular wall of the churchyard. Only 32km (20 miles) away is the Church of Llanfairpwllgwyngyll where a megalith lies under the pulpit. In Yorkshire, at Rudston (origin: 'Rude stone' or as some believe, 'Red-stone'), a tall gritstone menhir still dominates the churchyard (Fig. 95); this stone is associated with an old East Yorkshire legend similar to the Friar's Heel Stone legend of Stonehenge. The area round this church is extremely rich in prehistoric remains including three cursus-like features which, when viewed from the church tower, appear to lead into the valley of Rudston as trackways. The Rudston menhir is very similar to the three gritstone menhirs—the Devil's Arrows—at Boroughbridge, some 65km (40 miles) distant to the west. As the name implies, this is yet another monument dedicated to Old Nick himself. According to one local story, they represent three of his cross-bolts—turned to stone—which he shot at a nearby Christian missionary settlement.

One who looked closely into the question of British

95 The Rudston monolith, East Yorkshire.

pagan/Christian sites was Lyle Borst, an American professor of civil engineering and astronomy. He is yet another who was apparently motivated by Lockyer's and Penrose's earlier stellar alignment theories in addition to Thom's ideas for standard Megalithic units. Borst related that his interests developed during a visit to Greece in the 1960s where he initially travelled to study ancient metallurgy. One afternoon he and his wife (as tourists) visited the Temple of Hera at Argos, built $c. - 500$ and dedicated to the Vestal Virgins. He noted that the axis of the later temple was different from that of the earlier one destroyed by fire. This shift Borst claimed could be attributed to the precessional shift of the star Spica; for he concluded that both temples had been dedicated to the rising of this particular star, and the changes in axis were caused by the precessional shift between the two construction dates.

Borst, after having analysed the architectural plans of cathedrals at Canterbury, Wells, Winchester, Gloucester and Norwich, and the churches of Knowlton in Dorset and of Wing (Buckinghamshire), maintained he had discovered what he described as 'megalithic designs of an explicit kind'. His ideas follow much in the vein of Watkins' straight-track neo-disciples. In his Megalithic study he visited each site in turn and then came to the conclusion that the later Christain structures showed the same essential character as Stonehenge, Woodhenge, Arminghall (a Megaxylic henge site in Norfolk) and five lesser stone rings described by Thom as egg-shaped rings of Type I. He believed that Lincoln Cathedral showed evidence of a different Megalithic pattern, typical of Type II rings. He contended that his novel study of cathedral architecture shed new light on the geometry of henge monuments, and conversely believed that it is the study of henge monuments and long barrows which might explain the reasons for so-called peculiar features in cathedrals.

Borst's approach to the pagan/Megalithic site problem is certainly a novel one; unfortunately his ideas and methods rely on some rather slender or apocryphal evidence, and generally his thesis is unacceptable to those archaeologists who have specialized knowledge of churches and Megalithic monuments. Basing his study on an *a priori* acceptance of Thom's Megalithic yard, he claimed to have found unequivocal traces of it in all the sites chosen for study. However, only infrequently did he note traces of the half yard or quarter, or other fractions cited by Thom and others. Instead he claimed to have found the larger unit of 6 MY (5·03m; 16·2 feet). Borst maintained that this 6 MY 'unit' was no accident, for it relates very nearly to the length of the English rod of 16·5 feet (5·06m) and that for most purposes the two units could be used interchangeably.

He tried to show that the processional path of a cathedral is usually 1 rod wide, but that the distance between side chapels is an integral number of Megalithic yards—although rarely multiples of six. Leaning on Thom's evidence about the Megalithic use of Pythagorean triangles, he believed it indicated a ritualistic value to the Megalithic cultus, and those present in cathedral places provided the strongest evidence that Christian cathedrals rest on henge monuments.

He composed a list of both 'Megalithic Sanctuaries' and 'Church Sanctuaries' with all the supposed relevant inbuilt geometric qualities. Among the Christian Sanctuaries, Wing Church is the only one with a simple 3:4:5 triangle construction. Wing, even without Borst's ideas, is potentially a very interesting site in its own right. It is one among only three surviving Anglo-Saxon churches which show architecture based on the Roman *basilica*, or law court, where the apse is semi-circular or polygonal. Beneath the apse at Wing is a crypt of

Saxon date (probably fifth century or earlier). Borst contended that an oval based on a 3:4:5 MY triangle fits the crypt outline as well as any smooth figure could be expected to fit the irregular polygonal structure. The geometrical design at Wing is simple, and therefore he presumed it to be earlier than that of the more involved Megalithic geometry of the great churches.

The nub of Borst's thesis was of course that church builders followed the sanctuary pattern laid out by the Megalith builders, and in addition that they were frequently stellar orientated. Wing, he believed, was orientated to Bellatrix (Gamma Orionis) sometime between the dates − 2300 to − 1500, and Canterbury Cathedral to Betelgeuse (Alpha Orionis) at about the same time. Wing indeed may have been a pagan/Megalithic site, since there is good evidence of occupation in the area going back to well before Neolithic times, but the evidence for stellar orientation is very doubtful. Borst claimed that Wing was contemporary with the Megalithic (Megaxylic) site at Arminghall in Norfolk. This is another site which, like Woodhenge, was discovered by aerial photography. Excavations there have disclosed eight postholes in the form of a horseshoe with a circular inner and outer ditch and intervening bank. Borst considered the setting-out pattern to be based on a major radius of 8 MY of a 6:8:10 MY triangle—this fits the geometrical pattern reasonably satisfactorily. He admitted, however, that the pattern was not perfectly symmetrical, and some latitude was possible in positioning the oval. He believed that the Nidaros Cathedral at Trondheim in Norway—which has a similar octagon—was related to the Arminghall geometry.

Borst extended his studies of the Megalithic yard to chambered long barrows and, of even more interest, to discovering the so-called geometry hidden in Stonehenge. At Stonehenge his geometrical reconstruction, c. 1969, uses Stations 92 and 93 to form an isosceles triangle with the Heel Stone providing for Pythagorean triangles of 120:50:130 MY. He showed how the sarsen circle, the bluestone ring, the great trilithons and inner bluestones can be related by egg-shaped constructions and MY geometry (Fig. 97). It is of interest to compare his Stonehenge geometry with that of Thom's later attempts, c. 1974 (Figs. 91 and 92). Among the most remarkable triangles were 12:72:73 which Borst claimed to have found in the three English cathedrals of Canterbury, Norwich

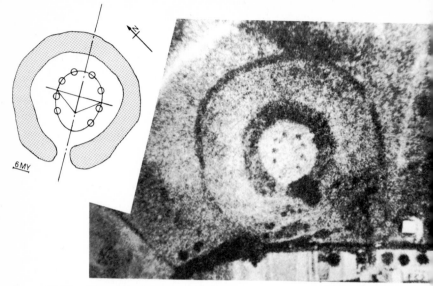

96 The Megaxylic site at Arminghall showing the location of eight (1m diameter) postholes discovered by aerial photography. The postholes have been radiocarbon dated to *c.* − 2490 (± 150 years). Reconstruction of Arminghall geometry is according to Lyle Borst, outer ditch omitted.

97 Stonehenge geometry according to the ideas of Lyle Borst.

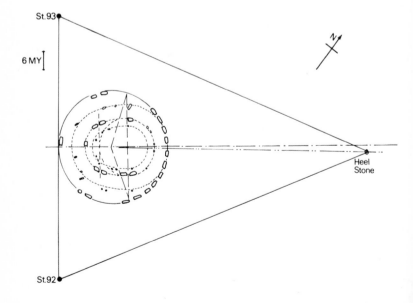

and Gloucester, and the Finnish cathedral at Turku.

According to his general ideas, Megalithic geometry could be expected to show progress from the simple to complex. The Trondheim Cathedral is representative of the oldest. The sites hidden below the church at Wing and the monument at Arminghall, and Turku Cathedral are supposedly of comparable age, *c.* − 2500; while the cathedrals using 12:72:73 (Canterbury, Norwich and Gloucester) were among the most recent. This finding led him to conclude that the Megalithic cultus was undoubtedly Scandinavian in its earliest form.

When D. Kendall, Professor of statistics at Cambridge, reviewed Thom's *Megalithic Lunar Observatories* in *Antiquity*, he described it as 'a remarkable book by a remarkable man' and considered it exceedingly difficult reading even for a mathematician. Kendall's review, however, was one of the most searching and definitive in the entire literature and put forward some highly original suggestions for checking out Thom's work. One suggestion was that it might be a good idea to reverse Thom's procedure which had been to go to a Megalithic site to note what orientations (declinations) appeared to be roughly marked and then set about measuring exact declinations of likely horizon notches. Kendall believed it would be useful to look out for environments with a suitably remote 'notchy' horizon and then attempt to find Megalithic sites that might fit them.

This, to some extent, had actually been done in the past by Watkins and his ley-hunting fraternity. In Central and Southern England truly 'notchy' horizons are comparatively rare phenomena, since there are few hills with rocky exposures. Most hills in these areas are well rounded and frequently covered with dense foliage.

Typical of the hills of Central Southern England are the chalk downlands of the Chilterns. The Chiltern Hills and the bordering plain of the Vale of Aylesbury to the west have long provided a happy hunting ground for Watkins-style ley hunters. This district also happens to be rich in astronomical associations of quite another kind—although I hasten to add no claim is made that the two phenomena are anything but remotely, and coincidentally, connected.

Since the whole area and surrounding hills were favoured by

early farming communities and had been occupied on and off from Upper Paleolithic times (and very likely from Lower Paleolithic too), it seemed a good area to check for likely skyline notches useful in establishing alignments. I was not so much looking for notches which would give precise values of the obliquity of the ecliptic—as Thom had done with the angular notches in craggy Scottish Highland sites—but for notches (or dips) which might prove useful to ancient farmers in following the shifts of the Sun to provide a workable solar calendar. In the Chiltern region the only likely areas for calendar sight lines are located in the Vale of Aylesbury lying to the west where the observer would then look eastwards across the Chiltern scarp. In theory the scarp features provide alignments for rising phenomena of the Sun, Moon, stars and planets.

Kendall's review had suggested sixty reversed sight lines (thirty declinations = sixty reversed sight lines) for each notch, but this is not realizable in the Chilterns, as the very nature of the topography allows only non-reversible (one-way) alignments.

There is solid evidence from many parts of the world that rudimentary solar calendars have been in wide usage at least since the onset of the Neolithic. One of the best documented ones is that of the Hopi Indians of the south-western United States. The passing seasons were measured by these Indians from the position of sunrise on the horizon. Important horizon positions were noted for festival days and events—especially those associated with seasonal tasks in respect to the agricultural year. For example, points on the horizon were known as 'work in fields begins' and 'corn may be planted', etc. The two points of the solstices were known as 'houses of the Sun', and altogether some thirteen horizon landmarks were significant when the Sun rose above them (Fig. 98).

Many similar examples can be found in both the Old and the New Worlds (*see* note 17); even the Eskimoes had analogous systems. In the Old World as late as the nineteenth century, this old pagan method was used to fix the solstices. On certain farms there was a definite stone buried in the earth from which the solar calendar observations were made. In mountainous districts the calendar was regulated to the Sun's rising or setting above certain mountain peaks, or when its last rays touched this or that summit. Some observed the length of the shadow on the face of

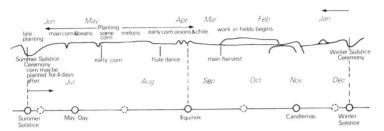

98 Horizon calendar of the Hopi Indians of the south-western United States.

a cliff, or noted when it touched the brow of a hill or a certain stone. In this way they were able to give the important days of the year.

The Incas in the New World erected artificial marks to perform the same task. At Cuzco there were supposedly sixteen stone towers, eight in the west and eight in the east, arranged in groups of four. The two middle ones were smaller than the others, and the distance between the towers was 8, 10 or 20 feet. The space between the little towers, through which the Sun passed at sunrise and sunset, was the point of the solstices. For observations of the equinoxes, richly ornamented stone pillars were set up in an open space before the temple of the Sun. When the time approached, the shadow of the pillars was carefully observed. Long experience taught them where to look for the equinoctial point, and by the distance of the shadows from this point they judged the approach of the equinoxes.

In the 'lost' city of Machu Picchu, discovered by Hiram Bingham in 1912, there was found the Inti-huatana ('the hitching post of the Sun'). This was a structure sculptured from the native rock which is believed to have served for the observation of the summer and winter solstices. Indications of such posts were found in all the major Inca sites, and their purpose was to regulate the farming calendar; but since the Conquistadors considered them central to the Incas' idolatrous Sun worship, they smashed them everywhere. But the one at Machu Picchu was fully preserved and persuasive proof indeed that the Spanish invaders never penetrated there.

In the *Odyssey*, Eumaeus remarked (in an account of his native land) about a certain island where the Sun turned, and this was the direction of the mark at which the Sun rose at the time of the solstice.

Greenland Eskimoes used a primitive horizon calendar which would provide them with important seasonal days in the year, but because of the high latitude, they also utilized stellar orientations—such as the heliacal rising of Altair.

In the Chilterns, several of Watkins' leys do actually give approximate reversed solstice sunrise and sunset alignments. A well-known ley between the churches of Aston Rowant and Marsworth indicates solstice sunrise and sunset. This alignment coincides with the approximate route of the Lower Icknield Way which, owing to the nature of the terrain hereabouts, follows the general line dictated by the strike of the Chiltern chalk scarp. The Lower Icknield Way is recognized as one of the oldest prehistoric tracks in Britain. It was in regular use in Neolithic times when it provided direct access from the Wash to the Berkshire Ridgeway and then to Avebury and south to Stonehenge. Apart from providing a fortuitous alignment for midsummer or midwinter travellers on the Lower Icknield Way, the Aston Rowant and Marsworth ley appears to have no other significance.

Looking eastwards from the flat-terrained Vale of Aylesbury towards the Chiltern scarp, there are several smoothed-out 'notches' and bumps which suggest good marks for the operation of a sun-calendar. The Vale is an area of rich agricultural land and littered with traces of its former Neolithic, Iron Age, Saxon and medieval agrarian populations. No known Megalithic (or Megaxylic) site falls within the area of the Chilterns. The nearest true Megalithic circle is at Great Rollright (Fig. 99) about 56km (35 miles) to the north-west (see note 18). This is too far away to be of significance to the Chilterns, but it does fall close to the ancient trackway known as the Jurassic Way (or Thoroughfare) which extends across England from the Bristol Avon to the south bank of the Humber in north Lincolnshire. This track is comparable in age with the Lower and Upper Icknield ways.

Among the many old church sites dotting the Vale and facing the Chiltern scarp is one at Stone (2 miles west of Aylesbury). At Stone are signs of yet another old track providing a cross-country interchange from the Jurassic Way to the Lower Icknield Way. Stone and district is one of the places significant in the earlier reference to the strictly coincidental astronomical associations. In the ancient churchyard is the resting place of Admiral W. H.

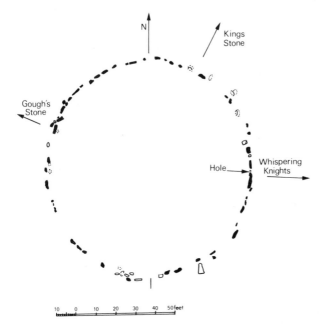

99 The concentric stone circle at Great Rollright, Oxfordshire (*see also* note 18).

100 An engraving of the Rollright Stones, Oxfordshire, *c.* 1777.

Smyth ('Mediterranean Smyth')—father of Piazzi Smyth—
and in the church itself is a splendid memorial to the Admiral.
Among the Smyths it is usually Piazzi who is remembered best
of all, but the Admiral was himself a famous astronomer,
geographer and antiquarian in his own right. His father was a
loyalist emigré who fled from New Jersey to England after the
American Revolution and was a direct descendant of the famous
Captain John Smith now remembered for his *History of Virginia*
(1624).

Admiral Smyth entered the navy as a boy and by
self-education and strength of character rose from the ranks—an
unusual accomplishment at that time. During the Napoleonic
Wars he was seconded to the Mediterranean, and it was this
which took him to Palermo in 1813 where he met and became
the good friend of Giuseppe Piazzi, discoverer of the first
asteroid (named Ceres at the insistence of Piazzi after the
Neolithic fertility goddess of Sicily). When a son was born to the
Admiral, it seemed natural he should name him after the great
Italian astronomer. Apart from his distinguished naval career,
Admiral Smyth has become one of the best remembered
amateur astronomers through his book *Cycle Of Celestial
Objects,* which still serves as a working handbook for stargazers.

Next door to the Admiral at Stone lived the wealthy Dr Lee,
who, like the Admiral, was to serve a term as President of the
Royal Astronomical Society. At Haddenham, some 3 ½ miles
distant, lived William Rutter Dawes—known as 'eagle-eye'
Dawes—who became one of the greatest observers in the
nineteenth century.

The church at Stone is very old, certainly pre-Conquest, but
its earliest history is lost in the mists of Saxon times. Significantly
perhaps, the church was erected on a mound whose nature has
been disputed, although many consider it to be artificial and
likely a pagan site in use long before the church was established
over it. Even more significant is the name of the village itself
which takes its name from 'the Stones', Old English *stānes*, for
at some unknown date the place was noted for its stones or
menhirs. But not surprisingly in an area scarce in good building
stone, the stones have long disappeared—some now perhaps
hidden in the church footings themselves. Two miles to the
south-east is the hamlet of Bishopstone—again no stones to be
seen nowadays and no known monument or pagan site. An

authority on Buckinghamshire place names attributes its present-day name as alluding directly to Odo, Bishop of Bayeux (Earl of Kent and half-brother to William the Conqueror) who, for a short time, held Bishopstone as part of the larger local manor.

If one wishes to speculate, and speculation it is I warn you, the ancient significance of Stone to Bishopstone may be the alignment = 131° = approximately sunrise point at winter solstice. If the alignment is continued southward in good old-fashioned Watkins-style, it *nearly* intersects the second highest beacon hill point in the Chilterns, Coombe Hill, 256m (852 feet), and to this day an important survey trig station. This old beacon site is within 'drum-beat' hearing of the British Prime Minister's country weekend retreat at Chequers. Of no *known* significance I hasten to add.

From Stone, with a little 'imagination', one can find several other solar calendar horizon markers, plus several Moon positions to add for good measure. Taken to its extreme (again Watkins-fashion) a whole latticework of Chiltern alignments can be drawn through Stone, Wing and many other ancient church sites scattered across the Vale; or they can be projected back on the skyline of the chalk scarp to mark out all manner of rising and setting points with astronomical significances. The strike direction of the Chiltern scarp itself, with its assembly of notches, humps and bumps, can be utilized as a large *in situ* computer to work out (in strictly arbitrary fashion!) any number of Sun, Moon, stellar or planetary alignments. . . .

Following up Kendall's earlier suggestion, nothing was proved for the Chiltern 'alignments' in relation to Thom's ideas—owing to the nature of the terrain I never really believed it could. However, my search for skyline notches proved beyond all doubt that the Chiltern Hills *did* likely provide sufficient distinctive horizon marks for ancient farmers to have defined their agricultural year and to have noted festival dates with comparative ease.

For the unwary the hunt for 'significant leys' and old pagan sites is fraught with many pitfalls. A healthy sceptical approach is the only sure way of separating fact from fancy. Consider, for example, the highly intriguing snippet of 'information' I found not too long ago in an article written in a local (Bucks) archaeological society magazine. It concerned an account of Penn Church (another Bucks church having very close links with early American history, viz: Penn of Pennsylvania, etc.). This again is an ancient church whose origins are undoubtedly pre-Conquest (*see* note 19). In the church tower are incorporated several sarsens, a fact in itself to rouse the curiosity in any student of Megalithology. The excerpt from the article relating to the history of Penn ran as follows: '... In a nearby village [to Penn] stood a Druid circle of Sarsen stones (shown on a map by John Speed) until the 14th century when they were taken down and hauled up the hill to form the foundation of the church tower. This involved terrific labour as every night most of the stones went back home. Finally they were all built in where they can be seen to this day: All except the biggest which was buried in the garden of a cottage. ...'

The legend concerning moving stones is a well known one and associated with scores of old churches. Indeed the same legend has been noted in connection with churches as far afield as Cornwall and Slagen *kirke** in Vestfold, Norway.

I did not know, nor could I contact, the writer of the article, but I knew the vicar of the church, and he even knew the site where the 'Druid circle' once supposedly stood. Even more intriguing, the very spot in question was marked plainly on the 6-inch Ordnance sheet as 'Church Knowl'. I almost began to believe that I now was on to something really significant. Finding the remains of a Megalithic circle not 25 miles from Piccadilly Circus would be a find indeed!

The vicar was able to elaborate further on the magazine story. It was held that the site Church Knowl, in a nearby dry-valley bottom, represented the earliest Saxon church at Penn. Legend had it that this early church had incorporated or been built over some pagan-cum-Druid remains. Later when it was decided to move the church up the hill to its present position, the sarsens had provided the foundations and part of the wall for the new church tower.

The first setback was not finding the John Speed map alluded to in the article as showing a 'Druid circle'. This was in spite of spending an afternoon searching out all the definitive Speed

---

* A church erected on an old mound which lies alongside the rich Oseberg Viking-ship burial believed to have been that of the legendary Queen Aase of Snorre Sturluson's *Ynglinga Saga*.

maps in the map room of the Royal Geographical Society. A visit to the site itself was more positive. Even from a distance Church Knowl was highly suggestive of an artifical mound, and near the centre of the site there were *three* large recumbent sarsens on the surface!

101a Recumbent sarsens at Penn, Buckinghamshire.

But first question: why hadn't these sarsens been noted previously? The vicar himself knew why. These stones had in fact been encountered by contractors some years earlier when a cable trench was excavated *across* the site. Indeed another story had it that many such sarsens had been encountered during the course of the excavations, many straddling the line of the trench, and this had necessitated their removal by explosives! Those that now remained on the surface had not been included when the contractors later backfilled the excavated trench material. . . .

The mystery of the sarsens began to deepen. There was the question of the cottage alluded to in the magazine article. Indeed, on the higher side of Church Knowl stood an isolated farm cottage which undoubtedly was the very one in question, for rumour had it that a previous occupier had found 'very large stones' when digging out the gardens. . . .

By sheer coincidence the cottage came up for sale soon after, and the new owner decided to enlarge it and excavate a new driveway approach through the old gardens. The new owner was sympathetic to antiquarian interests; and when the bulldozer arrived to do its work, we were told. Almost with its first scrape of the topsoil it hit several large sarsens lying just beneath the surface, and by teatime there were sufficient sarsens uncovered to form quite a respectable 'Druid circle'. I suddenly noted that one of the largest excavated sarsens looked ominously blackened. A montage of images momentarily flashed through my mind of Stukeley's rustic Avebury contemporaries with their fires a'roaring. . . . However, less dramatically, further and closer inspection showed that the black discoloration was nothing more than the stains of organic leaf-mould. Indeed, the bulldozer had amply confirmed what I had suspected *almost* from the start: what we had uncovered was a natural depository of sarsens which by some glacial-cum-fluvial whim of nature had assembled at this particular spot among the dry-valley gravels of Penn Bottom. . . . Without some experience in field geology, I might so easily have been misled, and later embarrassed. As it was, the sarsens looked quite at home in among the detritus of the Reading Beds, in almost the same *natural* geological context found farther westwards.

What then was fact and what was fancy? It was a fact that large sarsens existed *in situ* in goodly quantities. In spite of the evocative name Church Knowl, it was very unlikely that an earlier church had ever stood there. It was, however, likely that the early English church builders, on the hill overlooking, knew of the site as an excellent source of construction material and made use of it for the church tower footings and walls. Later, down below in the valley, the troublesome sarsens were covered by topsoil, but the name Church Knowl persisted.

Of the 'Druid circle', alas, there is still no trace, but to be scrupulously fair to the yarn spinner, much of the site is yet untouched. Moreover, I cannot say for certain that some ancient monument did not once exist there. Roundabout are no significant skyline notches, for the surrounding hills are covered and obscured by trees. John Speed's elusive map showing a 'Druid circle' still escapes my notice. In respect to this map, it is my own feeling that someone's overfertile imagination misinterpreted one of those decorative and palisaded circular enclosures which adorn the maps of Speed and his other contemporaries. Indeed it seems that the 'Druid circle' at Penn Bottom is as fictitious as the Norman castle shown on the skyline in early prints of Stonehenge (*see* Fig. 28).

Church Knowl provides a good example of a modern Megalithic mare's nest and should serve as a cautionary warning to all ley hunters and their like. Looking back I often wonder what Watkins, Michell and Lyle Borst would have made of it all....

101 The excavated sarsens of a supposed 'Druid Circle' at Penn, Buckinghamshire (*see* text).

CHAPTER XI

Megaliths Come of Age

Before the late 1960s the traditional archaeological view of British prehistoric culture was to attribute much of it to a European or Eastern Mediterranean influence via what was known as the invasion hypothesis. Many archaeologists and prehistorians could not believe in Stonehenge without invoking diffusionist influences from Mycenae (or elsewhere), consequently the thesis of 'Wessex without Mycenae' was held to be an archaeological heresy. As Grahame Clark has since argued, British archaeologists were so anxious to avoid ascribing any invention or innovation to their own forbears that there developed a kind of invasion neurosis. In the first half of the twentieth century especially, every change, every development of any kind was ascribed to overseas influence, preferably by invasion; culture contact was not deemed sufficient. It was this inhibition which prevented recognition of any kind of 'self-willed' prehistoric innovation in Britain.

The invasion-diffusionist hypothesis, however, was not formulated without good reason. After all within historical times Britain *had* witnessed several major invasions plus other minor infiltrations, and there was every reason to believe that in prehistoric times Britain had suffered similar incursions. The extreme hyperdiffusionist view of the origins of British culture was replaced in the 1920s by Gordon Childe's more sober, modified diffusionism with its thematic 'The irradiation of European barbarism by Oriental civilization'. But this still carried overtones of the older hyperdiffusionist ideas. Typical of the modified diffusionist point of view were J. F. S. Stone's remarks (*c.* 1958) in connection with the later construction phases at Stonehenge: '...I feel sure that we must look to the literal civilizations of the Mediterranean for the inspiration and indeed for the actual execution under the hands and eyes of some trader or mission from that region.' Stone's own view in this matter was no doubt strongly reinforced by the finding of the axe carvings at Stonehenge in 1953 (*see* note 20).

In the 1960s, the firmly entrenched diffusionist arguments began to be seriously questioned. This coincided with the gestation and birth of the so-called 'New Archaeology' which others more aptly nicknamed 'New-think' or 'New-speak' Archaeology. New Archaeology, like New Geology and all the other new -ologies, is a development of the widespread adoption of newer scientific techniques and technologies following World War II. This brought about a minor revolution in the whole field of scientific methodology. In particular, the enormous success of the International Geophysical Year (IGY) in 1957—8 led to the introduction of an interdisciplinary approach to the natural sciences and provided a model of scientific cooperation for the future. British archaeology began to move with the times in the early sixties.

New Archaeology owes much of its impetus to the new science of radiocarbon dating. No other new scientific tool had made quite such an impact on archaeology, and it is generally agreed it has provided the greatest major contribution to archaeology since the development of the stratigraphical techniques of the earlier 'New Geology' of 1780—1830.

Radiocarbon was discovered in the 1930s. This material has an atomic weight of 14 instead of the normal 12 of carbon, and for this reason it is referred to as carbon-14 (C-14). The first to find radiocarbon in nature was W. F. Libby, the American nuclear chemist. Libby knew that cosmic rays, which bombard the upper atmosphere, produce large numbers of neutrons. He reasoned that when these collide with nitrogen atoms in the atmosphere, some of them were transmuted into radiocarbon. Nitrogen is changed to carbon by replacing one of the positively charged protons in the nucleus of the nitrogen -14 atom with an uncharged neutron of almost the same mass. It was Libby's belief that radiocarbon combined with oxygen to form carbon dioxide which is diffused throughout the atmosphere. Plants absorb carbon dioxide by the process of photosynthesis. Plants in turn are consumed by animals and humans, and as a result radiocarbon is acquired in all their tissues.

But what happens to radiocarbon when a living organism

dies? It is obvious that death would stop further intake of radiocarbon. Libby found that what remained in the tissues after death slowly leaked away. The carbon-14 atom in fact is unstable and throws out its negatively charged electrons and becomes stable nitrogen. It was this characteristic which he realized could be put to good use.

Libby's value for the breakdown indicated a 'half-life' of 5,568 years. In this period half the radiocarbon in any given sample disappears. Half of what is left then disintegrates in the next 5,568 years, now leaving only one-quarter of the original; this disintegration then continues until all the radiocarbon is gone (in c. 70,000 years or more). Thus Libby realized that by determining the amount of radioactivity left at any point, and by measuring that amount against a calibrated scale based on the radioactivity of modern carbon, it is possible to gauge the age of the host substance. It was in this way that radiocarbon dating (C-14 dating) was born.

Any organic material is suitable for radiocarbon dating, such as wood, flesh, bone, antler, peat, excreta, grain, even beeswax. Each substance can be made to reveal its age. To check out the theory, Libby experimented with objects of *known* chronological age, but some early results were disappointing; eventually, however, as laboratory techniques improved, it was believed Libby's method could provide radiocarbon dates accurate to within a few per cent of the true value. One test was to attempt to date precisely when Hammurabi, the Babylonian king, lived; this is also a subject closely related to the controversial Venus tablets of Ammizaduga (*see* below). Libby's results in the 1950s finally gave a figure of c. – 1750 for Hammurabi—plus or minus a century. Libby also attempted to provide conclusive evidence for an exact correlation of the Western calendar to the Maya calendar which is still subject to controversy. His result (+451 ±110 years) indicated that the Spinden correlation of +481 seemed to be a better fit than the Goodman-Thompson correlation of +741 (*see* below).

In general usage Libby's radiocarbon dating method was subject to practical contamination problems that gave anomalous results. Again, however, as laboratory techniques slowly improved, it was accepted that the method was accurate enough. Libby assumed that carbon-14 had been in the atmosphere in similar amounts at different periods, or in other words, a more or less steady flux of cosmic rays has produced a constant proportion of carbon-14 relative to other isotopes of carbon. But this assumption proved to be an oversimplification. Cosmic radiation intensities likely varied in the past; for example, outbursts from the Sun and distant astronomical bodies such as novae, supernovae, pulsars, quasars and enigmatic X-ray bodies may have significant effects on the intensity of cosmic radiation. It has also been shown that lightning bolts can enhance the level of carbon-14 in wood. Dates via radiocarbon methods gave chronological fixes for Egyptian material which were *later* than historical calendar dates—this was both a puzzle and a nuisance. However, dates for European Megalithic societies seemed just right if equated with the *assumed* dates derived from prehistoric studies. For example, a date of about − 2400 seemed right for Iberia, and likewise dates of − 1620 and − 1720 for the main structure at Stonehenge. Carbon-14 dating also appeared valid to establish relative chronology. Nevertheless, it soon began to look suspect for *exact* chronological datings.

The solution to the difficulty was resolved by falling back on tree-ring dating. This proved to be the salvation for the radiocarbon method, particularly in the role played by the bristlecone pine (*Pinus aristata*) found in the White Mountains in California, the oldest living example of which is 4,600 years old. Earlier in the twentieth century, A. E. Douglass, an American astronomer, pioneered a method of tree-ring dating. Douglass noted that trees of certain species showed marked variations in ring width, reflecting wet and dry years. This he found especially true of the Rocky Mountain Douglas fir and some of the pines. By coring trees with a simple instrument, growth rings could be checked against those in neighbouring trees. It is possible to trace missing rings, extra rings and other growth irregularities and so date the rings exactly. By this method it was possible to date the time the prehistoric Indians built their pueblos.

The method was later applied to bristlecone pines; several of these are some thousands of years old. Long time spans can be cross-calibrated using many tree samples of old living trees and dead wood which overlap in age with samples from younger trees. This is possible because of the recurring characteristic recognition rings brought about by various weather conditions.

Trees in the same area are affected in much the same way, therefore all carry the same signature. In such a way the bristlecone pine has produced a chronology going back 8,200 years. The bristlecone rings provide samples of wood that can be dated by counting tree rings and by measuring their carbon-14 content, and the two results then compared.

These comparisons yielded results which were so surprising that the whole method was immediately called into question. If one accepted the C-14 correction indicated by the tree rings, the whole structure of prehistoric archaeology was upset.

A check was made: an independent tree-ring calendar was constructed using different wood samples. But the results were the same; the two calendars agreed exactly. These results also confirmed that contrary to the widely held belief, each tree ring does not correspond to one year. It confirmed, too, that large discrepancies observed between dendrochronological and radiocarbon ages could not be explained by major systematic errors in tree-ring dating.

For archaeology—for astro-archaeology—the consequences were far-reaching. Radiocarbon dates before – 1000 are too young. All corrections necessary are believed to be applicable uniformly on a world-wide basis. Nevertheless, there remain some minor anomalies to explain away, and it is not certain (c. 1975) that the calibration curve has yet reached its final, definitive shape. The Libby half-life of 5,568 years is thought to be in error. The magnitude of error is still not absolutely clear, but it appears that the Libby value is probably too small. Until everyone has agreed about the value of this all-important half-life, radiocarbon dates are still expressed in terms of the standard Libby figure. In the literature carbon datings have a special nomenclature such as bp (before present—reckoned as epoch 1950) and bc/ad (all lower case for carbon dates); these are cited as against BP and BC/AD notations for calendar years. With carbon-date citations the laboratory which published the radiocarbon data is also quoted whenever possible.

The new calibration curve has resolved the puzzling Egyptian radiocarbon dates; these have now fallen neatly into place with the traditional historical calendar dates. But for Megalithic Europe, the new calibration provided no such reassurances, for it put back many Megalithic tombs to a date earlier than the pyramids. It was found that an interval of 700 radiocarbon years is sometimes stretched to as much as 1,200 calendar years. Megalithic tombs like Newgrange in Ireland, now *c.* – 3100 (Fig. 93), are much older than previously considered; some of those of Brittany *predate* the pyramids by two millenniums. The dates for the late building phase at Stonehenge are not so dramatically affected but are reset around – 2000, at least four centuries before the Mycenaean civilization of the Aegean began.

Thus the chronology of prehistoric Europe has been turned upside down. Many of the so-called Mediterranean innovations supposedly carried into Europe by diffusion are now found *earlier* in Europe than in the East, and the assumptions that have grown over the last century are not substantiated. One principal effect of the upset chronology has been to invalidate each of the three routes by which these influences reached Britain and Europe, i.e. from the Aegean to Spain; from the Aegean to the Balkans; and from Mycenaean Greece to Central and North-West Europe. It is certain that by the fifth millennium BC, Balkan societies were as complex as any in the world.

One of the crutches on which the diffusionist origin of Megalithic culture rested was that the earliest Megalithic tombs in Europe were to be found on the Iberian peninsula. From here the Megalithic culture was believed to have spread northwards to Brittany and then to Ireland. The final stage of the northern arm of this diffusion movement was supposedly represented by the great Megalithic tomb at Maeshowe in the Orkneys. In Iberia the Megalithic settlements were considered to have been Aegean colonies that had become established after exploratory trading voyages. The archaeological evidence seemed to give ample support to this idea: they had similar knowledge about smelting ores; similar fortifications; and most significantly, burial in Megalithic tombs. Taken together the corpus of evidence seemed to provide an impressive dossier, and even the earliest C-14 dates did not conflict with it.

In Britain some of the strongest arguments for Mycenaean diffusion rested on artefacts such as dagger hafts of which similar patterns are also found in Mycenae. When Atkinson discovered the dagger carvings at Stonehenge, this seemed finally to clinch the theory. Additional evidence was the famous Rillaton cup from Cornwall that was very similar to two gold cups from a Mycenaean grave; and there were the blue faience beads and double axes long considered unquestionably Mycenaean.

After the new radiocarbon dating calibration, these artefacts were subjected to further examination. The Rillaton cup is now considered to be of local British origin, and the faience beads are of a different composition to similar style beads in the east Mediterranean. Actual undisputed Mycenaean imports in early Bronze Age contexts turn out to be very rare in Britain and in the rest of Europe, except for southern Italy. The famous double axes appear to have very doubtful pedigrees archaeologically and may have been brought from the Aegean area at a much later date; certainly none can now be admitted to have originated from prehistoric contexts in Western Europe. Almost overnight Gordon Childe's beautiful 'Oriental irradiation' theories that had swayed opinion for so long were found to be without substance. Today it is impossible to build up a reliable chronological development for the early Bronze Age of Central Europe on the basis of direct cultural links with the Mycenaean world. The so-called early Bronze Age Mycenaean-inspired Wessex culture, so closely associated with the later development of Stonehenge, seems without doubt to have evolved independently. Although radiocarbon dating indicates a chronological cultural overlap, it is apparent that Stonehenge III can rightly be attributed to a British inspired Megalithic culture, and indeed several now believe that Stonehenge III may have been completed in its final phase before the Wessex culture reached its peak. Thus the design of Stonehenge can be truly recognized as an original native innovation of the Neolithic aborigines of Southern Britain.

It is possible that European Megalithic cultures evolved independently in several centres—products of separate culture foci. The recalibration of radiocarbon dates has provided the necessary stimulus to look again for more profound prehistoric European societies. Archaeology, in the social context, is confronted with the problem whether the great tombs and other Megalithic monuments did indeed evolve independently as the evidence at present suggests, and whether this was possible in supposedly unsophisticated Neolithic societies. Egypt as a source of Megalithic inspiration can be dismissed, for nothing there is found in stone before −3000. A separate culture focus for each Megalithic centre is borne out by individual stylistic fashions reflected in Megalithic architecture. Brittany possessed

Megalithic tombs before – 4000, Britain and Denmark before
– 3000.

Few disciples of the New Archaeology would deny that some
diffusion via 'culture creep' or 'germinal-idea innovation' from
one group to another must surely have been influential in
Neolithic Europe. A parallel of this *modus operandi* model of
diffusion can be seen in the spread and influence of Babylonian
astronomical ideas, first to India and then to China. A more
modern parallel is how 'idea-stimulus-diffusion' provided
Galileo with his first telescope. He never saw the instrument
made by the Dutch spectacle makers, but when he *heard* about
the idea, he immediately saw its possibilities and then set to
work to make something much superior. But no one—except
perhaps the most ardent hyperdiffusionist—would claim that
almost identical methods practised by Mesolithic Lake Dwellers
in Europe and Polynesian races of more contemporary times of
tying together timber piles was anything more than human
minds—divorced in space and time—working alike to solve a
particular problem.

Archaeology is now faced with finding a Megalithic society to
suit its monuments. What kind of social organization was
necessary for such a society to function? Although not all
prehistoric societies with celestial-inspired calendars developed
for agrarian purposes were hierarchical, some evidence for
British hierarchical societies is certainly found in the archaeological record (*see* below). It would be interesting indeed if
native British Megalithic societies were one day proven to have
been egalitarian, but the well-documented evidence from
Egypt, Babylonia and the later neo-Megalithic societies of
Middle and South America shows these to have been strongly
hierarchical. Studies utilizing the comparative method might
indeed be fruitful. If the astronomical achievement is proved
valid, there is a need to establish that an elitist intellectual
astronomer-cum-priest class (provided by the Lockyer-Thom-
Hoyle model) could, *or would*, be supported by its peasant
farmers. Back in history elitist astronomer-priest classes are
certainly well documented in Egypt, Babylonia and the
Americas. Some of these men were undoubted geniuses such as
the shadowy Egyptian polymath-priest Imhotep, architect-
astronomer and father of medicine, who invented the science of

building in stone.* There is no valid reason why the British Megalithic culture was not also evolved and then maintained by astro-engineers of similar calibre.

A seated Imhotep and his scarab.

* Imhotep was vizier of Pharaoh Zoser of the 3rd Dynasty (c. − 2778 to − 2723). He supposedly designed and supervised the construction of the first Step-Pyramid at Sakkara where his name appears inscribed on Zoser's statue. He held many titles including 'supervisor of all that which heaven brings, the earth creates and the Nile brings'. He apparently stemmed from a priestly hierarchy, for Kanofer, his father, is recorded as 'chief of the works of the south and the northland'. Two thousand years later, in c. − 525, Imhotep appears as an Egyptian god.

CHAPTER XII

Astronomy, Metrology and Pyramidology

It is usually considered that archaeology can provide four kinds of evidence about a culture given the right artefacts: these can be formalized as technological (including numerate) evidence, economic evidence, evidence for social and political structure, and religious (mythological) evidence. The contemporary astro-archaeologist generally provides only numerate (and metrical) evidence, although along the way he might, unwittingly, supply significant clues about the rest.

It is not surprising that many attracted to astro-archaeology have a keen interest in pragmatic metrology often gained incidentally while following careers as architects, engineers, or land surveyors. Lockyer began his career as a War Office clerk but taught himself astronomy and then surveying. Penrose was an architect and an amateur-astronomer with an interest in sundials. Boyle Somerville was a navy man well versed in navigational theory and with a keen interest in maps and charts, as was also the Frenchman Lieutenant de Vasseau Devoir. 'Peter' Newham was an ex-Royal Flying Corps pilot and later a utilities engineer and surveyor who in his spare time designed novel sundials and perpetual calendar devices (see note 21). Thom was a professor of civil engineering at Oxford, and Borst is also a civil engineer. The Frenchman Charriere is an architect.

Lockyer, as a self-trained surveyor, took particular pleasure in noting the lack of metrical skills in his archaeologist critics and chuckled gleefully when they were caught out in debate while citing figures and not knowing whether a given azimuth was true or magnetic. It was not without some relish that he was often quick to point out that many previous archaeological surveys had been done in places where the magnetic variation was totally unknown so that any orientation in respect to a true azimuth was impossible to determine. What annoyed Lockyer was that astronomers were told to stick to astronomy and leave archaeology to the archaeologists. Indeed this same opinion was frequently sounded again in the contentious Stonehenge debates of the 1960s. Lockyer genuinely believed that astronomers should also be archaeologists and archaeologists also astronomers, and he thought astronomy and archaeology should be convertible terms. He was to voice his opinion about this matter on many occasions. Gerald Hawkins later echoed an updated version of Lockyer's remarks, believing that archaeologists should learn as much astronomy as the prehistoric peoples seemed to know. To this Glyn Daniel, for the archaeologists, was quick to retort that Hawkins and his fellows who call themselves astro-archaeologists should learn as much archaeology as a first-year undergraduate seemed to know in those universities which offer a degree course in archaeology. . . .

One exception among British archaeologists was Flinders Petrie who was not without considerable familiarity with *both* subjects and professed all his life a keen interest in astronomical and metrical problems. It is not generally known that Petrie started his career as a land surveyor. He had been inspired to take up this career by his father, a chemist and engineer, who, like countless other intelligent Victorians, had become completely infatuated and beguiled by Taylor's and Piazzi Smyth's pyramid theories. Perhaps this was not surprising in the context of the period, for Taylor, Smyth and their followers provided a strong religious background to the pyramid ideas—and thus the pious Victorians were only getting the pyramids they 'desired'.

At the age of twenty-two Petrie published his book, *Inductive Metrology*, and in 1880 *Stonehenge*, after having completed the most accurate survey of the monument to that date. His first trip to Egypt was strictly metrical in purpose. He remained in Egypt from 1880 to 1882, spending nine months in Gizeh, amassing the data that was to finally damn Smyth's Pyramid-inch theories to the discerning scientific public back home. Petrie's own pyramid labours resulted in the publication of *The Pyramids and Temples of Gizeh* (1887) which provided a landmark in the history of Egyptology. From then on he was an ardent archaeologist, but his early career in land surveying and interests in metrology stood him in good stead for the rest of his life.

In his autobiographic book, *Alms For Oblivion* (1966), Mortimer Wheeler recounts a fascinating anecdote about

Petrie's prowess as a surveyor as well as an improvisor. He recalled that in 1925 Petrie spent a holiday with him at Brecon in Wales while Wheeler was excavating a Roman fort. Petrie decided to busy himself surveying stone circles and other Megalithic monuments in the surrounding country. Wheeler asked Petrie how he proposed to do this work and with what instruments? Wheeler recalled: '. . . a look of ineffable cunning came into his eyes as he produced a single slender bamboo pea-stick and—a visiting card. The pea-stick, he said, planted in the ground gave him the line, whilst the visiting card, sighted carefully along two of its sides, gave him a right angle. At night after dinner, by the light of an oil lamp, he would get out a notebook containing lists of measurements resulting from his day's work in the field, and, with the help of a logarithm-table, would ultimately reduce them to a schematic diagram.'

Wheeler in recounting this anecdote said that it illustrated the paradoxical character of Petrie. By incredible ingenuity he was often able to solve complex problems and render them simple and surmountable; yet, at other times, simple problems might be tangled into inextricable complexities.

Today Petrie is best remembered as the British giant of Egyptology, and most archaeologists prefer to forget (or are unaware of) the great master's own metrical aberration: the so-called 'Etruscan foot'. This was the unit of measurement which he evolved to fit the theories surrounding his grand scheme for relating British hill figures. In his *Hill Figures of England* (1926) Petrie believed that the Whiteleaf and Bledlow crosses, the Long Man of Wilmington *and* Stonehenge could be shown to belong to the same primitive period and were set out with the same unit. For example, it was his notion that the base line of the Whiteleaf Cross, which he measured as 386 feet in length, was the exact diameter of the main sarsen circle at Stonehenge, approximately 400 Etruscan feet. Petrie had in fact simply fallen into the same obsessional trap as had Smyth with his Pyramid-inch theories.

It is round the evidence provided by precise measurements of Megalithic structures that the contentious debates have centred since Smyth's and Lockyer's time. It is the very application of metrology adopted by astro-archaeologists, plus the some-what austere scientific-method approach to archaeology, that has often upset and antagonized the less numerate socio-economic slanted archaeologists and made them mistrustful of the results.

The traditional picture of the North-West European Megalithic cultus is certainly at odds with the level of intellectual achievement required by astro-archaeological theory. The two models appear incompatible. Atkinson himself has gone on record as saying that if archaeologists accepted even part of Thom's conclusions (which he feels inclined to do), then they must alter radically their current view of the intellectual calibre of man in North-West Europe in the late third and second millennium BC; this would also include revising ideas of the accepted history of science in relation to geometry, mensuration, observational astronomy and the calendar in which primacy in invention is traditionally ascribed to the literate civilizations of the Ancient East.

But what level of attainment did the ancient astronomies outside Europe achieve? Ancient astronomy in the Near East has been studied during the last hundred years or so via extant clay tablets containing texts or mythological stories, through papyrus documents, monumental inscriptions, stelae and, in the case of Smyth's and Lockyer's Egyptian work, by field studies relating to the dimensions and orientation of monuments—Megalithic and otherwise. Meso-American and South American pre-Columbian astronomies have also been studied in a similar way.

It has long been held that scientific astronomy does not originate with recognition and grouping of irregular configurations of stars or the invention of celestial or astral deities which likely evolved back in Upper Paleolithic times. It does begin when attempts can be seen to have been made to predict, however crudely, periodic astronomical phenomena such as the phases of the Moon. In this context, Marshack's Upper Paleolithic lunar notations, if substantiated, qualify within the definition, as does much of North-West European Megalithic astronomy relating to Sun and Moon risings. In the context of ancient astronomy, North-West European Megalithic astronomy is unique in that we of the modern world have inherited the observatories—if observatories they are—without the backing of philological sources of any kind; whereas in the ancient Near East we have the philological sources but not the instrumentation and only the vaguest of references as to how the observations were carried out.

The classical writers relied much on Berosus as a source for their ideas about Babylonian astronomy. Berosus, a priest of the temple of Bel, was born in the reign of Alexander and was the author of several astronomical books and treatises including the history *Babyloniaka*, of which only fragments survive in the works of Josephus, Eusebius and Syncellus. However, there is little scientific astronomy in the surviving fragments; they consist mostly of astrological and mythological references relating the old cosmological legends. Berosus, nevertheless, has been extremely useful to historians in establishing the chronological order of the Babylonian king lists.

When George Cornewall Lewis wrote his definitive and influential *Astronomy of the Ancients* in 1862, the extent of scientific Babylonian astronomy was not yet appreciated. Although cuneiform tablets had arrived in France in 1846, having been excavated from the ruins of Khorsabad by Botta, and tablets from King Assurbanipal's library at Kuyunjik had been excavated by Layard in 1849/50 and sent back to London by the boxful,* the true content of many had not been recognized.

Some years later the Franco-German scholar Julius Oppert and the British scholar A. H. Sayce made cuneiform translations relating to so-called scientific astronomy of the Babylonians. But it was not until 1881, when the Jesuit fathers Epping and Strassmaier recognized sophisticated Babylonian lunar theory in cuneiform texts, that the real scientific astronomy of the ancient world came to light.

The interpretation of Babylonian astronomy has its own controversies. One of the earliest scientific texts concerns the Venus tablets of Ammizaduga (found in Assurbanipal's library), which are now counted among the treasured possessions of the British Museum. These tablets are closely involved with Immanuel Velikovsky's contentious theories. Among numerous hyperspeculations, Velikovsky proposed that two major catastrophes occurred sometime in the past owing to the Earth's dynamic interaction with a comet and then Mars. The comet encounter with the Earth supposedly took place about − 1500, and as a consequence the comet became transformed into the planet Venus; the Mars encounter supposedly took place in

* Many of these tablets, plus the thousands which followed, are still unpublished (*c.* 1975).

− 687. In both encounters Velikovsky claimed that the direction of the Earth's axial spin was switched plus the angle of tilt of the axis itself, resulting in a major change in the obliquity of the ecliptic.

These catastrophe theories of Velikovsky are in fact an updated interpretation of a fanciful seventeenth-century idea of Edmond Halley which he later revoked himself, and it was then taken up and developed by William Whiston in his *New Theory of the Earth* (1696).

If Velikovsky's ideas are correct, the proof would be forthcoming in Megalithic alignments. It follows that Stonehenge and other Megalithic monuments constructed before *c.* − 1500 would now not show positive alignments to the Sun and Moon. These colourful cataclysms have enormous dramatic appeal to a lay readership and in particular to some contemporary student bodies revolting against so-called traditional scientific dogmatism and teaching authoritarianism; by these Velikovsky is now considered something of a guru. In attempts to counter the damning positive Stonehenge alignment evidence, Velikovsky claims the monument was erected later than − 687; he maintains that radiocarbon dates are completely unreliable, the archaeological data wrong, and he is utterly convinced that artefacts originating from Stonehenge which had been dated as belonging to the early second millennium might easily have been placed there afterwards. Perhaps his views echo the instances of the British penny discovered in the lower levels of Harappa in the Indus Valley civilization, and the empty soda-water bottle found in a very ancient South African site!

The Venus tablets of Ammizaduga have also been drawn into these arguments. Several books and many contentious papers have been written about the Venus tablets. These have argued several premises but in particular the problem relating to their actual date which is believed at present to be *c.* − 1645 to − 1625; whereas Velikovsky's ideas would place them about a millennium later. All who have attempted to decipher the tablets have been faced with the problem of separating out misleading scribal errors. These errors have been manipulated and interpreted by Velikovsky and his acolytes in futile attempts to show that Venus has not always moved in the orbit she moves in today, and indeed they believe that the tablets justify and support the catastrophe theory.

The old diffusion-versus-independent-innovation arguments hound astronomy as much as they do archaeology. Perhaps even more so since astronomy is now beset with UFOism and Dänikenism and several other pseudological overspills from outer space. Several writers have long believed that astronomy can provide direct evidence to prove widespread diffusion of a specific culture in prehistoric times. Few would deny that both diffusion and local independent innovation have each played roles in developing particular cultures. The problem really is deciding which factor has been more influential in any particular locale. In the past, as we have seen, the diffusion idea was the easy option to explain the presence of ideas and artefacts otherwise difficult to explain away in the 'believed' context of a society.

Lockyer's ideas while firmly placing Stonehenge into its rightful prehistoric context, which had been misplaced by Fergusson and others opting for a more recent origin, also echoed the belief fostered in the second half of the nineteenth century that any sophisticated scientific thinking *must* have originated in the Ancient East. Lockyer's speculative thesis that Britain in early times, from about – 3600, was inhabited by a race connected by blood and cultural ties with Babylonia or Egypt, and whose contacts were maintained until at least – 1300, was typical of contemporary hyperdiffusionist arguments like those nurtured by the highly influential Panbabylonism school in Germany at the beginning of the twentieth century. The supporters of Panbabylonism concluded that most of the mythological narratives have an astronomical basis which contain hidden, elaborate and detailed astronomical information. Certainly few would deny that the earliest Sumerian myths, specially those concerning Inanna—Queen of the Heaven—are direct references to the movements of the planet Venus when it disappears for a time near the Sun at inferior conjunction. This sky myth predates the more scientific Venus tablets of Ammizaduga, describing the same phenomenon, by at least a millennium, but the information it contains is simple enough and comparable with the ingenuous mythical stories woven by the other ancient races to explain and justify the periodical disappearance of stars and planets and the occurrence of eclipses of the Sun and Moon.

The Panbabylonists also believed that all astronomical

knowledge could be linked back direct to the Sumerians who were supposed to possess an amazing advanced astronomical science. In other words, the Panbabylonists were hyperdiffusionists who argued that only in Mesopotamia did one find the required mathematical background for astro-mythology to be expressed so precisely in mathematical cuneiform texts. Like all hyperdiffusionists they cited unique world-wide similarities which they claimed could *only* be explained by evoking diffusion and not by independent innovation.

Franz Xavier Kugler (1862—1929), the great Jesuit scholar, was one of the few scholars in Germany who did not fall for this Panbabylonist view. He had begun his scientific career as a lecturer in chemistry, and when Joseph Epping died, Kugler continued Epping's pioneer astronomical and mathematical cuneiform decipherment. Kugler and others maintained that similarities among astro-mythologies—which the Panbabylonists cited as examples for diffusion—might easily be explained by the circumstances that all races witnessed the same events in the sky which made like impressions on the human mind.

The Panbabylonists, however, were highly influential in their time, and Alfred Jeremias' *Handbuch der altorientalischen Geisteskultur* gained a wide and popular audience much in the same way as the pseudo-scientific writers such as Velikovsky and von Däniken have in more modern times. It was Jeremias' thesis which evoked the so-called Babylonian 'Weltanschauung'. The Panbabylonists also believed that Babylonian texts showed that the ancient astronomers had discovered the use of lenses and had observed the phases of Venus; in fact every phenomena in classical cosmogony, literature and religion might be traced back to the so-called cosmic philosophy of the Babylonians. In the same vein as contemporary pseudo-scientific writers, they had complete disregard for textual evidence and cited misleading, apocryphal and antiquated translations.

For some of the Panbabylonist seminal ideas we can blame in part Sir Walter Raleigh's *History of the World* (1616) in which he wondered: 'How could it happen that the phases of Venus just discovered by Galileo seem to have been known to ancient authors.' We can also attribute part blame to the writings of Richard Proctor (1837—1888) who made out a similar case for Chaldean astronomy in a supplement to his *Saturn and its*

System (1865). Proctor also later had some strange ideas about the true purpose of the pyramids (*see* below). It is of interest that Lockyer and Proctor, the two prominent nineteenth-century astronomers who took up the study of astro-archaeological problems, should become sworn enemies. The cause of their dispute was *not* in astro-archaeological interpretations, but in other matters involving the little publicized personality clashes which dogged the Councils of the Royal Astronomical Society throughout the turbulent 1870s.

Almost in scholastic isolation Kugler demolished the great edifice of Panbabylonism theory piece by piece. The Panbabylonists had no answer to the criticism put forward in his books *Im Bannkreis Babels* (1910) and the monumental *Sternkunde und Sterndienst in Babel* (1907—13), both of which unfortunately were never translated into English. With the death of one of the movement's leaders, cuneiform philologist Hugo Winckler (1861—1913), Panbabylonism was scientifically dead by World War I and then banished for ever to the lunatic fringe of pseudo-scientific writings.

In archaeology, the Panbabylonist kind of hyperdiffusionist argument still turns up in what purports to be scientific literature. The Panbabylonist ideas were also fostered by Lord Raglan in *How Came Civilization* (1939) when he insisted that all higher culture and civilization came from southern Mesopotamia. Among similar well-known ones is the Elliot Smith and W. J. Perry Egyptocentric-hyperdiffusionism—known at one time as 'the Manchester school'—which held that all major inventions were made by the ancient Egyptians—the chosen people—and in turn were carried from land to land by migrations and by voyagers. The consequences of these ideas were that they advocate an Egyptian origin even for Asian cultures and, in the New World, for the civilizations of Central and South America. The Elliot-Smith school denied to all cultures and nations—other than Egyptian—any inventive capacity; thus everything of a culture higher than 'barbarian' must perforce be Egyptian. Any society which uses mummification must have been influenced by the Egyptians—even those found in the South Seas. The Elliot-Smith school went so far as to assert that the complex totemistic society of the Australian Aborigines was brought about by a visitation of

Egyptian 'Children-of-the-Sun' voyagers who arrived there looking for gold in about − 3000. It is interesting to reflect that Piazzi Smyth was brought up exposed to a similar hyperdiffusion thesis fostered by the British antiquarian Kingsborough—author of the nine folio *Antiquities of Mexico* (1831)—who had become obsessed with the idea that the New World had been reached by voyagers from the Old World long before Columbus set sail. Piazzi Smyth's father, Vice-Admiral Smyth, was a firm believer in Kingsborough's ideas. Piazzi, from childhood, was much under his father's influence, and at home the young Piazzi lived constantly exposed to the heady intellectual atmosphere of astronomy laced with Egyptology and diffusionism.

Piazzi Smyth was not the originator of the Pyramid theories—'the Bible in Stone'—he merely elaborated them. The principal originator was John Taylor, an eccentric London publisher who never visited Egypt but wrote a book to set out his ideas entitled *The Great Pyramid: Why was it Built? And Who Built it?* Taylor believed that the Great Pyramid was part of God's plan, for he supposedly found incorporated in its grand design all kinds of deliberate mathematical truths. The best known of these hidden truths was the value of *pi*: if one divides the monument's height into twice the side of its base, one actually does obtain a close approximation of *pi*. One of Smyth's key units of measurement was his so-called Pyramid-inch which he claimed represented one 500-millionth part of the Earth's polar diameter. The rest of the Pyramid's measurements, including the various internal passages, symbolized different periods of time in world history measured from the date of the building of the Pyramid, which on astronomical grounds Smyth assigned to − 2170, but so far no Egyptologist has conceived so recent a date for its construction.

Another nineteenth-century study of the pyramids, based on supposed astronomical evidence, was that of Richard Proctor in his *Myths and Marvels of Astronomy* (1878) and his *Great Pyramid* (1883). While not accepting all the Pyramid theories of Piazzi Smyth, Proctor nevertheless believed that there was little doubt that at least one purpose served by the Great Pyramid was astronomical.

The astronomical ideas had been fostered by several of the French savants such as Charles Frances Dupois (1742—1809)

102 (a) The Sphinx and the Great Pyramid. (b) The Great Pyramid drawn by Piazzi Smyth showing the Entrance Passage orientated towards the star Alpha Draconis c. – 2170.

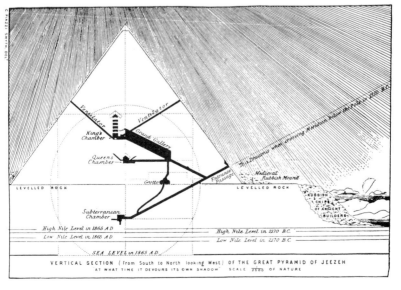

who had helped create Napoleon's commission to explore Upper Egypt. Dupois and others had been of the opinion that Egyptian astronomical science—with which they considered the pyramids had been involved—was of fabulous antiquity. However, when Champollion succeeded in reading the Egyptian hieroglyphs, this was shown to be unlikely. Jean Baptiste Biot (1774—1862), another of the Napoleonic French savants, also introduced several stellar alignment ideas. Biot was convinced that whatever its prime purpose, the Great Pyramid also served as an immense gnomon for the determination of the equinoxes. In 1853, Mariette, the great French Egyptologist, following Biot's instructions, supposedly used the Great Pyramid to determine the time of the vernal equinox within 29 hours.

It was the highly respected establishment figure Sir John Herschel who first introduced the next red herring into pyramidology (*c.* 1836) when he noted that the north-facing entrance of the Great Pyramid was aligned to the star Thuban (Alpha Draconis) about − 2160. Had Herschel known what was to follow, he might well have silently swallowed this innocent snippet of information. From Biot's and Herschel's ideas, I believe all the later cults for Megalithic stellar alignments can be traced. Proctor assumed Thuban to shine down the northern tunnel when culminating the lower meridian; but this was not all, for it was noted that a perpendicular line, set out from the Thuban-orientated entrance-passage slope, provided a further alignment for Alcyone (Eta Tauri, a star in the Pleiades—Fig. 37) at about the same date. Thus gestated a tangled web of hyperspeculation in which several influential astronomers all became involved, including Dr Brunnow, Astronomer Royal for Ireland. A later proponent of these Pyramid theories was the controversial figure of Percival Lowell, one of the champions for the existence of Martian canals, not finally discredited until the U.S. Mariner flights of the 1960s.

Proctor firmly believed that the Great Pyramid had been used as a kind of astronomical observatory. His theory was that the north-facing tunnel had played a role in finding true north and south when the building of the Pyramid took place. Much of his argument rested on the assumption that the ancient Egyptians had intended the Pyramid to be located exactly in latitude 30°N. Its actual position is 29° 58′ 51″. Refraction error resulting from the use of the pole-star method would push the

Pyramid *north* of the 30° parallel, but *south* if an alternative method, using Sun shadows, had been employed instead to orientate it. Proctor, in his *c.* 1878 speculations, also summarized what he considered were other plausible theories to account for the pyramids. He did not favour the tomb theory himself and trotted out ideas which even in his day were considered highly unlikely—ideas that they might have been used as defences against the sands of the Great Desert, that they might have been granaries like those made under Joseph's directions, or places of resort during excessive overflows of the Nile. Yet John Greaves, a professor of astronomy at Oxford, the first astronomer to dabble in Megalithology and who wrote *Pyramidographia* (1646), was under no doubts as to their rightful purpose—recognizing they were intended as tombs. He soundly dismissed the granary theory which had been in vogue earlier. Even in Greaves' day various astronomical observatory theories were freely bandied about. Greaves himself remarked: '...But that these Pyramids were designed for observatories (whereas by the testimonies of the ancients I have proved before, that they were intended for sepulchres) is in no way to be credited.... Neither can I apprehend to what purpose the priests with so much difficulty should ascend so high, when below with more ease, and as much certainty, they might from their own lodging hewn in the rocks, upon which the Pyramids were erected, make the same observations....'

But the ideas of Taylor, Smyth and Proctor, and all the ideas of others who have trotted out astronomical theories, continue to live on in current pseudo-scientific literature. One must not fall into the trap, however, of denying the ancient Egyptians a profound interest in the stars, particularly the northern stars. In the Pyramid Texts a king becomes a star as well as the Sun when he ascends the sky after death to gain union with the gods. The Great Bear known as the Bull's Foreleg and the 'Imperishable' was a very important asterism; important too were the entire northern circumpolar regions which were greatly revered. In the Pyramid Texts we read that the goal of the deceased was the region of Dat, in the northern part of the heavens. He who joined the circumpolar constellations (visible throughout each night of the year) would live for ever. A king's house in the sky could never be destroyed, and in the *Book of the Dead* we read that the stars themselves aided the dead man until Nut, the great sky goddess (Fig. 16), uncovered her arms to receive him.

Perhaps then, in the context of the Dead, there may indeed be significance in the entrance passage of the Great Pyramid *facing* northwards, since this was the most important direction for Heaven, and several of the other pyramids at Gizeh have north-facing passages. But the complete story of Egyptian astronomy and skylore requires the space of an entire book.

Smyth's own books went through many editions before they were replaced by those of his many disciples. The culmination of all that followed was *The Great Pyramid: its Divine Message* (1924) by D. Davidson and H. Aldersmith. This was indeed the very pinnacle of pseudo-pyramidology. Almost with pre-meditated cunning the authors cited and then manipulated Petrie's authenticated measurements rather than Smyth's suspect and mostly outdated ones, and it provided a whole new battery of geometrical geomancy and bizarre formulae for a new corpus of Pyramid prophesies. A great world war was predicted for 1928, and the Second Coming of Christ in 1936. When these prophesies were not fulfilled, Davidson, apparently unruffled, simply replayed his Pyramid numbers game and 'discovered' that 1953 was to be the actual year the world would end. We can now smile at this whole saga of Pyramidology, but a large audience took it (and apparently still takes it) seriously, and this gargantuan encyclopedic-style book passed through many editions.

Davidson's book also made reference to British circles, including Stonehenge, and the alignments in Brittany. Here Davidson fell back on Lockyer's work, and to support Lockyer's ideas of British Druid culture he dragged in for good measure the hyperdiffusionist ideas fostered by a D. A. Mackenzie (*Ancient Man in Britain*), who formulated the belief that the later-arrived Celtic peoples embraced the so-called Druidic system used by the earlier Iberians in Western Europe whose cultus in turn had been derived from Oriental colonists.

What real knowledge of scientific astronomy did then the ancient world possess? Indeed, when one gets down to the nub of the problem and isolates the true and proved scientific astronomy from the mythological-cum-astrological content, there is precious little left to flesh out the bones.

By tradition Babylonia has long been recognized as the home of astronomy. Mathematical texts have been recovered from the Old Babylonian Hammurabi period c. -1800 to -1600 and these indicate wide knowledge at this period of square and cube numeracy. Tablets are found that give examples of 'Pythagorean theorems' more than a millennium before Pythagoras. Nevertheless, all these tablets seem to have been written to help solve problems involving economic matters such as reckoning compound interest and calculating volumes of earthworks for canal and other municipal constructions. None have been found which relate to scientific astronomy. Not until one arrives at a date around the third century BC is scientific astronomy found unambiguously. It has been estimated conservatively that a quarter of a million tablets and fragments of the Sumerian period are in the hands of museums and private collections. Of these 95 per cent are economic in character—contracts of sale, wills and testaments, agreements, etc. The remaining consist of political, lexical, literary and mathematical texts. It always comes as something of a shock to students of the history of astronomy to be told that absolutely nothing is known about *astronomy* in earlier Sumerian times.

Epping, Strassmaier and Kugler were the first to explode the long-cherished myth of the supposed great antiquity of Babylonian scientific astronomy. The constellations had already been mapped out before the second millennium, and several examples of Babylonian star maps (planispheres) and texts exist for the second millennium. The movements of the planets and the Moon were well known (viz. the Venus tablets), and from earliest times (probably Sumerian) the Moon was the main basis for the calendar, but not until c. -700, under the Assyrian Empire, can one find texts that indicate true knowledge of why eclipses occur. Not until c. -250 to -50 do we find cuneiform ephemerides by which lunar eclipses might be satisfactorily predicted. As we have already seen (*see* above) the story of Thales predicting the solar eclipse of 28 May -548 is an historic myth long perpetuated even in serious astronomical literature, as is also the meaning of *Saros* (*see* above). It was from Kugler's researches in the early 1900s that we know how the astronomer-priests of the Seleucid period computed eclipses by careful attention to noting the latitude of the Moon in relation to syzygies. Before this it is likely that lunar eclipses were roughly predicted—or rather cycles of lunar eclipses—by means of the eighteen-year cycle, but how far this method dates back is not known.

The Moon determined the basis of the Babylonian calendar from earliest recorded times, the first day of the month beginning on the evening when the new crescent was seen shortly after sunset. If the crescent failed to appear when expected, that day was counted as the thirtieth day of the month. As a result of the synodic lunar month being 29½ days, the Babylonian month usually alternated between 29- and 30-day intervals. Occasionally two 29-day intervals follow and sometimes even three. Because 12 lunar months are about 11 days less than a true 365-day solar year, the months move out of proper sequence with the year. To prevent a complete breakdown an extra intercalary month was introduced every few years to balance things up.

Records of eclipses were kept by Babylonian 'astronomer-priest' scribes from the time of Nabonassar (-747). The names of a few of these scribes were recorded by the Classical writers, and some of them appear to have belonged to scribal guilds or families. Recognition of the 19-year Metonic cycle (235 lunar months = 19 solar years) dates from after $c.$ -450. It was also about this time that the zodiac—as we know it today—was invented.

In ancient Egypt we fare no better as regards our early search for true scientific astronomy. Eclipse prediction methods were not known at any period right up to the Ptolemaic period; indeed in all the written documents inherited from ancient Egypt there is very sparse reference to eclipses.

In all periods, however, the Egyptians were much concerned with calendars and time. From the earliest date we can glean references to the determination of time of night by star group risings from the decans. These are represented by the decanal (twelve-hour star-clock) paintings on coffin lids of the Middle Kingdom -2100 to -1800 (Fig. 17). Later, even more elaborate star-clocks appeared like those depicted in the Ramses' tombs. The early decanal star-clocks were continued as part of traditional decoration motifs long after their practical usefulness was lost for time-keeping. The old Egyptian star groupings are very difficult to reconcile with those inherited from Babylonia; only the constellations of the Great Bear and Orion, and the star

A facsimile of the round 'zodiac' or 'planisphere' of Dendera now in the Paris Louvre. This Egyptian star map, dating from the Ptolemaic period, provides a reconciliation of Greco-Babylonian constellation figures with ancient Egyptian asterisms (including the enigmatical decans), many of which go back to at least the third millennium BC. Much of this star map is schematic in form, but several Egyptian depictions can be identified. For example, the star Sirius is represented as a cow lying in a boat; the constellation of Orion is the royal figure standing under the Bull's hoofs. Note also the Ox's Foreleg (Ursa Major), *centre*. The position of the summer solstice is indicated by a hawk on a papyrus column. The decans (figures with stars) are seen portrayed along the circumference immediately inside the sky-sphere supported by gods and goddesses.

Sirius, have been identified beyond all reasonable doubts. The rest of the secrets of sky goddess Nut and her enigmatic decanal bands provide an interesting but at present unsolved puzzle to modern would-be decoders (Fig. 17).

The Egyptian calendar was strictly an agrarian one which consisted of three seasons each of four months. It began initially with the heliacal rising of Sirius because of the coincidence of the star's dawn rising with the flooding of the Nile—the prime event in Egyptian life. Although a rudimentary lunar calendar was also used in early periods, the year was based on the civil year composed of twelve months of thirty days each and five additional days at the end of each year. Sirius was known as Soth, and therefore the calendar based on it was called the Sothic year, or Sothic cycle. The trouble is that the 365-day calendar is really too short so that in an interval of 1,460 years the seasons shift entirely through the months. Nevertheless, it is from Egypt that we derive our modern calendar, but it is from Babylonian astronomy we derive the sexagesimal system (of minutes in the hour based on the number 60). The Egyptian calendar has been described as the only workable calendar invented by the ancient world. In Babylonian and even Hellenistic times, historians have great difficulty tracing back events because of calendar irregularities, whereas in Egyptian times the task is straightforward: one simply has to multiply the number 365 by the number of years required.

Contemporary with the Celtic-Druids of North-West Europe was the great period of Hellenic astronomy. It was the Hellenic period of science which provided a melting-pot for all the various astronomies inherited from the ancient world—chiefly those of the Near East.

The Greeks certainly had profound knowledge and interest in cyclic celestial phenomena and even constructed some fine differential planetaria-type machines to demonstrate the movements of celestial bodies like the ingenious device dated – 82 found by divers off Antikythera in 1900. Whether Celtic-Druidical calendrical astronomy was derivative of Central European, Greek or native British Megalithic astronomy no one can be sure. The later Anglo-Saxons are said to have gleaned their astronomy from Greek and Latin treatises which fell into their hands. Bede (the Venerable) showed great interest in astronomy, and his works were later translated by Alfred. One of the most intriguing astronomical references in Anglo-Saxon times is by Alcuin (+735 to +804), the Yorkshire-born adviser to Charlemagne, who described an astronomical diagram sent to him by Charlemagne 'which had a round form like a table, resembling the Sun'. Alcuin relates: 'it contained twenty-seven semicircles which if doubled would make fifty-four, and these were intended for marking out the lunar course'. Inside this was another circle supposedly representative of the rotundity of the Sun.

In ancient Chinese astronomy there is no scientific eclipse theory until Babylonian (and Greek) knowledge about lunar and solar ephemerides diffused, first to India and then to the East. However, with ancient Chinese astronomy we find a wonderful corpus of descriptive observational phenomena. Indeed, only from ancient Chinese records can we glean a clear record of periodic events and phenomena such as eclipses, comets and novae which are included in Sumerian and Babylonian astrological tablets but are there much garbled by astrological inferences.

In ancient China the Bureau of Astronomy was an integral part of a vast bureaucratic civil service whose traditions (fortunately) included a predilection for careful descriptive records. Eclipse records date back to − 1361, and these are the oldest eclipse records in any civilization that are verifiable. Between − 1400 and 1690 Chinese astronomers recorded details of more than ninety novae and supernovae. The earliest record is one preserved as a fragment of Shang oracle-bone (*c*. − 1400) which relates: 'On the 7th day of the month a *chi-ssu* day, a great new star appeared in company with Antares (Alpha Scorpius).' Comet records include more than 580 entries between − 1600 and 1600. Almost a millennium before the European astronomer Peter Apian noted that the great tails of brilliant comets always point away from the Sun, the Chinese had noted it in records dated +635. Apparitions of Halley's Comet have been traced back in Chinese records to − 467, and regular naked-eye sunspot observations were kept from − 28.

By *c*. − 1200 the Chinese were using a simple vertical pole (a gnomon) to measure the length of the Sun's shadows in order to determine the solstices and equinoxes. By night they observed star transits to fix the length of the sidereal year. It was also from about this period they began computation for the calendar.

Because China, like the other ancient civilizations, was an agrarian society, almost every Chinese mathematician and astronomer worked on calendar systems; between *c.* − 370 and 1742 about a hundred different calendars were developed, each one embodying astronomical events with ever-increasing accuracy.

Of the other great prehistoric civilizations such as that of the Indus Valley—which began between − 3000 and − 2500 and then inexplicably disappeared by *c.* − 1500—absolutely nothing is known about its astronomy. The pictogram script of the civilization itself still resists the combined efforts of international scholarship. Computer studies, however, have provided some provisional astronomical interpretations such as the signs for the planets linking them with signs for the gods. The early Indus Valley astronomy may have been incorporated into the later Dravidian astronomy of the Indian subcontinent. Nevertheless, so far these pictogram interpretations must be considered to be very tentative.

Finally, what knowledge of scientific astronomy did the civilizations of the New World possess? Once again when the corpus of evidence is stripped of its mythological and mystical trappings, there is precious little scientific evidence left. At least there is certainly nothing contained in New World astronomy to support the hyperdiffusionist theories of earlier Egyptian migrations. The wholesale destruction of Meso-American codices and stelae has robbed us of the key to gain real insights into pre-Columbian astronomy. We have seen that the Incas who had no writing had methods to determine a seasonal calendar according to the Sun (*see* above), but of all else such as the Inca star names and constellation patterns there are few records. The famous knotted cords—the quipus, or 'the recipes of the devil' as the Spanish priests called them—have frequently been cited as mnemonic devices which may hold profound astronomical and mathematical knowledge, but the sure interpretation of this so-called hidden knowledge has not been forthcoming.

One piece of unambiguous evidence in Meso-America is that provided by the great Aztec Calendar Stone, popularly known as 'Montezuma's watch', discovered near the cathedral in Mexico City. The stone is 3·6m (12 feet) in diameter and is both a magnificent piece of art and a marvel of primitive calendrical science (Fig. 103). It is cut from one large block of porous basalt and once took pride of place in a great Aztec temple. The stone shows a preoccupation with calendrical and life cycles which is the obsessional *leitmotif* running through the whole of Meso-American astronomy. It was believed that Nature operated in a

103 The Aztec Calendar (or Sun) Stone weighing over 20 tons and designed to symbolize the Aztec universe. Centre is Tonatiuh—the Sun, flanked by four cartouches providing the dates of the four previous ages of the world. Also included are the names for the twenty calendar days, symbols for the heavens, signs for stars, and two fire serpents representing the Year and Time.

series of rhythms or recurrences: night followed day; maturity, then death, relentlessly followed birth; there were the recurring seasonal cycles of spring, summer, autumn and winter that went on without stop; and in the sky the eternal swings of the Sun, Moon and planets personified the rhythms of the cosmos. The Aztec preoccupation was to discover all the rhythms and then study them; this led to a greater understanding of the purposes of all things; thus these rhythms were embodied in their calendar, and the stone itself reflected the whole of Aztec philosophy in its intricately carved face.

The great Aztec ceremonies took place in accordance with the rhythm dictated by the solar year consisting of eighteen months of twenty days and a five-day unlucky period. The preoccupation with an agrarian life is again manifest, for all the months had names relating to farming activities, e.g. Tlaxochimaco (IX)—the birth of flowers (22 July—10 August); Xocotlhuctzi (X)—the fall of the fruits (11 August—30 August). The great Calendar Stone shows lunar cycles: the Venus year of 584 days, which had important ritualistic significance, and several other planetary cycles. Aztec astronomer-priests knew the Pleiades well, and when these stars reached their highest point in the heavens, the priests would then declare it was a sign that the world would continue.

In the mythology of Meso-America, one of the most puzzling and confusing figures is that of Quetzalcoatl (the Feathered Serpent), god of Civilization and Learning and also identified with the planet Venus and the West. But just to confuse matters he is also depicted and interchangeable as a white Tezcatlipoca (the smoking Mirror) and associated with the East as the morning star. It is the ambiguous nature of Quetzalcoatl and his legend which led the early Spanish friars to formulate a myth that St Thomas the Apostle once visited Mexico in the guise of a white-bearded god. Much has been made of this legend and others like it involving a god from across the water and his subsequent promise to return one day (*see* note 22). Although Quetzalcoatl has been long associated with Venus as the evening star to the west and the morning star to the east, there is some probable confusion also with brilliant Sungrazing comets which suddenly appear near the Sun and often outshine Venus. Comet tails are often beard-like (the Greek name *kometes* means 'hairy star'); the dual association with the Smoking Mirror— Tezcatlipoca—is also indicative of a cometary association. In South America the Incas may sometimes have confused Venus with comets; they frequently spoke of the appearance of Venus as Chasca 'the Youth with the long and curling locks'—who was adored as a page of the Sun.

Among the Meso-American races the Maya probably had the most advanced astronomy which reached its peak between +250 and +1000. The Maya hieroglyphic script was highly developed; they had a notation for zero and a very accurate and elaborate calendar. Nevertheless, how the Maya actually made their observations has proved something of a mystery.

Only three Maya codices survive after the cultural rape of the Conquistadors. It is known that in July 1562, twenty-seven codices and 5,000 inscribed stelae were destroyed at the direction of Bishop Diego de Landa. The Maya are supposed for example to have had a glyph to signify a solar eclipse, but none has yet been deciphered. Only just over one-third of all the extant Maya glyphs have been interpreted with reasonable certainty. The Dresden *Codex* has been interpreted as containing part of a Venus tablet and/or a cycle of solar eclipses, but much of this codex is so obscure and overlain with mythological inferences that it is open to several interpretations (Fig. 104). It does, however, show that 405 lunar months = 11,960 days (present-day estimates = 11,959·1 days), demonstrating that Maya were only one day in error in thirty-three years. The Maya always used whole integral number

104 A facsimile rendering of the last page of the Dresden *Codex* showing three rivers pouring from the sky. The continuation of the crocodile body has been claimed to depict four constellation squares or possibly (left to right) the planets Venus, Mars, Mercury and Jupiter. At the start of the middle river may be the Maya glyph for a solar eclipse and from the right-hand river the glyph for a lunar eclipse. However, all the above interpretations are by no means certain.

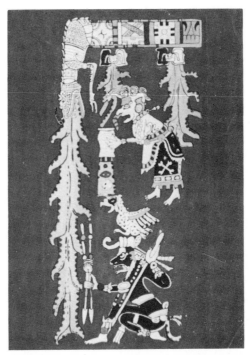

counts and had no fractions in their reckonings; this is again reflected in their lunar month count which was always twenty-nine or thirty days.

Through painstaking scholarship Maya lunar eclipse cycles have gradually been partly decoded. The Maya likely understood the regression of the lunar nodes and probably included a reckoning of node days when eclipses could occur. Indeed what we find in Maya lunar-eclipse-cycle reckoning (using whole day numbers) is at a level comparable to what one might expect to find in Megalithic societies in North-West Europe $c. -2000$. Further studies of Maya lunar-eclipse astronomy may be very fruitful in providing insights about primitive time-reckoning methodologies.

The Maya constructed remarkable cities and complex ceremonial centres with pyramids and so-called astronomical observatories staffed by an incumbent astronomer-priesthood. Whether their buildings were purpose-orientated to celestial bodies is far from certain. However, the Maya 'observatory' at Uaxactun in Guatemala does appear to be aligned for observation of the solstices and equinoxes. The 'observatory' at Chichen Itza is also supposed to be orientated so that specific celestial bodies made alignments to walls and passages.

The outstanding problem yet unresolved is to relate the exact dates of Maya and other pre-Columbian calendars to Julian dates. At present there are at least nine suggested correlation systems. Hopefully, perhaps somewhere in the jungles of Central America lies an inscription which when deciphered will enable this perplexing problem to be settled in a definitive manner.

Mixing metrology with archaeology has sometimes led to self-deception and untenable conclusions. Stukeley's 'Druid cubit', Smyth's 'Pyramid inch', and Flinders Petrie's 'Etruscan foot' are all examples where obsessional ideas took over in the face of common sense. Archaeology unfortunately is one of those disciplines vulnerable to the question: what is a fact? The nub of this problem was summed up by R. A. S. Macalister who wrote: 'Let an archaeologist once become obsessed with the idea that a defaced inscription must be read in a particular way... and he is lost, his eyes will follow the dictates of his mind.' For Macalister's archaeologist, one may substitute engineer,

astronomer, surveyor, mathematician or whatever other special
-ologist is appropriate to the situation. Petrie was fond of
recounting the story that he once found an enthusiastic disciple
of Smyth busily trying to file down the particularly significant
granite boss of the vestibule of the Great Pyramid to suit the size
that his theory demanded. Petrie, as we have seen, was himself
sometimes an over-enthusiastic metrologist tempted to play the
numbers game. On one occasion when recounting the
significance of the Egyptian royal cubit (20·62 inches) he threw
in for good measure the interesting fact that the diagonal of the
square of this cubit (the double remen) = 29·161 inches and 'is
almost exactly the natural length of a pendulum which swings
100,000 times a day; at the latitude of Memphis this would be
29·157 inches . . .'.

It was no doubt that this was the very story which gave rise to a
letter in *New Scientist* that suggested the length of the
Megalithic yard was perhaps determined by the discovery of
isochronism of the pendulum, i.e. employing suitable foresight
and backsight markers in the meridian for the successive
meridian passage of two specific stars. For example the MY
would give about 150 swings between the passage of Epsilon and
Zeta Orionis. In such a method the correspondent suggested
that the number of swings could be quoted for a rope of correct
length.

In an intentional anti-Pyramidological joke, Borchardt once
showed how to derive the base e of natural logarithms from the
angle of slope of the Sahure pyramid. Another numbers juggler
derived the Moon's diameter, the length of the lunar month,
plus the date of the building foundations by manipulating the
dimensions of the Temple of Artemis at Ephesos. Another well-
known numbers juggling trick is to show how frequently the
number 5 can be made to recur in facts and dimensions of the
Washington Monument. This kind of game can be played with
the architecture of any capital city in the world. Baring-Gould
wrote extensively on the fatality of numbers, and his fascinating
book, *Curious Myths of the Middle Ages* (1868), contains an
excellent nutshell study of this subject.

The coincidence-cum-numbers game can be played tongue-
in-cheek *or* deadly seriously as a matter of individual choice. At
Stonehenge, for example, the complex of stone circles and holes

provides several opportunities for speculation (refer to notes 23 and 24).

We have seen that a very strong case can be established for solar alignments in North-West European Megalithic monuments and some associated tombs. For the Moon also—especially at Stonehenge—alignments of a kind seemed proved beyond reasonable doubts. However, among the whole corpus of astronomical uses for Megalithic monuments the ideas advocating stellar alignments for star risings or settings seem to be the weakest of all. If we are to believe that the ancients knew the configurations of the stars and their risings and settings on very intimate terms—which I certainly feel can be assumed *a priori*—such permanent markers would have no practical use.

Nowhere else in the world can one find any real positive evidence for permanent alignments to *stars* for *practical* purposes. Dedication of a monument to a particular star rising, at a particular epoch, such as those cited by Lockyer and Penrose for Egypt and Greece, *may* be another matter, and this idea can perhaps claim a little verisimilitude on religious grounds. A star and planet spotter needs no horizon marker to guide him among the stars and help him anticipate the rising of any star or configuration still below the horizon. All necessary information can be quickly learned and then memorized. Any would-be stargazer sufficiently motivated can build up familiarity in a few seasons, and resort to star maps is only required to locate fainter objects not visible to unassisted eyes—even these fainter objects can soon be learnt with greater familiarity gained over several years.

In Egypt and Babylonia we find catalogues, pictorial star depictions and planispheres for time and calendar purposes which were the prototypes of modern star maps; but nowhere in Egypt and Babylonia can be found horizon azimuth markers for stars, and the same goes for both Middle and South America. The Australian Aborigines had a rich astro-mythological corpus and made wide usage of stars for calendar purposes simply by noting their presence and general orientation above or along the horizon, but neither these nor other Neoprimitives seemed to make use of man-made horizon markers (*see* note 25).

Looking back overall at Thom's work, several of his attempts at 'circle' reconstruction appear to be subjective exercises. With sites like Avebury, and if one assumes Megalithic units to have been more pragmatic modules such as the human pace, double pace, or fathom, alternative solutions readily offer themselves for consideration. However, it would be presumptious and premature for anyone yet to pass definitive judgement on any of Thom's work. No such judgement is possible until all his surveys and reconstructions have been repeated perhaps, independently, several times. Some of his ideas have great originality and provide well-reasoned solutions to long puzzled-over monuments. His ideas concerning solar and lunar alignments are the ones with most verisimilitude; his stellar alignments, like Lockyer's before him, have the least. But in spite of his immaculate methods, one is still left doubting the basic units he so readily manipulates—the Megalithic inch, yard, fathom, rod and their integral multiples that he uses in forming his geometric reconstructions. These have overtones of Stukeley's 'Druid cubit', Smyth's 'Pyramid inch', and Flinders Petrie's 'Etruscan foot'. The cautionary yesteryear warning of Macalister echoes repeatedly. Since studying Thom's work, it has always appeared strange to me that while the Egyptians and Babylonians were seemingly for ever chasing a more refined value of *pi*, Thom would have us believe that the Megalith builders would not face up to the reality of its incommensurability. Yet the recognition of incommensurabilies has always provided a singular challenge to the inquiring minds of *Homo sapiens*. Are we to suppose then that the Megalith builders were so different from the rest of mankind?

CHAPTER XIII

Megaliths in Retrospect

In the 1930s, the influential Gordon Childe fixed the beginning of the earliest European Neolithic about – 2700 and that of Britain and Scandinavia about – 2400. Thus after the long Mesolithic period, the Neolithic period for North-West Europe was but a short interval before the onset of the Bronze Age round – 1400. This idea became firmly entrenched for at least two decades.

However, on the evidence at present available it appears that farming arrived in Britain before – 4000. If large sea-going vessels were used by early Neolithic farmer-settlers to Britain, they have disappeared without trace, for remains of such vessels are unknown. Neither is it known how the new immigrants interacted with the incumbent Mesolithic population that had wandered in and out of Britain from mainland Europe until the landbridges were destroyed by the encroaching sea about – 6000.

Among Neolithic cultures in Northern Europe is the so-called Windmill Hill culture of Southern Britain, yet this certainly does not belong to the very earliest period of British Neolithic settlement. However, some of the earliest recognized British earthworks—the 'causewayed camps'—are certainly associated with the Windmill Hill peoples. These causewayed camps are somewhat of an archaeological puzzle. Although they are constructed as a large enclosure surrounded by interrupted ditches—which at first consideration is highly suggestive of a defence structure—they were more likely tribal gathering places, or enclosures (corrals) for keeping cattle. Also associated with the (longheaded) Windmill Hill people are the famous (orientated?) long barrows that contain multiple interments. The chalk Downs of Southern Britain were sites particularly favoured for long-barrow construction.

Other British Neolithic cultures have been termed Secondary Neolithic—a name coined to reflect the interchange of ideas, and domestic technology, between the incumbent 'native' British Mesolithic population and the 'primary' immigrant Neolithic Windmill Hill peoples. However, the basis underlying this idea has never been firmly established. Pottery attributed to the so-called Secondary Neolithic is often referred to as Peterborough ware, but there are several other pottery wares, subdivisions and styles detailed and described by archaeologists.

The great stone axe factory sites of Britain, best represented in Westmorland and Caernarvonshire, are also attributed to the Secondary Neolithic. The beginning of Megalithic tomb building is also placed within this period and was previously cited as being brought about by a generalized diffusionist-cum-religious influence. Even before the mid-1960s, several prehistorians were strongly advocating that the 'invention' of the idea of incorporating large stones in tomb construction in Europe had probably occurred independently to people more than once, and perhaps the first appearance in Northern Europe may have been a local innovation rather than something derived from an intrusive influence.

In the European Neolithic we still have the various mother-goddess fertility cultuses of the Upper Paleolithic and the Mesolithic. The tomb at Newgrange in Ireland shows various decorative spirals, chevrons and other motifs, but particularly significant are the lozenge oculi ('eye-goddess') motifs first manifest in an Upper Paleolithic context and suggesting a very long and widespread tradition of the earth-mother/nurse-cum-Venus-goddess fertility cults.

Between the British Neolithic and the Early Bronze Age Wessex Culture we find no sharp dividing line; instead there is at present an ill-defined transitional period which probably straddles the various construction phases at Stonehenge. The Bronze Age saw the so-called (round-headed) Beaker cultures and their barrows that are reckoned as defining the threshold of the Bronze Age in Western Europe. In particular the Beaker folk represent the transitional 'stone-to-bronze' horizon within the admittedly oversimple Three-Age system. It is believed that the Beaker folk first introduced bronze to Britain, but they are of course best remembered for their characteristic, attractively designed, fired drinking vessels found closely associated with

105 The West Kennet Long Barrow, Avebury. (a) Oblique aerial view from the south-east. (b) Interior, looking west.

Long barrows and other chambered tombs provide insight into the social/ funerary practices of the Megalith builders.

105c The Megalith facade of the Wayland's Smithy Chambered Long Barrow (Ashbury, Berks). Revised radiocarbon dates indicate an original construction date about − 3700 to − 3400.

105d Eye-goddess cult motifs engraved on drum-shaped chalk idols found in a round barrow at Folkton (East Yorks). *Inset right*: eye-goddess, lozenge, and spiral motifs from the chambered tomb at Newgrange.

their burials. Nevertheless, Beaker pottery is also sometimes contemporary with artefacts of the Secondary Neolithic, and the henge monuments.

The henge monuments are certainly some of the more puzzling features of the ancient British landscape. In 1963, the archaeologist Humphrey Case questioned the traditional interpretation of the so-called henges found in large numbers in Oxfordshire. Case believed that their primary use was as domestic settlements rather than ceremonial rings as the established view held them to be. It is often overlooked, however, that Gordon Childe, in the 1940s, had suggested habitation sites for the alleged 'ring-ditches'. In Oxfordshire alone there are several hundred henges-cum-ring-ditches, only recorded via the medium of air photography. The belief is now widely held that henges and ring-ditches likely represent settlement complexes of a kind relating to Late Neolithic seminomadic pastoral activities rather than to ceremonial features.* The problem of the henges and ring-ditches exemplifies the case that archaeologists as well as astronomers, in formulating ideas, often overlook the stark fact that the prime activity of most prehistoric societies was with economic/domestic matters. It seems that both archaeologists and astronomers are sometimes afflicted with the blinkered notion that almost everything ancient must have a ceremonial or be of a deeper 'scientific' purpose. This is nowhere more true than in studies of Sumerian, Egyptian and Babylonian societies where some astronomers see everything in terms of astronomy, mathematics and cosmology—while the texts themselves speak unambiguously and overwhelmingly of an ancient preoccupation with more mundane economic, domestic, or soci-political matters (*see* above).

The absence of dwellings on the British landscape suggests that pre-Bronze and later Iron Age Britons were pastoralists; the henges, ring-ditches and other large earthworks are the sole surviving traces of domestic/economic/agricultural activities. The undisputed fact that the once heavily grazed chalk Downs have eroded perhaps as much as 60cm (24 inches) in the last

---

*Construction-wise the ring-ditches were probably similar to ha-ha (hawhaw) sunken fence ditches (still encountered in some British country estates) which were dug to prevent cattle wandering about indiscriminately.

106 Silbury Hill, near Avebury: oblique aerial view from the east. Flinders Petrie once believed this to be a British pyramid.

4,000 years makes the search for British prehistory all that more difficult.

What then do the wood henges represent in the more ancient 'Megaxylic' culture which preceded and then overlapped with that of stone? Are henges 'observatories', temple sanctuaries, or dwelling places? What supreme purpose was played by the great Neolithic mound of Silbury Hill which Flinders Petrie once called, and truly believed was, a British pyramid: mute memorial to a chief, observatory platform, or special beacon site? Standing stones and circle stones may indeed be observatories in the manner suggested by various theories expressed in earlier chapters, but are there other, perhaps more plausible, suggestions for their usage? In spite of the corpus of evidence for the astronomical theories, no one at present can discount the ceremonial/phallic/fertility interpretations. Indeed comparative studies may weigh heavily in favour of these more simple, more mundane explanations (*see* note 26). The idea of connecting burial cairns and circles with phallic worship previously held wide support: it was believed that the circle itself could be interpreted as the yoni symbol and the menhirs composing it the linga. Megaliths found in Assam were certainly associated with a widespread fertility and phallic cult; alignments there have representations of male and female stones collected in groups. Menhirs in Assam are also associated with the dead and symbolic of the memory of the 'vital essence' of an enemy as well as that of a deceased clansman. In the same area it is of interest to note that the Cherama clan in the Naga Hills determined the calendar of their agricultural year by careful observation of the Sun rising along a distant range of jagged peaks which also enabled them to judge the solstices.

More than once the stone-laid great Avenue at Avebury has been given a sexual/fertility interpretation. The stones forming the Avenue have suggested selective pairings (male and female?)—each being of contrasting shape; a relatively upright pillar is opposed by a diamond-shaped one, erected with one of its points in the ground. The crudely carved mother or earth goddesses typified by those found at Windmill Hill, Grimes' Graves and Maiden Castle might also give support to an ancient preoccupation with sexual/fertility ideas. The Iron Age Hill-figure, the Cerne Man, has strong phallic/fertility overtones. However, in Western Neolithic Culutre such representations are rare, as are also chalk phalli closely associated with fertility cults. Archaeologists and anthropologists with a free-ranging imaginary apparatus akin to that of some of the astronomers feel equally entitled to indulge in speculative flights of fancy when they suggest that the Heel Stone at Stonehenge, and similar solar foresight markers elsewhere, are merely representative phallic symbols placed so to indicate the power of the Sun to rekindle life or stimulate birth when it rises above them at midsummer. In the same vein it has also been suggested that the trilithon and bluestone horseshoes at Stonehenge are symbolic of a womb with its opening orientated towards the Sun—the propagator of life; and that egg-shaped circles or 'rings' are built just so to represent eggs—the most original symbol of fertility and birth.

An archaeologist who could match the free-ranging imagery of astronomers was the late scholar T. C. Lethbridge who once taught Anglo-Saxon archaeology in Cambridge, and whom archaeologist colleagues now affectionately remember euphemistically as 'imaginative'. Some of his ideas were reminiscent of Alfred Watkins', especially those involving

107 A male and female pairing(?) in the West Kennet Avenue, Avebury.

108 b Menhir in Brittany.

Chalk fertility goddess of Neolithic age
a British site.

supposed discoveries of Hill-figures near Cambridge, plus other equally bizarre geomancies. In his last book, published after his death, *The Legend of the Sons of God* (1971), he put forward the suggestion that the sons of God cited in Genesis were Martians who landed (*Chariot-of-the-Gods*-style) at various places in the world and then were unable to get back home. According to Lethbridge, the Megalithic monuments of Cornwall and Brittany served as navigational beacons, and the Martians were guided to these by bioelectronic currents generated by excited human bodies engaged in ritual dance. But to be fair to Lethbridge, he did add the rider: 'This suggestion is probably quite enough to classify me as a "nut-case" to many readers. . . .' He also believed in the Geoffrey of Monmouth story about the bluestones coming from Ireland. Lethbridge claimed that the bluestones were from an outcrop of rock some 15 miles north of Dublin, but the original circle which they formed had been set up in Tipperary.

What the archaeological record can provide in a positive manner is an overall picture of the various funerary practices current in Neolithic society. In Western Britain the recurrent feature of graves is the provision of a stone or organic chamber, often covered by a large mound. This practice would have involved the community in a major call upon their manpower resources. However, it is obvious that many of the tombs were used in successive burials. Sometimes it is apparent that the tombs were remodelled to meet changing ideas and needs as occurred with henge and circle monuments. In Eastern England, where building stone was not normally available, the tombs were chambered with wood or turves. Both kinds of tomb, like the later Christian family vaults, permitted the deposition of bodies over a long period. As time went by, provision was made for more complex arrangements which probably reflect social changes rather than changes of fashion. These changes are manifest by an increase in the size of the chamber made by elongation and subdivision by pits, upright stones or posts.

The subdivided passage probably reflects ideas of new social divisions brought about by social evolution. What is conspicuously evident is that the burials show a selection of certain individuals. A statistical analysis of Neolithic burials has provided figures which, if taken at face value, would indicate only a few hundred people alive in Southern Britain at any given epoch. However, since the same epoch shows evidence of extensive farming—intensive enough in some locales to bring about widespread soil exhaustion and erosion—and evidence of vigorous communal activity, a much larger population is called for to account for it. From this it has been estimated that perhaps not more than 1 per cent of a given population at a particular epoch was privileged to be interred at death in a Neolithic monument. The rest presumably were disposed of after death in a manner not so far recognized through the archaeological field record.

Thus the evidence indicating tomb building for an elitist, privileged class reflects a strong motivation towards the maintenance of a hierarchical society. The skeleton material shows remains of men, women and children in numbers of roughly equal proportions. Infant remains are significantly few, which has been interpreted along the idea that very young children had no social status before reaching an optimum age. Based on the evidence above, it seems that some kind of dynastic society for North-West Europe is certainly a possibility. Beyond this, the archaeological record cannot help at present. But casting round for parallels in ancient Egypt, Babylonia and the Americas, it would not be unreasonable to assume that an important element of such a dynastic society might be an elitist astronomer-priest class whose intellectual level was similar to claims already made for the Megalith builders.

For the British Neolithic we have seen that some evidence for seasonal/fertility representations is provided by the 'Venus' figurines found at several localities (see above), but what about other evidence of the kind cited by Marshack for Upper Paleolithic sites—the so-called numerate evidence provided by representations on bone showing 'lunar counts'? In a numerate Neolithic British society as envisaged by Thom, Hawkins, Newham and Hoyle, one might expect to find some smaller artefacts which might support the ideas for the architectural evidence. It can be argued plausibly that any contemporary tallies made of wood would have long rotted away. But what about reindeer bone? Such bones have been recovered from Stonehenge and Avebury, but these are recognized as implements and show no indication of numeration.

However, at a henge site at Maxey, near Peterborough, two

decorated red-deer antlers were found. Both had been worked to some degree, and the signs of abrasion are still visible. Their most interesting features are criss-cross (chevron) decorations formed by shallow incisions with V-shaped profiles filled with red ochre; none of the patterns continue beyond the deliberately broken ends. A third object is an artefact made from the rib of a deer decorated on its inner and outer surfaces with incised chevrons containing carbonaceous paint-like material. On the rib are also found some scratches and other marks of abrasion which may be due to its preparation for a subsequent function.

When these objects were found, it was suggested that their association with a 'sacred' monument perhaps indicated they served some ritual purpose, but the chevron patterns are not very dissimilar to those found on prehistoric and modern artefacts claimed as representing notation aids. By stretching credulity to its limits, one may even go so far as to read into them representations of quarter or half lunar month counts. Although chevron motifs do not appear on isolated menhirs, in circles, or in avenues, they do appear on stones in several burial chambers.

Strong supporting evidence for a high level of social organization in the Megalithic culture of Britain has long been that provided by the transport of the bluestones from South Wales to Salisbury Plain. When in 1923 H. H. Thomas traced, in brilliant fashion, the *in situ* home of the bluestones to the Prescelly Mountains, everyone thought that Judd's old glacial theory had received its final death blow. In 1971, however, the issue was again raised in the pages of *Nature* when G. A. Kellaway—in a reassessment—maintained there was strong evidence to show that the bluestones had come to Salisbury Plain, and the sarsens to nearby Stonehenge, via ice deposition.

Kellaway had studied the various glacial problems in Southern Britain over several years and claimed that when the 'Anglian' (Elster) ice invaded the Bristol Channel, the Mendip and Cotswold hills were largely overridden. From this Middle Pleistocene ice-thrust, sarsens and other foreign erratics were deposited along and beyond a line joining the southern extreme of the Quantock Hills, Stanton Drew, Bath and the northern edge of the Marlborough Downs (Fig. 109). But Kellaway himself pointed out, 'Anglian' is a rather unfortunate name in this context owing to its link with the East Anglian succession.

The Anglian ice sheet also invaded the coastal region of Hampshire and Sussex *from the west* carrying sarsens and large 'foreign' erratics.

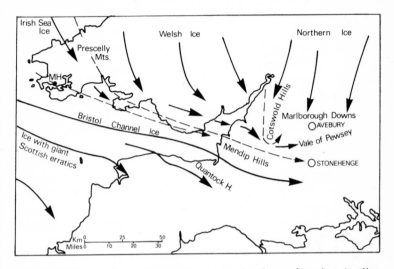

109 Sketch-maps of South-West Britain showing how advancing Anglian (Elster) ice may have brought bluestones and sandstones from the Prescelly Mountains and Milford Haven (MH) districts in South Wales to the Stonehenge area (after G. A. Kellaway).

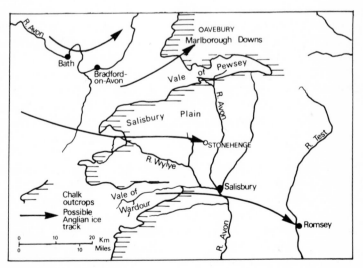

At one time a theory was forwarded that the bluestones once composed a venerated stone circle at Cil-maen-llwyd on the south-eastern slopes of the Prescelly Mountains. This idea was held by H. H. Thomas himself who speculated it was from this site the stones had been subsequently transported overland to Stonehenge. Later this earlier circle theory was abandoned, and the idea formulated that the bluestones had been loaded on some kind of raft at Milford Haven and from there transported by sea to Stonehenge via the Bristol Channel and River Avon (Fig. 45).

In addition to the ideas for the mode of transportation for the bluestones, Kellaway also strongly challenged the idea that the sarsens forming Stonehenge had been dragged cross-country from the Avebury area. One plausible belief long held was that the overland transport of sarsens might well have been eased by hauling them during winter over frozen ground, but the knowledge that during the later Neolithic the winter climate was substantially warmer than at present did not lend much support to this idea.

Archaeologists as a body are strongly attached to their now traditional idea that the bluestones were brought by sea from Milford Haven and they would be extremely reluctant to see it superseded. From a geological point of view Kellaway's ideas do have some verisimilitude and at present cannot be entirely discounted. In dismissing Kellaway's ideas out of hand, as some archaeologists have been inclined to do, they seem unaware of or ignore the very sketchy dry land record of the Pleistocene—especially of the Lower and Middle Pleistocene. Only the last glaciation, the Devensian, or Weichselian, is reasonably well known; those that went before it and the long, warmer interglacial periods between the various great ice thrusts are in some respects lost in antiquity as much as the great ice ages of remoter Precambrian time.

In the context of Megalithic prehistory the late Bronze and Iron ages appear less important, except that it is in the Middle or Late Bronze Age when perhaps a cultural decline overtook British society, and the traditions of the early Megalithic culture—including its astronomical knowledge—were lost. For the prehistorians the problem of demarking the Middle Bronze Age is focused on pottery and bronze weapons. It was often suggested in the past that the key to understanding the Middle and Late Bronze Age in Britain, and penetrating the obscure mists surrounding it, is the sudden end of the Mycenaean civilization around – 1200. But now that Britain has been divorced from Mycenaean influence by the New Archaeology, one has to think again. It is probable the prehistoric British societies were affected by the gradual decline of the climate that had reached its thermal optimum (several degrees above that of the present) $c.$ – 4000. This certainly would influence Late Bronze Age farming activities which in conjunction with two or three millenniums of overgrazing and over-intensive agricultural pursuits on the cleared uplands of Britain brought about a deterioration in the fertility of the soil. There is indeed strong evidence that the moors and uplands now encroached by bracken, heather and peat-bog were once areas subject to intensive prehistoric agrarian activities. . . . It was at the end of the British Neolithic and the beginning of the Bronze Age when great changes occurred in the British landscape. When Neolithic man began to farm the uplands of Britain $c.$ – 4000, some of these regions were not the bleak heaths and moorlands that we know today. At this time Britain was covered by a great primeval forest which extended to a height of 540m (1,800 feet). In Ireland and Scotland particularly there are remains of trees much larger than any now found in the neighbourhood. Apart from secular climatic changes that brought a deterioration, Neolithic farmers likely helped along the metamorphosis of woodland to peatland which, when it ran its full course, drastically changed the British landscape. Peat accumulates when fibrous vegetable matter is not broken down by microorganisms such as happens when the soil becomes waterlogged. This probably occurred on the uplands in prehistoric times as rainfall increased and the tree-cover disappeared both through man's intervention and climatic factors. This decline began when the British climate was becoming wetter and colder—a period now known to palaeoecologists as the 'elm decline'. The intensification of farming, the effects of ploughing, cattle overgrazing and population pressures were all likely contributory factors.

In Europe generally excavations today down through the peat to the old forest level reveal many articles dating from the Bronze Age, including dwellings and timber corded roads. In Ireland, Bronze Age cairns are frequently found resting on bedrock covered by several feet of bog. Recent field excavations in the west of Ireland have brought to light a whole complex of field systems complete with stone walls dividing off separate fields, all of which had been hidden by a peat-bog for over three millenniums.

This discovery suggests that stone circles at present encumbered by peat deposits might provide suitable subjects for careful excavation. Here tell-tale information about how circle geometry was established may still be present—cocooned below protective layers of peat. At the Callanish monument the depth of accumulated peat removed in 1858 was 1·5m (5 feet). It completely buried the cairn which shows that the accumulation followed the erection and then probably the abandonment of the stones.

When the British farming economy collapsed, did its long-established chieftainships and elite priestly hierarchies also collapse with it? Or was a cultural decline induced by other factors such as outbreak of plague or disease which decimated a native population?

Voltaire's quip 'History is a fable which has been agreed upon' is probably nowhere more true than in respect to traditional accounts of British prehistory. Colin Renfrew, an ardent disciple of New Archaeology, believes that the whole of British prehistory needs to be completely rewritten. But the interpretation of the New British prehistory must rest firmly on chronology rather than speculative fancies. Megalithic astronomy via Thom's work on solstitial and lunar sites has already provided, independent of radiocarbon dating, several epochs when sites were supposedly in operation. Nevertheless, for good reason archaeologists are reluctant to accept construction dates based on astronomical alignments. It seems likely that Thom's early estimates are too recent when related to the newer radiocarbon dates. At the same time archaeologists themselves must not forget that astronomy can play a key role in chronological dating. It was Epping and Strassmaier who determined (via the decipherment of astronomical tables in cuneiform tablets) the correct zero point of the Late Babylonian Seleucid Era and that of the Parthian Era and provided historians for the first time with a real chronological basis for the history of Mesopotamia after Alexander the Great.

One of the outstanding puzzles of later British prehistory

concerns the role of the Iron Age Celtic Druids who arrived in Britain late in the first millennium BC. Were they heirs-apparent to a decadent British Megalithic astronomy as some would still have us believe? The discovery of Iron-Age pottery at Stonehenge has in the past suggested even to sceptical archaeologists that in a dying phase Stonehenge was administered by an immigrant Celtic priesthood. It would be ironic indeed if Stukeley's long-discredited, romantically inspired Druidical incumbancies at Stonehenge and Avebury were one day proved real enough.

Although in the future some of the lost or now obscure British and European Megalithic prehistory might well be resolved into a more factual picture by the combined interdisciplinary efforts of archaeologists, astronomers and others, the human ingenuity which created the system as a whole may always lie beyond conjecture simply because the creative orderly minds that evolved it have quitted the landscape for ever. It is difficult to follow the workings of the human mind even when the man is alive and in the flesh before us. It is infinitely more difficult then to reconstruct his mind when the skull that held his brain has been empty for upwards of five millenniums. In the end our twentieth-century enquiry, like that of Aubrey before us, is still, alas, 'a gropeing in the Dark'.

finis

Supplementary Notes

Note 1   p. 12

When necessity requires it, celestial orientation is an art quickly learnt even by modern Europeans. In the Australian Outback the stars were frequently utilized by early prospectors and overlanders to guide them over large tracts of difficult, waterless terrain when travelling in the cool of night. In Western Australia, the township of Southern Cross was founded by gold-miners who had learnt to use the Southern Cross as a directional aid. Today all the streets retain astronomical names to perpetuate the township's origin. In Ballarat, Victoria, it was the familiar Southern Cross which was symbolically raised on the miners' standard during the incident of the Eureka Stockade and the reason why this configuration of stars now dominates the Australian national flag. Elsewhere in Australia the Magellanic clouds (Nubecula Major and Minor) are still known—more familiarly—as 'the Drovers' Friends' because they unerringly helped guide the overlanders when they moved their herds at night to escape the heat of the day.

Note 2   p. 29

It is interesting to note that mnemonic devices made of wood and similar in appearance to Upper Paleolithic 'tallies' were well-known objects during the eighteenth and nineteenth centuries at the time of the great canal- and railway-building projects in Britain. Gangs of Irish navvies bought their own food and contracted cooks to prepare it. These cooks were usually quite illiterate people and kept track of individual ownership of victuals by an elaborate system of nicks cut into a wooden slat. In this way the cook knew at any time the ownership of every item of food in the communal store-cupboard under his charge. The question arises, what will future archaeologists make of such interesting finds lying uncatalogued in the dusty vaults of some industrial archaeological museum!

Note 2a   p. 29

Inscribed tally marks from European Upper Paleolithic contexts certainly also remind one of the oghamic inscriptions which later appear to have been peculiar to the Celtic populations of the British Isles. The origins of the oghams are uncertain. Some believe it was a criptic script imported from the east, or from Iberia. Others subscribe to the idea that the whole of the oghamic alphabet was invented (or utilized) by the Druids as a secret code for private signalling. There appears to be some affinity between oghams and the telegraphic signalling system used by Roman armies, and oghams also seem allied to the later runes of North-West Europe.

302

The oghams were employed for writing messages and letters usually on wooden staves, occasionally on shields, and for carvings on tombstones. The alphabet was very simple and consisted of twenty letters represented by straight or diagonal strokes. Many of the oghamic inscriptions surviving are bilingual (Latin/Celtic), and oghams were written with Roman characters alongside. There is also an interesting runic/oghamic inscription from the Isle of Man. However, with only one exception, Irish inscriptions are in oghams only. Both oghamic and later runic inscriptions were frequently involved in a kind of 'number magic' which so far has remained incomprehensible to modern epigraphists. It is of interest that the use of rune characters for calendar sticks was maintained in Scandinavia until comparatively recent times. It is an intriguing thought that the Celtic-Druid oghams may trace their origin to a distant prehistory—back to the European Upper Paleolithic. There is scope in this direction for some enterprising student of epigraphy to re-examine the whole question of the origins of oghams.

Oghams inscribed on an artefact from a British site.

Note 3 p. 44
One of the earliest references to Greywethers is contained in Colonel Richard Symonds diary in the year 1644, when in November the king's army was camped near Marlborough at Fyfield '. . . a place so full of a grey pibble stone of great bigness as is not usually seen . . . the inhabitants calling them Saracen's stones; you may goe upon them all the way. They call that place the Grey-wethers, because a far far off they looke like a flock of sheepe'.

Note 4 p. 53
John Webb was Inigo Jones' son-in-law. It was John Webb who collected and published his father-in-law's notes and drawings in book form three years after Inigo Jones' death in 1655. When in 1663 Walter Charleton forwarded the idea that Stonehenge was built by the Danes, Webb returned to the attack and two years later published his vindication for a Roman origin.

Note 5 p. 56
Among classical references, Caesar, in *De Bello Gallico*, book 6 (borrowing from Posidonius $c. -135$ to -50), attributed much knowledge to the Druids. They taught 'many things concerning the stars, and their motions; the size of the world and its countries; the nature of things; and the force and power of the immortal gods'.

In Pliny's account we learn that mistletoe was sacred if it 'vegetated from the oak' (see also Frazer's *The Golden Bough*). The Druids selected groves of oaks, and thought everything was sent from heaven which grew on this tree. Pliny writes that on the sixth day of the Moon—which began the Druids' months and years and their 'long count' period of thirty years—they came to the oak 'on which they observed any of the parasitical plant which they called all-healing'. Under the venerated tree they prepared a sacrifice and feast. Two white bulls were brought forth, whose horns were first tied. The officiating Druid in a white robe climbed the tree and with a golden knife pruned off the mistletoe, which was received in a white woollen cloth below. The victims were then sacrificed, and the Druids addressed their gods to make the mistletoe prosperous for those to whom it was given. Pliny recounts that they believed it 'caused fecundity' and was an amulet against poison. He says that the Druids were superior in knowledge to the rest of the nation; they were present at all religious rites; they obeyed one chief who had supreme authority over all; and some Druids took twenty years to acquire their education. It was conceived unlawful to commit their knowledge to writing. As a font of Druidical knowledge and customs, Pliny tells us they taught that the soul never perished but passed at death into other bodies—thus all fear of death in them was removed.

Note 6   p. 60
Penrose was twenty years Lockyer's senior. At Cambridge, in the 1840s, he was friendly with the author Charles Kingsley, the prominent Christian socialist J. M. Ludlow and the mathematician John Couch Adams who, independent of the Frenchman Leverrier, predicted the planet Neptune discovered in 1846. By training, Penrose was primarily an architect, but his many interests took in archaeology, sundial construction and astronomy, all of which provided a stimulus for his later work on determining the so-called astronomical orientations in Greek temples.

Note 7   p. 66
(*Note clarifying the relationship of declination to observed horizon azimuth*):
The rising or setting azimuths measured (clockwise) from true north for an astronomical body for a particular observer are determined primarily by the observer's latitude and by the declination of the body.

The declination (Dec) of an astronomical body is the celestial analogue of terrestrial latitude (the celestial analogue of terrestrial longitude is Right Ascension (RA) which can be measured in hours, minutes and seconds (time) or in angular measure (*see* Star map Fig. 37)). Declination is measured as an angular measurement above (+ plus) or below (– minus) the celestial equator (0°).

Because of the inclination of the Earth's axis (the obliquity of the ecliptic), the Sun appears to move annually (owing to the revolution of the Earth round the Sun) between the two tropics—from declination $+23 \cdot 5°$ in the northern mid-summer to a declination of $-23 \cdot 5°$ in the northern midwinter along a path traced out by the ecliptic (shown in Fig. 37). This has the effect of changing the position of sunrise and sunset (rising and setting azimuths) for an observer at any point on the Earth's surface. To an observer at Stonehenge (latitude 51° 11′ N) these shifts show as a sunrise shift from true azimuth 129°

(at midwinter solstice; Sun declination − 23·5°) to true azimuth 51° (at midsummer solstice; Sun declination + 23·5°). Thus in *six months* the sunrise point swings along the horizon at Stonehenge by 78°. Since the Moon's orbit is inclined to the ecliptic by a little over 5°, the Moon's rising and setting points show even greater extremes of horizon azimuth swing during the Moon's monthly journeys round the sky and the slow regression of the nodes over 18·61 years (*see* Fig. 52).

Over the short time-scale, stars rise and set at a fixed azimuth for an observer. However, a shift of the star sphere, altering a star's declination, does occur, i.e. over 26,000 years giving rise to the precession of the equinoxes (*see* Figs. 32, 36 and 37), but such star declination shifts cannot be detected by the visual observer over a single human life-span.

The true azimuth at which any celestial body will rise and set at any latitude, given its declination, can be calculated by the use of simple trigonometric formulae (viz. the astronomical triangle Z.P.S.) found in standard astronomical textbooks. However, field corrections need to be applied such as refraction, parallax, elevation of horizon, air temperature and, in the case of an observation relating to the upper or lower limbs of the Sun and Moon, the semi-diameter.

Note 8   p. 62

J. W. Judd was Lockyer's colleague at the Normal School of Science (later the Royal College of Science) at South Kensington where Lockyer was Director of the Solar Physics Observatory. Judd wrote a popular book on volcanoes and was the author of the best-selling *The Students' Lyell*, which went through edition after edition.

We can gain a glimpse of Judd through the eyes of H. G. Wells who, while himself a student at the Normal School of Science, studied geology under him. In his *Experiment in Autobiography* (1934), Wells relates that Judd was an amateur in teaching science and bored him 'cruelly'. He described him as 'a slow, conscientious lecturer with a large white face, small pale blue eyes, a habit of washing his hands with invisible water as he talked, and a flat assuaging voice'. Unlike T. H. Huxley—another of Wells' lecturers—whom Wells greatly admired as one of the giants of the nineteenth century, 'Judd insisted not merely on our learning, but learning precisely in his fashion . . . just as a Judd would have done'. It was Judd, Wells recounted, who killed off further ideas of his following a scientific career, but trying to be fair recalled: 'I am told that not only was Judd's work in stratigraphy sound and patient and excellent but that he was a very good and pleasant man to know. But I never knew him and my antipathy was immediate.'

Note 9   p. 83

The Golden Bough grew on a certain tree in the sacred grove of Diana at Arica, and the priesthood of the grove was held by the man who succeeded in breaking off the Golden Bough and then slaying the priest in single combat.

The priest in question represented the god of the grove—Virbius—and his slaughter was regarded as the death of the god. It was this that raised the question about widespread customs of killing men and animals regarded as divine. Frazer collected many examples of this custom and proposed a new explanation of it. . . . It was Frazer's belief that the Golden Bough was mistletoe, and the whole legend could be connected with the Druidical reverence for mistletoe and the human scarifices which (supposedly) accompanied their worship; it could also be connected with the Norse legend of the death of Balder. Frazer used his Golden Bough researches to lead on to a new explanation of the meaning of totemism, ancient mythology and custom; he introduced subjects such as taboo exogamy and the worship of Nature. He showed the origin and source of divine kingship and other long-standing human customs in the context of widespread social and cultural patterns. When published, Frazer's *The Golden Bough* marked a turning point in anthropological studies. It forced the scholars of the older literary tradition to enlarge their vision and look afresh at classical writings.

Note 10   p. 87
Because of his consuming interest in Celtic-Druidical matters, Lockyer attended the 1907 Eisteddfod—the Welsh national bardic congress—held in Swansea. The organizers were so pleased with Lockyer's interest that they conferred on him the title 'Gwyddon Prydain', Britain's Man of Science. It was also about this time that someone suggested that he might be addressed as 'Your Solar Prominence'.

Note 11   p. 123
That the Celtic-Druids possessed 'scientific' calendars now seems beyond doubt. One of these, the Coligny Calendar, consists of fragmentary remains of a great bronze plate measuring 150cm × 100cm (5 feet × 3½ feet) engraved with a sequence of sixty-two consecutive lunar months and two 'intercalary' months. This plate was found at Coligny near Bourg-en-Bresse (Ain) and is believed to be Augustan in date. Although the letters and numerals are in Roman characters, the language employed is Gaulish.
    In format it reckons by the night and includes lucky and unlucky days and is divided into half-months. The incommensurability of the lunar and solar year is adjusted by the insertion of intercalary months of 30 days at alternate 2½- and 3-year intervals. Claims have been made that it either relates to the 30-year cycle cited by Pliny (*see* note 5) or the Greco-Babylonian 19-year Metonic-style cycle.
    The Celtic peoples of Central Europe also possessed circular calendrical monuments and devices which appear to have been destroyed in Roman times.

Note 12   p. 128
A Babylonian tablet containing a prayer of Ashurbanipal (*c.* – 668) relates: 'O Adad, the prince of heaven and earth, at whose command mankind was created, speak thou the word and let the gods take their stand by thee . . . I make my petition unto thee and I ascribe praise unto thee because the evil which followeth the eclipse of the Moon and the hostility of the powers of heaven and evil portends are in my palace and in my land. . . .'

Note 13   p.162
Boyle Somerville, in 1912, recounted that he himself had been led into the investigation of Megalithic monuments chiefly through reading Sir Norman

Lockyer's well-known book *Stonehenge* at a time and place he wrote:
'. . . when I was within easy reach of several prehistoric monuments, being
then engaged on a hydrographic survey of Lough Swilly, on the north coast of
Ireland, the shores of which offer a rich field for archaeologists. This was in
1908; and, since then, I have had opportunity of examining over 60 of these
ancient ruins, of all descriptions, in Scotland and Ireland, with the result that I
am now fully convinced of the reality of the existence of orientation. I will even
go further, and say that in my belief no one with a technical knowledge of
practical astronomy and surveying, who takes the trouble to go into the field to
examine for himself, could long remain in doubt on the matter.'

Near Lough Swilly, Drumhallach, Somerville found a remarkable group of
avenues at a place called the Giant's Bed. The Giant's Bed consists of a ruined
chambered tomb, and Somerville claimed that the remains of the five avenues
associated with it were supposedly orientated to sunrise at the summer solstice.
He also claimed the construction of the avenues indicated a date of – 1400 if
these were related to the first gleam of the Sun.

Note 13a   p. 162
At Callanish (Callernish), Somerville noted five avenues, one of which points
true north, another west. Two avenues, or stone rows, are orientated to the
north-east, and a single row to a lower point in a north-easterly direction.
Lockyer had several passages referring to this monument in his *Stonehenge*. He
related how in 1858 Sir James Matheson took steps to remove the peat which
had accumulated on the site after it was abandoned in prehistoric times. The
measurement of the accumulated peat-depth at a monument suggests itself as
a novel method of dating British and Irish Megalithic monuments—analogous
with the varve method used in establishing Alpine and Scandinavian
chronology. At Callanish the depth of accumulated peat was up to 1·5m
(5 feet); in the process of removing it the workers uncovered the remains of a
circular chambered cairn (a circle of thirteen stones with an orientated stone).
Lockyer believed that the cairn was related to an alignment for the Pleiades in
– 1330; this he claimed would give an advance warning of the May sunrise by
1¼ hours.

Stukeley, who believed that all avenues were related to serpent worship, also
interpreted a snake configuration at Callanish (as he had done at Avebury). He
wrote: 'I saw another [avenue] at Shap, in Westmorland . . . There is another,
as I take it, at Classeness [Callanish], a village in the island of Lewis between
Scotland and Ireland. I took a drawing of it from Mr Lwydd's travels; but he
was a very bad designer . . . a part of the snake remains going from it, which
he calls an avenue. He did not discern the curve of it any more than that of
Kennet Avenue which he also has drawn in the same collection as a straight
line.'

Both Thom and Hawkins also surveyed Callanish—which has been
nicknamed the 'Stonehenge of the North'. At Callanish, Hawkins measured
ten alignments with the Sun and Moon at their extreme positions. Callanish is
a remarkable site in many ways. By virtue of its high latitude the Full Moon
stands only 1° above the southern horizon once in eighteen or nineteen years.
After his own survey, Hawkins claimed that the alignments at Callanish are set
out more accurately than those at Stonehenge.

Note 14   p. 162
Before Lockyer's interest, A. Lewis had paid close attention to British stone circles and wrote voluminously about them in several journals particularly the *Archaeological Journal*, the *Journal of the Royal Anthropological Institute* and *Nature* in the period 1878—1914. Lewis was one of the first to introduce a system of circle classification. He recognized three main types of stone rings, but in addition he also cited Sun and star circles and temples. Lewis was one of the first to draw attention to a great preponderance of outlying stones positioned towards the north-east quadrant of circles. It is unfortunate that much of Lewis' pioneer field work has been overlooked by those who followed him.

Note 15   p. 208
Sabine Baring-Gould (1834—1924) was one of those remarkable larger-than-life individuals that enriched the Victorian scene. He was a polymath with some very diverse talents which in more modern times would have damned him in academic circles. As an author he was responsible for at least 140 books. At various times he was parson, squire, traveller, archaeologist, folksong collector, historian and popular novelist. Between 1872 and 1889 he laboured continuously on his seventeen-volume project *The Lives of the Saints*. As a lyricist he wrote the words to the famous hymn 'Onward Christian Soldiers' and the well-known evensong 'Now the Day is Over'.

Note 16   p. 228
Somerville investigated the orientation of numerous barrows—particularly chambered barrows—including several in Brittany. In Britain the largest barrow is the West Kennet chambered long barrow south of Silbury Hill. Lockyer himself was sure that this was another example of orientation with the May and August sunrise and the May year, and he believed it provided another argument in favour of Avebury and the whole region hereabouts having connections with the May year.

   The barrow was excavated in 1955—6 by Stuart Piggott and Atkinson. The gallery is walled and roofed with massive slabs of sarsen 2·4m (8 feet) high, extending 12m (40 feet) into the mound. In the gallery more than thirty skeletons were found. Unlike the barrow at Newgrange (Fig. 93) the sarsens are undecorated.

Note 17   p. 228
Of great interest in a similar context is the Big Horn ('Megalithic') Medicine Wheel located in the Big Horn Mountains of northern Wyoming whose construction has been attributed to earlier nomadic Plains Indians (either the Crow, Sioux, Arapahoe, Shoshone or Cheyenne). The so-called wheel consists of an imperfect circle of loose stones *c*. 25m (80 feet) in diameter. The central cairn is the 'hub' of the wheel from which twenty-eight unevenly spaced spokes are connected to the outer rim of stones. In addition five smaller cairns, each consisting of an open circle 1 to 1·5m (3 to 5 feet) in diameter and several stone courses high, are spaced at irregular intervals along the circumference of the wheel. A sixth cairn of similar construction is located *c*. 4m beyond the larger rim on an alignment extended from a south-westerly

directed spoke (Fig. 110).

In 1974, John A. Eddy published an intriguing account (*Science*, 7 June 1974, Vol 184, Number 4141), in which he claimed that the Big Horn Wheel might be astronomically orientated. As a result of surveys he made in 1972—3, Eddy derived possible alignments for the Sun (solstice sunrise and sunset), Aldebaran (a heliacal rising for summer solstice), and others for Rigel and Sirius. The twenty-eight spokes he believed could have been significant in use as day counters to track lunar months.

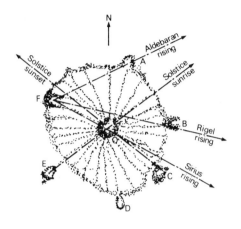

110 The Big Horn Medicine Wheel, northern Wyoming. (a) Plan view showing a summary of possible azimuths through various cairns (A; B; C; E; F; and O). (b) View of the Medicine Wheel horizon azimuth in direction E—O (± 1°5).

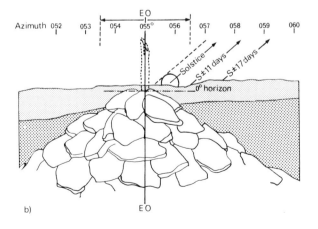

b)

Eddy claimed that the Big Horn Wheel, as a two-dimensional interpretation, resembles the well-known Sun Dance Lodge (the Medicine Lodge [Medicine synonymous with 'magic' or 'supernatural']) where the Indian Sun Dance was traditionally performed in June at the time of the summer solstice (interpreted by the Indians as the time when the Sun was highest and the growing power of the world strongest).

Nevertheless, strong doubts about the archaeological origins of the Medicine Wheel have been forwarded. Eddy, from the evidence, cited a date of around 1700 (dendrochronological evidence indicates 1760). However, others have suggested whatever its antecedents, the entire structure was redesigned and relaid by U.S. Forest Rangers using different stone, sometime between the period 1931 and 1955. Some have questioned whether the nomadic Indians of the Plains knew enough astronomy to design such a structure. It has been argued that perhaps this knowledge came north from Mexico by an *infusion* of astronomical ideas; then later, during the nineteenth century, with the spread of white settlers into the northern plains, the Indian culture declined and with it was lost the method of using this Megalithic calendar monument.

In the follow-up correspondence to Eddy's account in *Science*, one writer suggested intriguingly that the twenty-eight spokes in the wheel might possibly have functioned in a similar manner to the fifty-six Aubrey holes at Stonehenge—as a kind of eclipse-season computer operated by the Plains Indians—but no one has yet shown convincingly how this would function.

Note 18   p. 242

The legend associated with the Rollright stones is that a certain king set forth at the head of an army to conquer England, but as he advanced up the hill, the witch who owned the ground appeared. Just as he approached the crest of the hill from where the village of Long Compton should have been visible—she halted him with the words: 'Seven long strides shall thou take' and—

> *If Long Compton thou canst see*
> *King of England thou shalt be*

At this the King cried out:

> *Stick, stock, stone*
> *As King of England I shall be known*

. . . and strode forward seven paces. However, instead of Long Compton there rose up before him a long earthen mound, and the witch replied:

> *As Long Compton thou canst not see*
> *King of England thou shalt not be*
> *Rise up, stick, and stand still, stone,*
> *For King of England thou shalt be none;*
> *Thou and thy men hoar stones shall be*
> *And I myself an eldern tree*

Thus the King became transfixed into a single stone (the 'King Stone') and his men formed a circle. The stones of the neighbouring burial chamber, the 'Whispering Knights', are said to be 'traitors' who, when the King with his army hard by was about to engage with the enemy, withdrew themselves privily apart and were plotting treason together when they were turned into stone by the witch.

An alternative version has it that all the stones are at prayer. Yet another story says that they cannot be counted. At midnight the 'King Stone' and the 'Whispering Knights' are supposed to go down to drink at a spring in Little Rollright spinney. At precisely the same hour the stones of the circle are said to become men again, join hands and dance in the air.

Note 19   p. 246
Penn parish church has been added to over nine centuries and includes in its structure sarsen stone, Roman brick and flints and clunch from Saxon and Norman times. Among famous families associated with it are the Spencer-Churchills, the Hampdens and the Penns. It has royal connections with William the Conqueror, his half-brother, Bishop Odo of Bayeux, Henry VIII, Elizabeth I, Edward VI, Queen Anne, William IV and Queen Adelaide.

William Penn, the founder of Pennsylvania, claimed Penn as his ancestral village. The Penn family have been buried for over six centuries in the vaults below the chancel. William Penn's sons, Thomas and Richard, buried six of their children in another large family vault below the church.

Note 20   p. 251
In his book *Stonehenge of the Kings* (1967) Patrick Crampton wrote in similar vein. After discussing various ideas that Stonehenge was probably laid out using the ancient Greek foot as the unit module (via an idea of Newham who in turn had been influenced by Atkinson's similar beliefs on the subject!) he wrote: '. . . the Parthenon of classical Greece and Stonehenge seem to have been laid out using the same unit of length. This further link to the Greek world increases one's respect for the builders of Stonehenge, and appears to project a certain unity of thought into ancient Europe. . . .'

Note 21   p. 259
Newham was also interested in historical metrology. Having been greatly influenced by Atkinson's ideas about the probable origins of Stonehenge III architecture, he had looked closely into the question of the ancient Greek metrical units. He believed (somewhat obsessionally) that at Stonehenge at least nine linear measurements correspond in round numbers with the use of the ancient Greek foot (= 12·16 Imperial inches). For example: from the centre of the Heel Stone to Aubrey hole 28, the distance scaled is 400 ancient Greek feet; and a quarter chord of the Aubrey circle measures 200 ancient Greek feet. The definitive measure for the Greek foot is reckoned to be the measurement of the platform of the Parthenon at Athens which is 100 ancient Greek feet in width and 225 ancient Greek feet in length.

Note 22   p. 280

Nineteenth- and twentieth-century literature is cluttered with discussions and fantastic theories about connections between pre-Columbian civilizations and Sumer and Egypt, complete with all the apparatus of sunken continents and mandatory bearded strangers as culture bearers—usually white for preference. At least with the recognition of sea-floor spreading and the understanding of plate tectonics, the sunken-continent theories have been truly scuttled for all time.

Note 23   p. 284

Playing with Stonehenge numbers. Arbitrary Game (1): At Stonehenge it has been recognized that the monument might have been utilized as an eclipse predictor. The Metonic cycle may be a previously unrecognized cycle to aid in predicting eclipses (Hawkins' method). The Metonic cycle was the only useful method in ancient and medieval times of following the Moon's phases for calendar purposes, i.e. Meton noted that 235 lunar months equal 19 solar years, so that after one cycle of 19 years the Full Moon occurs again on the same calendar date (*see* also p. 112).

Now, keep in mind the significant number 235. At Stonehenge the inner bluestone horseshoe has 19 stones, each one can be reckoned as representing a solar year (i.e. 19 bluestones = the Golden Year numbers). The trilithons have 10 uprights; the outer bluestone circle is attributed with 60 stones (but also remember opinion ranges 59—61); the sarsen circle numbers 30 stones, while the Z- and Y-hole counts are 29 and 30 respectively; finally we have the 56 Aubrey ('computer') holes.

Now add up all the holes and upright stones beginning from the outer circle: 56 Aubrey holes; 30 Y holes; 29 Z holes; 30 sarsen stones; 60 bluestones; 10 upright trilithon stones and 19 horseshoe bluestones. Total holes and stones = 234.

Hole position number 8 in the Z circle (not included in the above count) was never dug. This is significant (and intentional), for it provides, by its conspicuous absence, a natural starting *and* finishing point for the cycle count. By recognizing the position as significant, we can add it to the total which is now 235.

Or alternatively, supposedly there were only *59 bluestones*, this gives a total of holes and stones numbering 234. Because hole position number 8 in the Z circle was never dug, it seems that the builders intended it as the starting point for the count and *also* the finishing point and should therefore be counted *twice*, thus we have a total which now reads 235.

Again, alternatively, supposing there were *61 bluestones*, since this provided a total of holes and stones numbering 235, it indicates that the omission of hole position number 8 in the Z circle was intentional to the astronomer-priests' purpose of providing the correct significant number 235.

Thus in addition to the presently accepted 29- or 30-day lunar-month counts, the 59—60 double lunar-month count and the 19-year solar-year count supposedly hidden in the Stonehenge circles, the astronomer-priests possessed a built-in means of keeping tabs of the entire 235 lunar-month count of the Metonic cycle.

Arbitrary Game (2): 19 synodic revolutions of the node of the Moon = 6585·78 days (important in the so-called Saros eclipse cycle); 233 lunations = 6585·32 days.

Problem: find a Stonehenge count to follow 223 lunations (6585·32 days) ∿ to 19 synodic node revolutions (6585·78 days).

Keep in mind the significant number 223. Add up all the holes and stones (beginning from the outer circle) but not the horseshoe trilithon upright stones which in this game are *not* significant: 56 Aubrey holes; 30 Y holes; 29 Z holes; 30 sarsen stones; 59 bluestones and 19 horseshoe bluestones. Total holes and stones = 223. Thus the Stonehenge astronomer-priests had a built-in method of keeping count of both the 223 lunations *and* the 19 synodic (node) revolutions connected with eclipse cycles.

Note 24 p. 284

The power of chance has figured prominently in discussions about Megalithic alignments. Both Hawkins and Thom have argued persuasively that statistical studies of their own claims for positive astronomical alignments of Megalithic configurations show they can safely be dismissed as examples of pure chance.

Nevertheless, one is constantly reminded of the so-called mysteries of the powers of chance and coincidence long familiar to readers of Arthur Koestler's and Alister Hardy's books. While actually writing the present book, I had an interesting first-hand experience of the remarkable workings of chance and coincidence which concerned the Hurlers Megalithic monument situated on the edge of Bodmin Moor, Cornwall (p. 75). Working in my study, I was actually tracing across the map the line of Lockyer's alleged sight line to the November sunrise when at that instant the postman delivered a letter. Breaking off to open the letter, I found it was from a property agent offering me a country cottage in the West Country. Included with the particulars was a map showing the exact location of the cottage known as 'Gable Hid', lying a few hundred yards from the Hurlers monument, through which Lockyer's November sunrise alignment passed within a few feet!

Note 25 p. 284

The Australian Aborigines used several stars and asterisms for economic-cum-calendrical purposes. For example, in south-east Australia, Arcturus was used as a guide to the wood-ant season, for the larvae of the wood-ant were a prized delicacy. When Arcturus rose in the north in the evening (winter), the larvae were coming into season; when it set shortly after the Sun, the larvae were finished. The Aborigines of Victoria knew Arcturus as *Marpeankurrk* and believed she was a female ancestor who had first discovered the larvae long ago; then when she died she became a star so that she could remind the people when the larvae were ready. The presence of Vega in their sky indicated that the eggs of the mallee-hen could be found; and when Canopus rose before dawn, it was the signal to collect the eggs. Other stars seasonally important were Achernar, Alpha and Beta Crucis, and Alpha and Beta Centauri (*see* Fig. 37).

To the Aborigines, the Pleiades, used as a time-gauge, were especially important as the bringers of heat. When they set, they heralded winter; and when they reappeared early in the evening in the eastern sky, it was reckoned that the warm weather was not far away. The Aborigines felt a very close affinity with all celestial bodies, and in common with several other primitive races they believed that the stars and planets represented great people who once lived on Earth and then after death had risen to the sky to continue their lives there. Many of the stars important in Aboriginal legend and cosmic mythology are still depicted on traditional Arnhem Land bark-paintings. The Aborigines evolved simple practical explanations for the things they saw. For example, one tribe who lived on the banks of the river Darling explained that Mars was a red colour simply because while he was a man on Earth, he spent too much time over the fire cooking his favourite foods!

To the Aborigines, the Pleiades, as an asterism, represented a group of young women, the *Karat-goruk*. This is a remarkable interpretation and is practically a carbon-copy of the Greek legend of the 'Seven Sisters' and the story of 'the company of Maidens' as the Pleiades were known to the Florida Indians. It has always surprised me that the hyperdiffusionists of the Elliot-Smith school apparently overlooked this most remarkable coincidence in astronomical mythology as ammunition to support their crank theories (*see* p. 267). Another remarkable astro-mythological coincidence is the independent adoption of the Bear Legends for Ursa Major by the Greeks and the North American Indians.

Note 26 p. 291
Worship of fertility (fetish) symbols of many kinds has been very common throughout the world in all ages. Among the most bizarre was an old Dutch shore-defence cannon—the Holy Cannon, Kyai Satomo—at Bantam, to which women long offered flowers and prayers for fertility. Nowadays the cannon has been removed to a local museum.

Select References

Hawkins, G. S., 'Stonehenge Decoded', *Nature*, Vol 200, 306—8

Hawkins, G. S., 'Stonehenge: A Neolithic Computer', *Nature*, Vol 202, 1258

Hoyle, F., 'Stonehenge—An Eclipse Predictor', *Nature*, Vol 211, 127

Hoyle, F., 'Speculations on Stonehenge', *Antiquity*, Vol 40, 262

Colton, R. and Martin, R. L., 'Eclipse cycles and Eclipses at Stonehenge', *Nature*, Vol 213, 476

Hawkes, J., 'God in the Machine', *Antiquity*, Vol 41, 174

Hawkins, G. S., Atkinson, R. J. C., Sadler, D. H., Thom, A., Newham, C. A. and Newall, R. S., 'Hoyle on Stonehenge: Some Comments', *Antiquity*, Vol 41, 91

Atkinson, R. J. C., 'Moonshine on Stonehenge', *Antiquity*, Vol 40, 215

Atkinson, R.J.C., 'Decoder Misled?', *Nature*, Vol 210, 1302

Newham, C. A., 'Stonehenge: A Neolithic "Observatory"', *Nature*, Vol 211, 456

Sadler, O. H., 'Prediction of eclipses', *Nature*, Vol 211, 1120

Borst, L., 'English Henge Cathedrals', *Nature*, Vol 224, 335

Neugebauer, O., 'Tamil Astronomy', *Osiris*, 10, 252

Long, W., 'Wiltshire Archaeological Magazine', Vol 16, 1876

Kellaway, G. A., 'Glaciation and the Stones of Stonehenge', *Nature*, Vol 233, 30

Thom, A. and A. S., 'The Astronomical Significance of the Large Carnac Menhirs', *Journal for the History of Astronomy*, Vol 2, 147

Thom, A., A. S. and A. S., 'Stonehenge', *Journal for the History of Astronomy*, Vol 5, 71; Vol 6, 19

Patrick, J., 'Midwinter sunrise at Newgrange', *Nature*, Vol 249, 517

Emmott, D., 'The Mystery of Hole G', *Yorkshire Post*, 16 March 1963

Kendall, D., 'Megalithic Lunar Observatories: Review', *Antiquity*, Vol 45, 310

See also text, *passim*

Select Bibliography

Atkinson, R. J. C., *Stonehenge*, London, 1956

Hawkins, G. S., *Stonehenge Decoded*, London, 1966

Newham, C. A., *The Enigma of Stonehenge and its Astronomical and Geometrical Significance*, Leeds, 1964

Newham, C. A., *Supplement to the Enigma of Stonehenge*, Leeds, 1970

Newham, C. A., *The Astronomical Significance of Stonehenge*, Leeds, 1972

Frazer, J. G., *The Golden Bough* (Abridged Edition), London, 1922

Thom, A., *Megalithic Sites in Britain*, Oxford, 1967

Thom, A., *Megalithic Lunar Observatories*, Oxford, 1971

Renfrew, C., *Before Civilization*, London, 1973

Lockyer, J. N., *The Dawn of Astronomy*, London, 1894

Lockyer, J. N., *Stonehenge and Other British Stone Monuments*, London, 1909 (2nd Edition)

Marshack, A., *The Roots of Civilization*, London, 1972

Neugebauer, O., *The Exact Sciences in Antiquity* (2nd Edition), New York, 1969

Michell, J., *The View Over Atlantis*, London, 1973

Watkins, A., *The Old Straight Track*, London, 1925

Smyth, Piazzi *Our Inheritance in The Great Pyramid*, London, 1864

Smyth, Piazzi *Life and Work of the Great Pyramid*, London, 1867

Newall, R. S., *Stonehenge, Official Guide Book*, London, 1959

Lancaster Brown, P., *Measuring Length: The History of Methods and Units*, London, 1971

Lancaster Brown, P., *What Star Is That?*, London and New York, 1971

Lancaster Brown, P., *Comets, Meteorites & Men*, London, 1973; New York, 1974

Baity, E. C., 'Archaeoastronomy and Ethnoastronomy So Far', *Current Anthropology*, Vol 14, 389. (In this useful contribution the author includes the most comprehensive bibliographical compilation of Megalithic astronomy source-material yet published.)

See also text, *passim*.

Index

Figures in italics refer to page numbers of selected illustrations.

ERRATA

p. 51 line 2 from bottom: for parellel read parallel.

p. 58 line 2 from bottom: for ouput read output.

p. 135 line 9 from bottom: for correction read correct.

p. 179 line 2 from bottom: for of some, read of some of.

p. 211 line 19: ''Soudardet san Cornély'' [sic] translate to 'Soldiers without St Cornély'.

p. 224 line 20, p. 225 line 1 and p. 225 line 6: for Metheun read Methuen.

p. 225 line 22: for landcape read landscape.

p. 232 line 14 from bottom: for Litchfield read Lichfield.

p. 262 line 11: for millennium read millenniums.

p. 285 line 4 from bottom: for incommensurabilies read incommensurabilities.

p. 292 line 21: for Culutre read Culture.

p. 316 line 12 from bottom: for *of The Great Pyramid* read *at The Great Pyramid.*

p. 318: for Dendrochronology *see* Radicarbon, read Dendrochronology *see* Radiocarbon.